MODERNIST WRITING AND
REACTIONARY POLITICS

In *Modernist Writing and Reactionary Politics*, Charles Ferrall argues that the politics of Yeats, Pound, Eliot, Lawrence, and Wyndham Lewis were a response to the increasing separation of art from a society undergoing a second industrial revolution. Fascism became attractive to these writers because it promised to reintegrate art into society while simultaneously guaranteeing its autonomy. As a kind of parodic avant-garde, it therefore allowed the reactionaries to be both 'primitive' and 'modern' at the same time. Yet with the exception of Pound and Yeats, these writers all finally rejected fascism preferring instead to see the aesthetic as a sphere in permanent opposition to liberal democracy, rather than the basis for a new social order. Individual chapters focus on Yeats and decolonisation, Pound and 'the Jews', Eliot and the uncanny, Lawrence and homosexuality, and Lewis and the Cartesian primitive. Ferrall's account of why some of the greatest writers of the early twentieth century became involved in reactionary politics offers new insights into the relation between modernist aesthetics, technology and avant-gardism.

CHARLES FERRALL is Lecturer in the School of English, Film and Theatre at Victoria University of Wellington. His articles have been published in *Yearbook of Research in English and American Literature, University of Toronto Quarterly, English Studies in Canada*, and *Modern Fiction Studies*.

MODERNIST WRITING AND REACTIONARY POLITICS

CHARLES FERRALL

Victoria University of Wellington

CAMBRIDGE
UNIVERSITY PRESS

PUBLISHED BY THE PRESS SYNDICATE OF THE UNIVERSITY OF CAMBRIDGE
The Pitt Building, Trumpington Street, Cambridge, United Kingdom

CAMBRIDGE UNIVERSITY PRESS
The Edinburgh Building, Cambridge CB2 2RU, UK   www.cup.cam.ac.uk
40 West 20th Street, New York, NY 10011–4211, USA   www.cup.org
10 Stamford Road, Oakleigh, Melbourne, 3166, Australia
Ruiz de Alarcón 13, 28014, Madrid, Spain

First published 2001

Printed in the United Kingdom at the University Press, Cambridge

Typeface 11/12.5pt Baskerville   *System* 3b2   [CE]

A catalogue record for this book is available from the British Library

ISBN 0 521 79345 9 hardback

For Rebecca

Contents

Acknowledgements

I would like to thank Robert Kroetsch, Harry Ricketts and Kim Worthington for reading early chapters of this book; David Norton and Sue Wilkins for their computer expertise; Brian Opie for his support as Chair of our Department; the editors of *Yearbook of Research in English and American Literature* for permission to reprint in a revised form 'W. B. Yeats and the Family Romance of Irish Nationalism'; but above all Jane Stafford, colleague and dear friend, for her constant encouragement during the difficult time in which this book was written.

Introduction

Someone said: 'The dead writers are remote from us because we *know* so much more than they did'. Precisely, and they are that which we know.

T. S. Eliot, 'Tradition and the Individual Talent'[1]

The idea of the modern has always harboured its opposite. If the Judaeo-Christian awareness of history as moving towards an end implied some kind of progress or, more apocalyptically, a notion of Redemption, it also presumed a sense of degeneration or, more catastrophically, of Fall. Similarly, when Bernard of Chartres used the term 'modernus' in the twelfth century to claim that the Moderns could see further than the Ancients, he also pointed out that it was only because they were dwarfs standing on the shoulders of giants. Two centuries later during the early Renaissance, the division of history for the first time into the three eras of antiquity, the immediate past of the 'dark' Middle Ages and a 'luminous' future expressed a similar paradox or doubleness since the arrival of this 'luminous' future depended upon a revival of antiquity.[2]

By the seventeenth century, however, the Ancients and the Moderns were less aligned against the 'dark' ages than involved in a *querrelle* or 'battle' with each other. And with the emergence of a modern capitalist economy and the doctrine of aesthetic autonomy towards the end of the next century, this 'battle' became one between two competing modernities: an aesthetic modernity which attempted to marry the primitive or medieval with originality and spontaneity and the modernity of laissez-faire economics and liberal democracy.[3] Thus when T. S. Eliot refigured the Ancients and the Moderns in his famous 1917 essay as the Tradition and the Individual Talent, his implicit adversary was as much laissez-faire individualism

as the Romantic cult of what he calls 'personality'. Indeed upon
revisiting the principles propounded in 'Tradition and the Individual
Talent' six years later in 'The Function of Criticism', he suggested
that 'we may give a name' to 'the Inner Voice' of Romanticism: 'and
the name . . . is Whiggery'.[4]

In essays such as 'The Function of Criticism' Eliot distinguished
himself from his nineteenth century predecessors by situating the
latter within the 'bourgeois' modernity to which they were and are
customarily opposed. This is perhaps not surprising given that every
generation must, arguably, consign their immediate predecessors to
a kind of 'dark' age. Yet what is striking about Eliot and the other
subjects of this study – W. B. Yeats, Ezra Pound, Wyndham Lewis
and D. H. Lawrence – is, I will argue, the extent to which they
combined a radical aesthetic modernity with an almost outright
rejection of even the emancipatory aspects of bourgeois modernity.
Like the late eighteenth- and nineteenth-century tradition charted
by Raymond Williams in *Culture and Society*, the reactionary modernists expressed their hostility towards what was variously called
'liberalism', 'democracy', 'industrialism' and 'progress' in terms of a
nostalgia for the cultures of premodernity while at the same time
feeling compelled, in Pound's famous phrase, 'to make it new'. As
Eliot maintained in his review of Lewis's *Tarr*, 'the artist . . . is more
primitive, as well as more civilized, than his contemporaries'.[5]
However unlike such conservatives as Edmund Burke the reactionaries were drawn to revolution while at the same time generally
opposing, unlike later socialists such as William Morris, any process
of democratisation. All five writers were, I will argue, attracted
towards various fascist ideologies (although some finally rejected
them), because such ideologies provided a kind of parody of 'revolution' which reflected their own ambivalence towards modernity.

Perhaps the most crucial aspect of the historical predicament of
Anglo-American modernism was that it came into existence at a
moment when the rift between the two modernities was, arguably, at
its greatest. As Peter Bürger observes, with the Aestheticist and
Symbolist movements of the late nineteenth and early twentieth
centuries, '[t]he apartness from the praxis of life that had always
constituted the institutional status of art in bourgeois society now
becomes the content of works'.[6] Shelley's 'unacknowledged legisla-
tors' had, we might say, ceased to recognise their own legislative
potential. The doctrine of *l'art pour l'art* was a form of social protest

but it was also an acknowledgement of temporary defeat. After all, as Eric Hobsbawm argues, following the revolutions of 1848

the prospects of bourgeois society and its economy seemed relatively unproblematic, because their actual triumphs were so striking. For either the political resistances of 'old regimes' against which the French Revolution had been made were overcome, or these regimes themselves looked like accepting the economic, institutional and cultural hegemony of a triumphant bourgeois progress. Economically, the difficulties of an industrialization and economic growth limited by the narrowness of its pioneer base were overcome, not least by the spread of industrial transformation and the enormous widening of world markets. Socially, the explosive discontents of the poor during the Age of Revolution were consequently defused. In short, the major obstacles to continued and presumably unlimited bourgeois progress seemed to have been removed.[7]

Although Hobsbawn does point out that contradictions within this progress became more apparent after the Depression of 1870, its forward momentum was nevertheless such that the post-1870 period is often described as one of a 'second industrial revolution'.[8] Thus the final decades of the nineteenth century saw the emergence of various cults of 'efficiency' (such as that of the 'pilgrims' in *Heart of Darkness*) culminating in Taylorist principles of economic management and, finally, the Fordist production line. The same period also saw the European colonial project taken to its geographical limits and 'Victorian' gender roles (exemplified by Mr and Mrs Ramsay in *To the Lighthouse*) reach their point of most rigid opposition.

However while many of the movements of the *fin de siècle* and early twentieth century insisted on the 'autonomy' or 'purity' of their art as a way of resisting many of the aspects of this 'second industrial revolution', they did not necessarily desire to escape the exchange values of the broader capitalist marketplace altogether. As Lawrence Rainey argues, '[L]iterary modernism constitutes a strange and perhaps unprecedented withdrawal from the public sphere of cultural production and debate' but this was a retreat into a world where writer-promoters such as Pound could sell limited or deluxe editions of books like *Ulysses* as investments or commodities to a new elite of 'patron-investors' such as John Quinn. Just as, in the words of Rainey, '[M]odernism and commodity culture were not implacable enemies but fraternal rivals',[9] so the two modernities, for all their mutual hostility, were both the offspring of an earlier modernity.

Thus Andreas Huyssen's earlier and influential proposition that '[m]odernism constituted itself through a conscious strategy of exclusion, an anxiety of contamination by its other: an increasingly consuming and engulfing mass culture'[10] is qualified but not contradicted by the recent scholarship of those such as Rainey who describe the marketing of the modernist text. Modernist culture was constituted through its resistance to 'mass' culture but this resistance also constituted, in Pierre Bourdieu's terms, its high 'cultural capital' and therefore, paradoxically, the considerable 'economic capital' for which it could be, at least eventually, exchanged.[11] Similarly, although the reactionary modernists were 'elitist' to the extent that they despised the emerging 'mass' culture and by implication the 'masses' who consumed it, they were also 'populist' to the extent that they dreamt of a popular audience in the future or, as Yeats puts it, of writing a 'cold and passionate' poem for a fisherman 'who does not exist'.[12] Ironically, this modernist dream was eventually realised in the post-war universities.

The reactionary modernists did, therefore, frequently and sometimes obsessively gender 'mass' culture as feminine but such a culture was also frequently seen as the product of an industrial society which, because of its cult of science and technology, could only be gendered as masculine. Alternatively, the pre-modern, the primitive, or the tradition could also be gendered as either feminine or masculine. The Tradition in Eliot's 'Tradition and the Individual Talent,' for example, is certainly a source of patriarchal authority but the way in which the individual talent 'surrender[s]' to it suggests a kind of primitive or oceanic merging of self and other.[13] Thus not only could a writer such as Lewis attack 'mass' culture in the name of a tradition of high masculine culture or critique like Yeats the instrumental reason of bourgeois modernity by invoking the 'primitive' and feminine other but he could also identify with the Madame Bovarys of a feminised cultural sphere like Lawrence or in Poundian fashion promote his writing in the cultural market place like some kind of Yankee entrepreneur. It is probably impossible to ascribe a gender to modernism.[14]

Nor is modernist withdrawal from the public sphere, resistance to 'mass' culture, or advocacy of autonomous art fundamentally opposed to any avant-gardist attempt to bridge the great divides of the early twentieth century. Bürger argues that

[o]nly after art, in nineteenth-century Aestheticism, has altogether detached itself from the praxis of life can the aesthetic develop 'purely.' But the other side of autonomy, art's lack of social impact, also becomes

recognizable. The avant-gardiste protest, whose aim it is to reintegrate art into the praxis of life, reveals the nexus between autonomy and the absence of any consequences.[15]

Although Bürger does point out that the 'aesthetic experience' which the historical avant-garde directed towards 'the praxis of life' was one which Aestheticism itself had 'developed', he nevertheless interprets avant-gardism largely as a critique of modernist or aestheticist doctrines of aesthetic autonomy. While this is to a large extent true, it could also be argued that the avant-gardist impulse was already harboured within the concept of *l'art pour l'art*.[16] For example in 'Arnold and Pater' (1930) Eliot derided the nineteenth-century poets not only for their social isolation but also, paradoxically, for meddling with social affairs. '[T]he dissolution of thought' in the nineteenth century, he argues,

the isolation of art, philosophy, religion, ethics and literature, is interrupted by various chimerical attempts to effect imperfect syntheses. Religion became morals, religion became art, religion became science or philosophy; various blundering attempts were made at alliances between various branches of thought. Each half-prophet believed that he had the whole truth. The alliances were as detrimental all round as the separations.[17]

Thus the theory of 'Art for Art's sake', which apparently valorises the autonomy of art and its separation from life, is actually, Eliot argues in 'Baudelaire' (1930), 'a *theory of life*' and its best known proponent, Pater, is 'primarily' a 'moralist' concerned that, in the words quoted by Eliot in 'Arnold and Pater', we ' "treat life in the spirit of art" '.[18] The impulse to separate art from life always generates a contrary impulse, the desire to imitate art and thus close the art/life divide.

Alternatively, the aestheticisation of life does not abolish aesthetic autonomy but only establishes it at a higher level. When Marcel Duchamp painted a moustache on the Mona Lisa it was not on the original, obviously, but a mass reproduction. Critics usually interpret this as an attack upon what Bürger calls the 'institution of art' – and so it was – but it could just as readily be seen as a defence of the authentic masterpiece against its banalisation by mass culture. Lewis's *Übermensch* of early modernism, Tarr, notices with distaste, for example, that his 'bourgeois-bohemian' mistress, Bertha, has 'a photograph of Mona Lisa' in her Paris apartment.[19] Similarly, when Bürger observes that Duchamp chose to sign his famous mass-produced urinal with the signature of R. Mutt so as to mock 'all claims to individual creativity', he does not mention that 'Mr Mutt's fountain' is displayed in an inverted position unlike any actual urinal.[20] As Duchamp himself pointed out, when he 'took an ordinary article of life, placed it so that its useful significance disappeared under the new title and point of view', he 'created a new thought for that object' – or, we might say, a new art object.[21] The fact that such 'provocations' are now exhibited in museums is in part, as Bürger argues, a sign that the 'historical' avant-garde failed, but it is also in keeping with the original impulse of the historical avant-garde to turn life into art.

Avant-gardism can be regarded, then, as the most radical of modernities. By attacking the 'institution of art' it not only re-establishes aesthetic autonomy at a higher level by reconstituting the 'world' or 'life' as an aesthetic object but it also reproduces, again at a higher level, the undifferentiated cultural conditions of premodern, 'organic' or 'primitive' cultures. Jean Arp's collages and Tristan Tzara's poems are, according to the former, 'like nature . . . ordered "according to the law of chance"' but this 'nature' or 'life' is characterised, unlike the 'nature' of cultures which experience only cyclical time, as a place of pure freedom and spontaneity.[22] In a sense, the avant-gardist impulse was an attempt to transcend the primitive/modern dichotomy.

Yet while the avant-garde's exemplary movement, Dada, was over almost as soon as it began, its capacity for self-negation could be interpreted as both a refusal to descend into self-parody and a recognition, as W. H. Auden puts it, 'In Memory of W. B. Yeats' (1939), that 'poetry makes nothing happen'.[23] Bürger makes one passing reference to the fact that 'the fascist politics of art . . . liquidates the autonomy status'[24] of art but he does not discuss Walter Benjamin's famous dictum in the epilogue to 'The Work of Art in the Age of Mechanical Reproduction' that 'Fascism is the introduction of aesthetics into political life', nor does he mention Futurism, the movement which for Benjamin exemplifies this ten-dency.[25] Nevertheless like the avant-garde fascism both 'liquidates' aesthetic autonomy and provides according to Benjamin 'the con-summation of "*l'art pour l'art*"'.[26] By aestheticising politics fascism conflates the autonomous spheres of art, morality and science, thereby negating what historians and philosophers from Max Weber to Jürgen Habermas have regarded as the defining characteristic of the Enlightenment project.[27] However by doing so politics is also transformed or reborn as a spectacle or an aesthetic object defined by its autonomy. As Benjamin concludes, '[m]ankind, which in Homer's time was an object of contemplation for the Olympian gods, now is one for itself'.[28] Fascism can be described as a parody of the avant-garde because whereas the latter, at least according to Bürger, reintegrates art into a 'new life praxis' rather than the current 'means–ends rationality of the bourgeois everyday',[29] it achieves its effects as Benjamin points out 'without affecting the property structure which the masses strive to eliminate'.[30]

Furthermore if avant-gardism is the most radical of modernities then fascism also has a parodic relationship towards not just what Habermas calls 'the project of Enlightenment' or 'modernity' but towards that broader form of modernity which, at least according to my brief description, encompasses both the 'modern' and the 'mythic'. In an early and influential post-war analysis, the German historian Ernst Nolte interpreted fascism as a 'resistance' to 'transcendence', both of the 'practical' kind or that which has gone by such names as 'Enlightenment, technologization, liberalism, secularization, industrialization', and of the 'theoretical' kind or 'the reaching out of the mind beyond what exists and what can exist toward an absolute whole'.[31] But George Mosse replied that 'Fascism was a new religion . . . and it gave to its followers their own feeling of transcendence'.[32] Since then historians have been divided on whether or not fascism was a form of resistance to the 'modern' or 'modern' transcendence. Henry A. Turner, for example, argues that the Nazis only 'practiced modernization out of necessity in order to pursue their fundamentally anti-modern aims'[33] while other recent analyses have tended to interpret fascism as a product of rather than a resistance to the Enlightenment tradition. However even the latter concede that at least certain forms of fascism had strong anti-modern tendencies. Renzo De Felice, for example, interprets Italian fascism as a 'revolution of the middle classes' with its origins in the principles of 1789 but he also argues that in the more industrialised and modernised Germany '[n]azism sought a restoration of values and not the creation of new values'.[34] Similarly, Stanley G. Payne argues that '[f]ascism was nothing if not modernist, despite its high quotient of archaic or anachronistic warrior culture'[35] and Roger Griffin defines generic fascism as 'a palingenetic form of populist ultranationalism' which seeks to establish the 'new order' only 'within a secular and linear historical time' while conceding that '*etymologically* "palingenetic political myth" could be taken to refer to a "backward-looking" nostalgia for a restoration of the past' (my emphasis).[36]

These are only a few of the more influential historians of fascism and there are many, such as A. James Gregor and Walter Laqueur, who believe in the words of the latter that 'an ideal generic definition covering every aspect of the phenomenon does not exist'.[37] Nevertheless if there is any validity to the view that modernity considered as a dialectical phenomenon embraces both the 'modern' and the 'ancient', then it may be unnecessary to take sides in what might be regarded as another version of the seventeenth-century Battle of the Books. For as Jeffrey Herf argues, '[t]he paradox of [German] reactionary modernism is that it rejected reason but embraced technology, reconciled *Innerlichkeit* with technical modernity'.[38] Thus in another context Marinetti represents his automobile in *The Founding and Manifesto of Futurism 1909* as both the symbol of the new century and as some sort of mythological beast while at the same time proclaiming that the Futurists will 'glorify war, the world's only hygiene – militarism, patriotism, the destructive gesture of freedom-bringers, beautiful ideas worth dying for, and scorn for woman'.[39] Similarly in *On the Boiler* Yeats writes that with the

multiplication of the uneducatable masses, it will become the duty of the educated classes to seize and control one or more of those necessities. The drilled and docile masses may submit, but a prolonged civil war seems more likely, with the victory of the skilful, riding their machines as did the feudal knights their armoured horses.[40]

Yet whereas the avant-garde attempts to re-establish life as an autonomous aesthetic sphere drained of instrumental reason, fascism reconstitutes the political arena as an aesthetic spectacle at war with the progressive and enlightened aspects of modernity. Yeats's and Marinetti's war machines fuse the mythic and the modern but they only do so by declaring war on women, untidy democracy, and the masses. Whereas the avant-garde desires to transcend instrumental reason, fascism reifies technology and thus negates the emancipatory aspects of the larger reason which produced it.

In its most radical aspect this fusion of the mythic and the modern can be described as a parodic messianism. George Steiner in *In Bluebeard's Castle* interprets German fascism as a form of resistance to the almost unbearable transcendental demands of 'the monotheistic idea' whose 'three supreme moments . . . in Western culture' are Sinai, primitive Christianity and nineteenth century messianic socialism.[41] However as the character A. H. says to his Israeli captors in Steiner's later novel, *The Portage to San Cristobal of A. H.*, '[w]hat is a thousand-year *Reich* compared to the eternity of Zion? Perhaps I was the false Messiah sent before. Judge me and you must judge yourselves. *Übermenschen*, chosen ones!'[42] Of course A. H.'s point of view is not Steiner's. Nevertheless, there is a sense in which the *Führer*, *Volk* and *Reich* of Nazism could not have existed without the God, Chosen People and Promised Land of Jewish messianism. In its theological form – i.e. whether or not God is in some sense 'responsible' for Satan – this idea has concerned not a few theologians and I certainly find aspects of the idea that German fascism was a kind of demonic parody of Judaism deeply troubling. Nevertheless A. H.'s question can probably be answered in the negative only if we accept either or both of the following propositions: that the highly industrialised death camps did not in some way exemplify certain aspects of modernity and that the idea of modernity is entirely secular.

In any case, I will later argue that Pound's attempt to 'make it new' by a return to the 'pagan' produces a kind of parodic modernity which is grounded in symbolic violence towards 'the Jews'. Yet while this in part justifies describing much of his writing during his residence at Rapallo as 'fascist', 'reactionary' is a more suitable political label (if one exists!) for all but some of Yeats's later texts and most of the writing of the other subjects of this study. Not only does this writing tend to resist the kinds of parodic messianism described by Steiner but it also tends to affirm various kinds of separation between aesthetic and bourgeois modernity. Indeed, resistance to such messianism and the assertion of aesthetic autonomy may well be two aspects of the same phenomenon if it is true that the messianic desire to locate the kingdom of heaven on earth is also what drives the avant-garde's attempt to conflate these two modernities.

But if such assertions of aesthetic autonomy are what distinguish reactionary modernism from fascism, other criteria must be used to distinguish reactionary modernism from the many other varieties of 'progressive' modernism. While the most obvious criterion is the stance taken towards the democratising and generally emancipatory aspects of bourgeois modernity, this criterion can nevertheless only be applied loosely. James Joyce's *Ulysses*, for example, probably defies political and aesthetic taxonomy. On the one hand the series of comic correspondences between Leopold Bloom's peregrinations about Dublin and Odysseus's adventures clearly deflate the revolutionary pretensions of those such as the Citizen in the 'Cyclops' chapter who identifies a future Irish state with the heroic and therefore aestheticised past of Celtic Ireland. On the other hand, the text's vast assimilation of contemporary print media and its status as a self-contained Book resembles the vaticinations of the avant-garde or the aesthetic corollary of the Citizen's violent modernity.

But even aside from such potentially unclassifiable texts, the boundary between a progressive aesthetic modernity and the negative aspects of the bourgeois modernity it critiques are by no means always clear. In Joseph Conrad's *Heart of Darkness*, for example, Marlowe is horrified by the fact that Kurtz's report for the International Society for the Suppression of Savage Customs, which begins by communicating 'the notion of an exotic immensity ruled by an August Benevolence', is terminated by the 'terrifying' 'post-scriptum' ' "Exterminate all the brutes!" '. We might say that in the terms of Adorno's and Horkheimer's *Dialectic of Enlightenment*, he is terrified by the way in which 'enlightenment reverts to mythology'.[43] Yet just as Marlowe begins his journey up the Congo with the intention of returning Kurtz to 'civilisation' only to discover that he is 'thrilled' by the thought of his 'remote kinship'[44] with the people of the Congo, so upon his return he tells the Intended that Kurtz's last words – in actuality 'The horror! The horror!' – were her name[45] thus ensuring that barbarism and enlightenment or death and the 'idea' which he thinks 'redeems' European colonialism remain irrevocably entwined. Similarly just as Marlowe is unable to distance himself from the charismatic Kurtz, so the anonymous narrator observes at the novel's conclusion that the Thames – whose change of tide is about to carry himself, Marlowe, the Director of Companies, the Lawyer, and the Accountant, away from the world's dominant commercial metropolis – seems 'to lead into the heart of an immense darkness'.[46] The narrative's insistent doubling of characters, places and events, its atmosphere of psychological claustrophobia, its circular plot, and the embedding of its story-tellers like so many Chinese boxes – all suggest that even the most progressive or enlightened critiques of colonialism cannot escape the nightmare of modernity.[47]

Few other canonical modernist texts match the pessimism of *Heart of Darkness* but then few others are as damning in their critique of bourgeois modernity. Virginia Woolf's *To the Lighthouse*, for example, affirms the redemptive powers of art but, significantly, only by coming close to committing the kind of symbolic violence whose very real consequences in a different context Conrad so powerfully describes. The abstract, post-Impressionist painting completed at the end of the novel by the resolutely unmarried painter, Lily, exemplifies an aesthetic sphere which transcends the oppositions within the Ramsays' marriage between the public and private spheres, masculine reason and feminine intuition.[48] Like so many modernist writers, Woolf represents aesthetic transcendence as a resolution of oedipal conflict: Lily completes her picture, begun before the war, of Mrs Ramsay and her youngest child, James, just as an older James and his sister Cam reach the lighthouse and reconcile themselves with a domineering father who had, at least in the case of James, imposed his own demands upon his wife and therefore interrupted James's idyllic relationship with his mother. Woolf claimed not to have read Freud until 1939, 'a deferral that must have required some effort', Elizabeth Abel notes,[49] since the Woolfs' Hogarth Press began publishing the English translation of Freud's complete works three years before the publication of *To the Lighthouse* in 1927. Nevertheless, 'Freudian' readings of *To the Lighthouse* are almost unavoidable because the Ramsays' marriage approximates so closely the kind of marriage which must have generated many of the patients of early psychoanalysis. Oedipus might not be ubiquitous, but the Victorian middle-class private/public division could not but have produced some very distant fathers and extremely close mother–son relationships (complicated in many cases, of course, by the existence of servants).

Nevertheless it could be argued that this dual form of oedipal resolution and aesthetic transcendence is achieved at some cost. Apart from the housekeepers Mrs Bast and Mrs McNab – whose domestic drudgery, incidentally, allows Lily and the other upper-middle-class occupants of the house to engage in aesthetic and intellectual labour of one kind or another – Charles Tansley is the only character in the novel who does not belong to the upper-middle class.[50] Although the son of a chemist and someone whose class resentment rankles nearly all the other characters in the novel, Tansley is nevertheless not unlike an adopted son. As someone at the beginning of his academic career, he is probably in his mid-twenties whereas he speculates that Mrs Ramsay 'was fifty at least'.[51] Tansley is about the right age for a son whereas Mrs Ramsay's own eight children, none of whom have reached adulthood, are rather young for a woman of her age. Of course Tansley might be wrong about her age but if that were so his speculation that she 'was fifty at least' sounds like the hyperbole of a child or young adolescent. Thus whatever her real age Tansley feels, like a son, an 'extraordinary pride' walking with Mrs Ramsay, 'the most beautiful person he had ever seen'[52] and according to Mrs Ramsay parodies her husband's behaviour.[53] Nevertheless, his 'odious' prediction in the first section of the novel that there will be '[n]o going to the Lighthouse' causes Mrs Ramsay to think that '[i]f her husband required sacrifices (and indeed he did)' she would 'cheerfully' offer 'up to him Charles Tansley, who had snubbed her little boy'.[54] But Tansley is also old enough to be James's father. Indeed he is called 'the atheist' by the children not just because he wants to kill God-the-Father (as well as to succeed academically their own ageing father) but because he exaggerates or parodies Mr Ramsay's sceptical rationalism. In a sense Tansley is both a resentful son and a paternal wrecker of childhood illusions. Thus James and his father can only be reconciled and Lily achieve her vision if Tansley is sacrificed. Oedipal conflict is resolved by being displaced on to the only character in the novel other than the servants who does not belong to the upper-middle-class intelligentsia.

Such a reading of the novel could be used to support Lyotard's contention at the end of *The Postmodern Condition* that 'the price for the nostalgia of the whole and the one' and 'the transcendental illusion' of modernity is inevitably repression or 'terror'.[55] However in their different ways, Mrs Ramsay, her husband, their children and Lily all struggle to overcome their aversion to Tansley and Woolf's narrative dips into his consciousness and explains the source of his class resentment as though Woolf were also valiantly attempting to like the kind of man who could receive the university education she herself was denied. Tansley is never entirely a scapegoat figure. Towards the end of the novel, Lily remembers that he 'had got his fellowship. He had married; he lived at Golder's Green'.[56] Certainly, his success is due to hard work unlike that of the other members of the extended Ramsay household, August Carmichael and William Bankes, who succeed professionally with no apparent effort. It is also significant that Tansley now lives in the partly Jewish suburb of Golder's Green, one of the suburbs from which creep '[t]he red-eyed scavengers' of Eliot's 'A Cooking Egg'.[57] But he *does* succeed and Lily presumably does include him in her vision. Woolf's vision is almost but not quite grounded upon symbolic violence.

Although upwardly mobile, Tansley is from the same broad lower-middle class as Eliot's 'young man carbuncular . . . A small house agent's clerk' in *The Waste Land*[58] and the shopkeepers in Yeats's 'September 1913', who 'fumble in a greasy till'.[59] Thus just as Lily's vision of aesthetic transcendence requires a degree of animus towards Tansley, so the '[t]he pleasant whining of a mandoline' which issues from the fishermen's 'public bar in Lower Thames Street' immediately succeeds Eliot's assault on the 'young man carbuncular' and 'Romantic Ireland' lives again in Yeats's verse as he accuses the shopkeepers of forgetting the heroic sacrifices of the past. Indeed it might be argued that the ideological fiction of the 'masses' was primarily a response to the cultural demands of the lower-middle classes rather than the working classes. However not only do Eliot and Yeats never question their own animosity but the class and general milieu to which these characters belong is seen as having no redeeming features. By 1913 Yeats had severed virtually all ties with the nationalist movement and the 'small house agent's clerk' and typist are the only characters in *The Waste Land* who can with any certainty be described as lower-middle-class. Certainly, Tansley grew up within this class but if he stands for all those men who, as a consequence of recent educational reforms, were gaining access to higher education then Lily is one of the New Women whose political demands had recently succeeded in extending the franchise to women.[60] By contrast the reactionary modernists were a part of a larger political culture which rejected even the emancipatory aspects of 'liberalism', 'progress' and 'democracy' while at the same time, paradoxically, being drawn to various kinds of revolutionary politics.

II

Before the First World War the main forum in England for writers and intellectuals hostile towards 'liberalism', 'progress' and 'democracy' was the *New Age*.[61] This weekly paper played a crucial role in the formation of reactionary modernism because it was one of the few places where those such as Lewis, Pound and Hulme could publish before little magazines like the *Egoist* and *Blast* were founded. Essentially, the *New Age* was home to three main varieties of anti-liberalism: Nietzscheanism, Guild Socialism and what would later become known as Distributivism. Each of these movements was largely a reaction to the wave of 'progressive' and 'liberal' opinion which swept through Britain following the landslide victory of the Liberal Party and its Labour allies in the general election of 1906. From 1909 onwards, the Liberal government introduced a range of legislation called the New Liberalism to which most historians now trace the origins of the Welfare State. In a series of articles published in the *New Age*, Hilaire Belloc argued that the New Liberalism would produce

a State in which the few are left in possession of the means of production while the many, who are left without such possession, remain much as they were save that they have their lives organized and regulated under those few capitalists who are responsible for the well-being of their subordinates.[62]

These articles were later published as a book called *The Servile State*, arguably the most influential anti-liberal and anti-socialist tract of its time.

As an alternative to this 'servile state', Belloc and G. K. Chesterton advocated a return to a largely agrarian society of small landholders. By contrast, the Nietzscheans favoured the kinds of 'aristocratic' society which flourished before Christianity, Protestantism, 1688, 1789 and other numerous 'slave' revolts. One of their number, J. M. Kennedy, even advocated the creation of an actual slave class![63] And the Guild Socialists argued for a form of economic democracy which would marry the concept of the medieval guilds with the contemporary trade unions, a Ruskinesque medievalism with French Syndicalism. All of the members of these three movements were opposed to parliamentary democracy; most were hostile towards the Suffragists; and many were virulently antisemitic and enthusiastic about eugenics. Furthermore, although the editor of the paper, Alfred Orage, and all but the modernists amongst his stable of writers had quite conservative literary tastes, all expended considerable energy attacking the socialist politics and the literary realism of Britain's three most prominent writers, George Bernard Shaw, H. G. Wells and Arnold Bennett. As one contributor later remembered

No one . . . can look at the journals and memoirs of that half-dozen years from 1909 without getting the impression of something exceptionally alive and kicking about it. These were the days when Shaw and Wells and Bennett were really formative influences . . . It was . . . the age of the counter-offensive against them.[64]

This counter-offensive did not enlist modernist and post-Impressionist literature and art into its ranks but its attacks upon the literary realism of the Shaw–Wells–Bennett triumvirate did help clear the way for several varieties of anti-realist art and literature. For example Orage maintained that the writer should not just 'reproduce' the 'vulgar' conditions of contemporary commercial reality but mount some kind of 'heroic resistance'[65] whereas one of the Nietzscheans, J. M. Kennedy, argued that there were 'two publics – one the small artistic public, and the other the great uncultured middle-class public'.[66] Although Orage and Kennedy had little in common aesthetically with Pound and Lewis, they nevertheless shared the same enemies. A few years later Orage's caricature of the realists as commercial advertisers would reappear as Pound's Mr Nixon in *Hugh Selwyn Mauberley* and Kennedy's 'two publics' would be personified in Lewis's 1914 'play' *Enemy of the Stars* as Arghol and Hanp.

The *New Age* did, however, directly influence the party politics of the reactionary modernists. It was the first paper to propagate the Social Credit doctrine which would captivate Pound after the war; Lewis later admitted that 'Nietzsche was . . . the paramount influence, as was the case with so many people prior to world war I',[67] and Eliot, who described Orage as 'the best literary critic of that time in London',[68] became a Vice President of the Distributivist League in 1936.[69]

Although there were considerable differences between the *New Age*'s various contributors nearly all advocated the (sometimes violent) overthrow of liberal democracy while rejecting virtually every emancipatory aspect of modernity. For example the Nietzscheans' call for a return to some kind of aristocracy precluded sympathy for just about every aspect of the modern world. Even the Distributivists with their advocacy of the rights of the small property holder saw no essential difference between capitalism and its modern adversaries. In *The Servile State*, for example, Belloc writes dismissively that 'the stupider kind of Collectivist [or socialist] will often talk of a "Capitalist phase" of society as the necessary precedent to a "Collectivist phase"' as though he were someone 'working *with* the grain of that society'.[70]

The Guild Socialists could be viewed as an exception to this rejection of bourgeois modernity since most of them did advocate utilising the militant aspects of the existing trade union movement. Thus Orage remembered that

During the period 1906–12 . . . the idea of the *national* guild was first brought into relation both with historical and with recent economic development . . . The tide of Collectivism . . . was then . . . too powerful to admit of even the smallest counter-current. Some experience of collectivism in action and of political methods as distinct from economic methods was necessary before the mind of the Labour movement could be turned in another direction. This was brought about by the impulse known as Syndicalism which, in essence, is the demand of Labour to control its industry. At the same time that Syndicalism came to be discussed, a revival of trade-union activity took place, and on such a scale that it seemed to the present writers that at last the trade unions were now finally determined to form a permanent element in society.[71]

However it should be remembered that the founder of French Syndicalism, Georges Sorel, advocated the 'myth' of the General Strike as a form of 'creative violence' which would culminate not in a classless society but one in which the proletariat and bourgeoisie would maintain a healthy antagonist separation. Thus according to Sorel

proletarian violence confines employers to their rôle of producers, and tends to restore the separation of the classes, just when they seemed on the point of intermingling in the democratic marsh. Proletarian violence not only makes the future revolution certain, but it seems also to be the only means by which the European nations – at present stupefied by humanitarianism – can recover their former energy. This kind of violence compels capitalism to restrict its attentions solely to its material role and tends to restore to it the warlike qualities which it formerly possessed.[72]

As Lewis pointed out much later, 'it was a matter of complete indifference to [Sorel] which class got charged with hatred first: bourgeoisie or proletariat, it was all one'.[73]

Such sentiments were not necessarily shared by all at the *New Age*. Nevertheless there are striking similarities between the *New Age* circle and the French alliance between Sorel's Syndicalists and Charles Maurras's *Action Française*. Both brought together members of the radical right and radical left; both argued that the revolutionary energy of the working classes had been recuperated and emasculated by socialist or labour parliamentary parties; and both advocated forms of direct action, in particular the General Strike.[74] Of course in England there was no equivalent of the Dreyfus Affair (the nearest equivalent was probably the Marconi Scandal) and the *New Age* circle did not spawn a fascist movement. Nevertheless, according to T. E. Hulme the 'obscure figures' involved in the Dreyfus case 'all have their counterparts here, and . . . the drama they figure in is a universal one'.[75]

The defining characteristic of the protagonists on one side of this universal drama, according to Hulme, is that they deny the 'essential connection' between 'the working-class movement' and the ideology of 'democracy'. Whereas the two-hundred-year-old ideology of 'democracy' is 'liberal', 'progressive', 'pacifist', 'rationalist' and 'hedonist', Sorel's 'contrasted system' is 'classical' and 'pessimistic' because it springs from

the conviction that man is by nature bad or limited, and can consequently only accomplish anything of value by discipline, ethical, heroic, or political. In other words, it believes in Original Sin. We may define Romantics, then, as all who do not believe in the Fall of Man. It is this opposition which in reality lies at the root of most of the other divisions in social and political thought.[76]

Thus the ideology advocated by Hulme is a form of counter-revolution which uses the energy of the working-class movement to reinstate an authoritarian and hierarchical society. To define fascism (of which there were several varieties) as a parody of revolution by no means exhausts all the ways in which it can be described. Nevertheless if this is at least partially an adequate definition then Hulme's politics can certainly be described as fascistic.

These comments of Hulme's are taken from his 'Translator's Preface to Sorel's *Reflections on Violence*', first published in the *New Age* in October 1915. The crucial 'turn' in Hulme's politics, however, had occurred several years earlier. Hulme originally made his name as a promoter of Henri Bergson, believing that his vitalist philosophy was the most recent and successful attack on materialism and nineteenth-century mechanistic world views but by 1911 he had begun to assert that a particular 'type of mentality' had recently associated itself with Bergson and that such a 'mentality' was

at the back of all forms of romanticism. Translated into social beliefs, it is the begetter of all the Utopias. It is the source of all of the idealist support of Revolution.[77]

In 1911, Hulme met Pierre Lasserre, a literary critic and member of the *Action Française*, and was impressed by both his anti-romanticism and his attack on Bergson.[78] The year is significant, because as Alan Robinson demonstrates, after the Parliament Bill of 1911 (designed to curb the power of the Lords), the promotion of 'classical' aesthetics was virtually synonymous with support for the defeated Lords or for Tory and radical Right politics in general.[79] Like the English Nietzscheans, Lasserre believed that all philosophy, literature and the other arts had been predominantly 'democratic', 'liberal' and 'progressive' since 1789. Thus Lasserre divides all history until the present into two aeons:

Il y a deux 'passés'. Il y a celui des institutions et des organisations decal la Revolution valet abolir tout vestige. Mais il y a celui qu'une siècle de Revolution constitue aujourd'hui. Voici cent dix-huit ans que les principes des 'Droit de l'Homme,' les idées de 'Contrat social' et de 'Démocratie' sont un object de piété, aveugle ou non, en tout cas respectable, de passion religieuse même pour de trés nombreux Francais.[80]

[There are two 'pasts'. There is the past of those institutions and organisations of which the Revolution wanted to abolish all trace. But there is also the past constituted by a century of Revolution. For a hundred and eighteen years the principles of the Rights of Man, the ideas of the Social Contract and of Democracy have been an object of piety, blind or not, but definitely respectable, of religious passion even, for vast numbers of French people.]

Even if this were an accurate description of French history, it could hardly be applied to the English history. Nevertheless virtually everything Lasserre has to say in this text, *Le Romantisme Français*, is repeated by Hulme in his famous essay 'Romanticism and Classicism'. Thus Hulme contends that the final goal of Romanticism is Progress even though such a *telos* is precisely what is contested by the tradition of anti-liberalism charted by Williams in *Culture and Society*. Essentially, by labelling bourgeois modernity 'Romanticism' and defining it as the belief 'that man, the individual, is an infinite reservoir of possibilities',[81] Hulme is able to empty the idea of revolution of any emancipatory content. As Orage pointed out, Hulme's insistence on the dogma of Original Sin is never balanced by any doctrine concerning itself with redemption.[82]

In 'Romanticism and Classicism' Hulme is unable to find any examples of contemporary 'classical' verse. However after the first Post-Impressionist exhibition in London towards the end of 1910, there was a striking body of visual art to which he could apply his cultural politics. Most of what Hulme has to say about the new art derives from Worringer's theory that the entire history of art can be reduced to the expression of two basic *Weltanschauungen*. Because the new art is 'abstract', 'geometrical' and 'mechanical' it must therefore, according to Hulme, also be an expression of the 'dread of space', 'agoraphobia' and spiritual alienation which Worringer thinks is characteristic of medieval and primitive art.[83] Thus for the first time in English cultural history, a writer describes the revolt against bourgeois modernity, not in terms of the 'vital', 'organic' or 'unified', but in terms of the 'geometrical', 'mechanical', 'dead', 'lifeless' or 'discontinuous'. Like every revolutionary movement since the Renaissance, Hulme calls for a break with the immediate past (which begins with the Renaissance) in terms of a return to the 'medieval' and 'primitive' but this is a break which will allow humankind, to use a phrase coined by Chesterton to describe Orage, to be 'emancipated from emancipation'.[84] Although Hulme's advocacy of the art of the new industrial and technological era failed to impress his colleagues at the *New Age*, it nevertheless closely resembled their own support for the new militant unionism. Just as Hulme reifies the machinery of the modern industrial world as a form of resistance to the very reason which produced it, so the *New Age* political writers sought to harness the militant energy of the increasingly radicalised industrial working class and turn it against a more than century-long tradition of democratic and emancipatory politics.

Significantly, most of the members of the *New Age* circle and reactionary modernism were from class backgrounds which, although considerably varied, either excluded them from the radical working-class movement or the progressive upper-middle-class intelligentsia. Ironically most of the *New Age* contributors came from class backgrounds not entirely dissimilar to the writers they most despised, Wells and Bennett.[85] According to one memoir, Orage's father died at an early age after dissipating his inheritance and his son was only able to continue his education past the minimum leaving age because of a family friend's generosity.[86] Hulme went to and was sent down from Cambridge, but his father owned a ceramic manufacturing business in Staffordshire, the county of Bennett's Five Towns.[87] Appropriately, in the debate published in *Cambridge Magazine* during early 1916, his pacifist adversary is Lord Bertrand Russell. Lewis received his education at Rugby and later the Slade but he did so with little economic support from his absent American father and impoverished but doting mother. William Chace describes Pound's family as 'nouveau-poor: refined, with pretensions to gentility, with a memory of rather better times, with little room for social mobility'.[88] Pound's Vorticist ally, Gaudier-Brzeska was French and his father a carpenter. The other soon-to-be-Vorticists who seceded with such acrimony from Roger Fry's Omega workshop in 1913 were, as Charles Harrison points out, 'mostly the children of working men, shopkeepers, foreigners or the nouveau riche'.[89] Eliot was a graduate of Harvard but his father had acquired most of his wealth making bricks in St Louis, still a 'frontier town' during Eliot's father's adolescence.[90] Of all the reactionary modernists, Eliot maintained the most cordial relations with 'Bloomsbury' but if nothing else his friendship with Lewis, who made a career out of baiting Bloomsbury's 'bourgeois-bohemians', ensured that he could never be entirely assimilated into such an upper-middle-class liberal culture. Lawrence was closely associated with many of the leading members of Bloomsbury but after a serious bout of homosexual panic induced by seeing John Maynard Keynes in his pyjamas at Cambridge in early 1915, his relations with Bloomsbury became increasingly strained. And while Yeats's father was an artist he was not from that strata of the Anglo-Irish which included his son's much later friends, Lady Gregory and the Gore-Booths.

Thus much of modernism was not just, as Eagleton argues, 'the work of foreigners and émigrés'[91] but also of those who were working-class but upwardly mobile, lower-middle-class, déclassé or, like Eliot and Yeats, on the margins of the beau monde. Because these writers came from quite a diverse range of class and cultural backgrounds, generalisations should only be made quite tentatively. Nevertheless we can say that none either kept or established any permanent connection to either the radical working class or the culturally progressive aspects of the upper-middle class. Theirs was a literature without roots in any larger progressive socio-economic class and for partly that reason it was one which expressed an extremely ambivalent relationship to modernity. Ironically, the reactionary modernists were barely less culturally marginalised than some of their targets, primarily women, the lower-middle class and Jews. Their disenchanted modernity required sacrifices, as perhaps does even the most progressive of modernities, but they tended to be sacrifices of the weak rather than the strong.

CHAPTER I

W. B. Yeats and the family romance of Irish nationalism

Yeats has essentially three political identities: radical nationalist, defender of Anglo-Irish or Ascendency culture and fascist. While each identity has its various critical advocates, there tends to be a reluctance amongst many critics to concede that Yeats's political life might have encompassed all three such apparently contradictory identities. Defenders of Yeats have rejected the charges of fascism first made by George Orwell and then later and more controversially by Conor Cruise O'Brien, claiming that the poet was either an 'aristocrat who looked to an eighteenth century aristocratic Ireland',[1] a writer of 'unrepentant solitude',[2] an authoritarian anti-democrat,[3] an Anglo-Irishman whose 'aristocracy is really a meta-phor, or image'[4] or a combination of aristocratic liberal and 'nationalist of the school of John O'Leary'.[5] More recently, Yeats has been assimilated into a postcolonial tradition, the fascist charge either rejected outright[6] or reduced to something which 'one can quite easily situate and criticize . . . without changing one's view of [him] as a poet of decolonization'.[7]

But if Yeats's defenders are sometimes reluctant to recognise what Orwell called 'his rather sinister vision of life',[8] then his detractors tend to be suspicious or even dismissive of his nationalist credentials. Thus Yeatsian Irishness was an 'adaptation' of Matthew Arnold's Celt,[9] 'an attempt to reconcile on the level of myth what could not be reconciled at the level of politics'[10] or one aspect of the Ascendency's 'means of attaching themselves to their native country and at the same time of holding at arm's length the English connection'.[11] Whether he was a nationalist or fascist, however, all agree with O'Brien that 'at the bottom of it all was the Anglo-Irish predicament'.[12]

Any attempt to show how, as the class to which he belonged inexorably declined in political and cultural influence, Yeats moved from nationalist revolutionary to defender of a minority culture to fascist counter-revolutionary, would require a book-length study. Nevertheless, it is possible in a smaller space to describe some of the ways in which he constructs these three identities through his personification of Ireland as a woman. Yeats confessed in a letter that all his poetry 'becomes love poetry before I am finished with it'[13] and claimed in his public diary, 'The Bounty of Sweden', that 'we Irish . . . good lovers of women . . . had never served any abstract cause, except the one, and that we personified by a woman'.[14] As C. L. Innes shows, in his 'later poetry the desirable female body and the desirable body politic become analogous', an observation we might extend to all Yeats's writing.[15] Yet if all desire is 'triangular' as René Gerard for one has argued,[16] then the ways in which Yeats's love for Ireland is mediated through his various political rivals must also be considered. In what follows, I will argue that three forms of triangular desire correspond to Yeats's main political identities: during his radical nationalist phase, political desire is, as Joseph Chadwick argues, figured in oedipal terms, Yeats's love for Mother Ireland inseparable from his hatred for paternal England;[17] later, as the Catholic middle classes occupy the position of rival originally held by the English, Yeats attempts to consummate his political ambitions by refiguring the radical nationalist women whom he has lost as Anglo-Irish aristocrats; and finally, as the Irish Free State is succeeded by the Republic, his imaginative repossession of the body politic is so violent as to constitute a form of fascistic desire.

Furthermore while these three political identities are to some extent discrete there is nevertheless a logic to their development. As a revolutionary nationalist, Yeats not only desires that the sons of Ireland should supplant their English fathers and thus marry a modern and independent Ireland to the Mother Ireland of Celtic tradition, but he also writes explicitly for the nationalist cause thereby renouncing, if only briefly, any strong claim to aesthetic autonomy. During his Anglo-Irish phase, however, he celebrates the 'ceremony' and 'innocence' of the Anglo-Irish tradition both as a way of renouncing the Mother Ireland of the new ruling Catholic middle classes and because he believes that such 'ceremony' and 'innocence' is a necessary social condition for the flourishing of autonomous art. Thus Yeats's third phase reconciles his two previous ones. Not only does it repeat the nationalist revolution by sup-planting a ruling class just as the nationalist revolutionaries had

previously supplanted the English while at the same time renewing
the political virility of the conservative Anglo-Irish class, but it also
aestheticises politics thereby reconciling the need felt during his first
phase for a political art with the imperative for aesthetic autonomy
expressed during his second. Since this reconciliation of art and
politics, aesthetic modernity and bourgeois modernity, is explicitly
and violently anti-emancipatory, it can be described as a parody of
the avant-garde and therefore as fascistic.

In his Nobel Prize acceptance speech Yeats dates his active
involvement in Irish cultural politics from the fall of Parnell in 1891
when a 'disillusioned and embittered Ireland turned from parliamentary politics'.[18] In the decade which followed, he helped establish two Irish literary societies and a national theatre, joined the Irish
Republican Brotherhood, helped organise the centenary of the 1798
Uprising, and protested against both British involvement in the Boer
War and Queen Victoria's Jubilee. His increasing engagement in
nationalist politics during this period can be measured by the
ideological distance between *The Countess Cathleen*, published in its
first version in 1892, and the play which best exemplifies his radical
nationalist phase, *Cathleen Ni Houlihan*, first performed in 1902. In
both plays there is a female character who personifies the Irish
nation, a peasantry characterised by their grasping materialism and
a plot which culminates in an act of personal sacrifice. Only the later
play, however, makes the role of self-sacrificing nationalist available
to a character from the Catholic peasantry. In the earlier play, the
Countess Cathleen is both a personification of Ireland and the figure
who rescues the starving Irish peasantry from the clutches of the
Devil's emissaries, the merchants, whereas the peasantry remain
passive throughout as the Countess and the merchants struggle for
their souls. When the play was first performed in 1899 there was, as
Yeats reports, a 'very vehement opposition', the playwright being
accused 'of blasphemy . . . because I made a woman sell her soul,
and yet escape damnation, and of a lack of patriotism because I
made Irish men and women, who, it seems, never did such a thing,
sell theirs'.[19] Put in a slightly different way, however, these accusa-
tions are not without some foundation: the aristocrat of the play, no
matter how much associated with actual traditions of Anglo-Irish
nationalism and radicalism, has no capacity for wrongdoing whereas
the Irish peasants, no matter how implicated in their own oppression
historically, are accorded virtually no capacity for resistance, only

one of them, Mary, refusing the merchants' offer, an action which precipitates her death and saves no souls other than her own. Needless to say, the fact that the Countess's coffers are full when the peasantry are famine-struck simply draws attention to her capacity for endless beneficence rather than a grimmer and more obvious irony.

But in *Cathleen Ni Houlihan* the triangular structure is significantly different. The merchants' position is now occupied by the English, the feminine figure of Ireland calls others to action rather than acting herself, and the adversary of evil or injustice is now a peasant, Michael Gillan, a son, unlike his equivalent in the earlier play, in conflict with his father. Cathleen Ni Houlihan might be a more conventional since more passive figure than the Countess, but the later play is more conventionally radical, shifting as it does the capacity for political action from the aristocracy to the peasantry. However, if Michael chooses what Chadwick describes as 'an idealized fulfilment of Oedipal desire: a Poor Old Woman who is also a queenly young girl, a mother who is also a lover'[20] then the play is considerably less revolutionary than Yeats, who famously worried that it might have sent out '[c]ertain men the English shot',[21] and others believed. Michael's rejection of his fiancée, Delia, and embrace of an idealised maternal figure, his inability in other words to choose a lover outside the confines of his own 'family', means that he has simply taken the place of the colonial father. Of course Yeats glamorises Michael's sacrifice and by implication all those who died and were defeated in the 1798 rebellion but such a sacrifice also amounts to what might be described in other terms as a kind of massive repression. Because it ends with Michael rushing off to follow Cathleen Ni Houlihan, the play does incite contemporary Irishmen to repeat his action and consummate their own nationalist desires but because we know that the Irish and French were defeated such a consummation must also be deathly.

Cathleen Ni Houlihan could be read in terms of Yeats's own family history, knowing as we do that the 'old songs and stories' which inspired the play and which he first heard in Sligo as a boy in the countryside surrounding his maternal grandfather's house[22] he elsewhere associates with his mother[23] while his father is repeatedly associated with the kinds of 'Victorian science' which the young romantic nationalist grew 'to hate with a monkish hate'.[24] However the biographical connection which Yeats himself invited audiences to draw was not with his immediate family but with his beloved, Maud Gonne. Audiences at the play's first production would have known that the prominent nationalist playing Cathleen was also the muse and beloved of Yeats's poetry. (What most would not have known, however, was that Maud Gonne had refused again his offer of marriage, an offer we might add made by a man who had lost his virginity only seven years earlier at the age of thirty during a particularly harrowing relationship and who had remained celibate ever since.) Thus Cathleen's transformation within the play from mother to lover is to some extent repeated by the actor playing her, Gonne moving from a public arena strongly determined in Ireland by familial relations, an arena where on several occasions Yeats figures her as a mother to the radical nationalists (no doubt facilitated by her Anglo-Irish background and maybe even her great height), to the comparatively more private space of the theatre, a move which the audience would assume was at least in part motivated by her personal and romantic relationship with the poet. Similarly, just as the audience never witness Cathleen Ni Houlihan's transformation but only infer that the 'young girl' with 'the walk of a queen'[25] whom only Patrick sees must have been the Old Woman, so they also needed to remember actively how the actor '"made up" centuries old' was also '[t]he most beautiful woman of her time'.[26] These transformations partly reverse Yeats's own relationship with Gonne, her refusal of marriage requiring Yeats to reimagine her not as a lover but as a friend.

Yeats's conflation of mother and lover in *Cathleen Ni Houlihan* is in part the culmination of a tradition of *aisling* poetry stretching back to the seventeenth century in which, according to Yeats in an article published in 1889, 'Ireland becomes [the poet's] . . . Kathleen, Ny-Houlanhan, or else his Roisin Dubh, or some other name of Gaelic endearment' so as to conceal 'his sedition under the guise of a love-song'.[27] But while Yeats may have self-consciously situated *Cathleen Ni Houlihan* within this tradition, there are, as many critics have noted, less positive myths and figures upon which the play draws: the 'Devouring Female'; the *femme fatale*, particularly as she is con-structed in the 1890s; and the Leanhaun Shee, whom Yeats describes as 'the Gaelic muse' whose 'lovers waste away, for she lives on their life'.[28] According to Patrick Keane, for one, 'beneath the appeal to romantic Nationalism . . . the primordial form of the Terrible Mother and Devouring Female persists',[29] an interpretation which intends to rescue the play from propaganda only to damn it for its anti-feminism. In fact the Terrible Mother is but the repressed aspect of the idealised Mother of romantic nationalism. As Yeats became disenchanted with romantic nationalism he tended to emphasise the terrible aspects of Ireland rather than her beauty but the terror and the beauty are both faces of the same woman.

In any case, after the marriage of Gonne to Major John MacBride in 1903 and after the Nationalist movement's *rapprochement* with the Catholic clergy following the reunification of the Irish party in 1900, Yeats is able to give full expression to what was previously a submerged hostility towards Gonne and her idealistic nationalism. In the first draft of his Autobiography begun in 1915, Yeats remembers how during the nineties he 'came to hate her [Gonne's] politics, my one visible rival', observing also that those nationalists such as believed that the literature of Young Ireland was 'great lyric poetry . . . could not escape from England even in their dreams'.[30] By the mid-1900s these nationalists have replaced the English as Yeats's main rival and he fears for Gonne's

renewed devotion to an opinion. Women, because the main event of their lives has been a giving of themselves, give themselves to an opinion as if [it] were some terrible stone doll . . . opinions become as their children or their sweethearts, and the greater their emotional nature the more do they forget all other things. They grow cruel, as if [in] defence of lover or child, and all this is done for something other than human life. At last the opinions become so much a part of them that it is as though a part of their flesh becomes, as it were, stone, and much of their being passes out of life. It was part of her power in the past that, though she made this surrender with her mind, she kept the sweetness of her voice and much humour, yet I cannot but fear for her. Women should have their play with dolls finished in childish happiness, for if they play with them again it is amid hatred and malice.[31]

Yeats will later use the image of the stone, of course, in 'Easter 1916' and his infantilisation of Gonne as a child playing with a doll anticipates, I will argue, many of his later political lyrics. But this passage from his personal journal of 1909 is also apposite to the two plays of his nationalist phase. Gonne resembles both the Countess Cathleen, since she is an active lover rather than the beloved, and Cathleen Ni Houlihan, the mother and lover of those who are figured here by the metonymy 'opinion'. Curiously, Gonne does not so much give birth to these opinions as reverse the act of parturition: instead of her body producing life, something lifeless is assimilated by her 'flesh'. Thus Gonne is both the victim of her nationalist children and, since she plays with them 'amid hatred and malice', their cruel mother/lover. By representing Gonne's relationship to her nationalist allies as irremediably oedipal, Yeats renounces his own former political desire and in the process reinterprets the nationalist myth of heroic self-sacrifice which he in part created as a kind of life-denying hatred.

In the same month as this entry from his journal, March 1909, he also observes that

The root of it all is that the political class in Ireland – the lower middle class from whom the patriotic associations have drawn their journalists and their leaders for the last ten years – have suffered through the cultivation of hatred as the one energy of their movement, a deprivation which is the intellectual equivalent to the removal of the genitals. Hence the shrillness of their voices. They contemplate all creative power as the eunuchs contemplate Don Juan as he passes through Hell on the white horse.[32]

This later became the poem 'On Those that Hated *The Playboy of the Western World*, 1907', Don Juan being of course John Synge and the eunuchs the nationalists who protested against the play. Presumably, these lower-middle-class nationalists have not castrated themselves. While neither this entry nor the poem names who has emasculated them, we can infer that their self-professed love of Mother Ireland cannot be fully consummated because they are incapable of fully displacing an emasculating English father. The 'great Juan' of the 'sinewy thigh' who rides through Hell, Synge the Anglo-Irishman, appears oblivious to these eunuchs as though he were able to love without regard to any rival.

Thus in one of the other three great public controversies of this decade, Yeats admonishes the 'Wealthy Man who promised a second Subscription to the Dublin Municipal Gallery if it were proved the People wanted Pictures' to give without considering whether 'enough of Paudeen's pence/By Biddy's halfpennies have lain'.[33] 'What the exultant heart calls good' is not, in more prosaic terms, mediated through an 'other'.[34] During this decade of withdrawal from nationalist politics, Yeats finds for the first time a social correlative to aesthetic vitality and autonomy, noticing '[e]very day . . . some new analogy between [the] long-established life of the well-born and the artist's life'.[35] Essentially, what Yeats means is that 'where all must make their living they will live not for life's sake but the work's,' a misfortune spared the artist and the well-born.[36] The journal entry in which he makes this observation also contains an early draft of 'Upon a House shaken by the Land Agitation,' a poem which begins by asking

> How should the world be luckier if this house,
> Where passion and precision have been one
> Time out of mind, became too ruinous
> To breed the lidless eye that loves the sun?[37]

To which we are meant to have no reply. However as Yeats notes in his journal entry, the poem was written 'on hearing the results of reductions of rent made by the courts' to the Gregory estate,[38] a fact which rather indicates that the 'high laughter, loveliness and ease'[39] of the Anglo-Irish aristocracy is dependent upon – rather than the antithesis of – Paudeen's pence and Biddy's halfpennies. Just as Yeats projects his own oedipally unresolved emotions towards Ireland on to his nationalist rivals, so the kind of economic dependency which most characterises the Anglo-Irish landowners is attributed to the Catholic middle classes.

The famous conclusion to this long period of disillusionment with nationalist politics is 'September 1913', a poem which reverses the transformation scene of *Cathleen Ni Houlihan*. Whereas Michael rejects the woman whose relationship to him was mediated through his father's financial bargaining so he can love and die for another, in 'September 1913' the Irish nation have renounced the 'delirium' of their nationalist martyrs to 'fumble in a greasy till'.[40] Michael turns his back on his new adult responsibilities and becomes 'a man that has got the touch'[41] whereas the shopkeepers of the poem have 'come to sense' and forgotten '[t]he names that still your childish play'.[42] The association in both texts of adulthood with some kind of reality principle and childhood with the higher world of dreams is, however, more complex in the later text, Yeats conceding that '"Some woman's yellow hair/Has maddened every mother's son"',[43] the substitution of 'mother's son' for a proper name suggesting childlike vulnerability as much as radical innocence or heroic self-sacrifice. Nevertheless, Yeats is still a long way from renouncing his nationalist commitments: 'Romantic Ireland's dead and gone' for the loveless shopkeepers but she still lies 'with O'Leary in the grave'. Just as the nationalist shopkeepers have won the nation only to lose Romantic Ireland, so the school of John O'Leary has lost the nation only to win the deathly love of Cathleen Ni Houlihan. Like *Cathleen Ni Houlihan*, 'September 1913' is a love song for defeat.

When Cathleen Ni Houlihan demanded another sacrifice from her sons in 1916, Yeats, although never a player in the ensuing drama, was nevertheless too generous not to concede that its main protagonists were capable of extraordinary love. In 'Sixteen Dead Men' the martyrs of the Uprising 'converse bone to bone' with 'Lord Edward and Wolfe Tone'[44] while their blood sacrifice in 'The Rose Tree' is depicted as a kind of Frazerian vegetation ceremony. However while 'Easter, 1916' retains the triangular structure of *Cathleen Ni Houlihan* it is now strained to its limits:

> Too long a sacrifice
> Can make a stone of the heart.
> O when may it suffice?
> That is Heaven's part, our part
> To murmur name upon name,
> As a mother names her child
> When sleep at last has come
> On limbs that had run wild.
> What is it but nightfall?
> No, no, not night but death;
> Was it needless death after all?
> For England may keep faith
> For all that is done and said.[45]

The rebels' sacrifice is a denial of natural vitality and the English, whose sudden violence is never mentioned in the poem, have, like some stern but fair father, kept faith on their pre-war promise of Home Rule. The only position left for Yeats to occupy is that of mother murmuring 'name upon name' to the exhausted rebels, a position which he initially rejects as too sentimental only to assume again when, in a more displaced way, he 'names' the litany of nationalist heroes at the end of the poem. 'Man is a woman to his work', Yeats notes in his Journal,[46] and in a sense his 'work' in this poem is the Uprising. By murmuring the rebels' names Yeats not only establishes a generative relationship to an event from which he was initially excluded but in conventionally colonialist fashion subtly infantilises nationalist Catholics such as 'MacDonagh and Mac-Bride/And Connolly and Pearse'.[47]

By the following year, however, Yeats has almost entirely distanced himself from the triangular structure of his nationalist phase. In *The Dreaming of the Bones* (1919), the Young Man in hiding who fought in the Post Office is confronted with the ghosts of Diarmuid and Dervorgilla, the legendary Irish lovers who, so it is said, first invited the English into Ireland. If the Young Man can forgive the lovers their treachery, then their lips will be able to meet for the first time in seven centuries. According to Chadwick, the Young Man's refusal to forgive amounts to a 'denial of the lovers' parental relation to him' and

perfectly complements Michael Gillane's Oedipal devotion to the Poor Old Woman in *Cathleen ni Houlihan*. By combining the psychic situations of the two plays, one can construct a single family romance in which the repression of the primal scene of parental intercourse results in an idealization of one parent – the mother, Cathleen ni Houlihan – and hostility toward the other – the father, John Bull.[48]

There are two related difficulties with this interpretation: not only is *The Dreaming of the Bones* the later play but *Cathleen Ni Houlihan* approximates far more closely the primal scene of Irish history. For surely the primal scene of Irish history is not an act of illicit love between two Irish parents but the rape of Mother Ireland by the English Father. Whatever their subsequent complicated relations, the original act of union between Ireland and England was hardly one of love. Freud argues that the young boy actually misinterprets 'the [parents'] act of love as an act of violence',[49] but in terms of Irish history this violence is not a fantasy but real. Thus we should not read the psychic scenario of *Cathleen Ni Houlihan* as a reaction to the scene recounted in *The Dreaming of the Bones* but the other way around. This accords with Yeats's own biography because of course the later play is at least in part a rewriting of the earlier one. The triangular structure of Yeats's Anglo-Irish phase is not yet present in *The Dreaming of the Bones* but the play does significantly revise all the axes of the nationalist triangle. An Irish woman (Dervorgilla) still occupies one axis but unlike Cathleen Ni Houlihan she is complicit in the colonisation of Ireland; the mythic Father (Diarmuid) is still a colonising figure but he is Irish rather than English; and the revolutionary son (the Young Man) still harbours oedipal fantasies because he is unable to forgive his parents but, unlike Michael Gillane, is incapable of acting them out. Michael commits parricide whereas the Young Man is merely emasculated. If the Uprising has lost its terribleness it has also lost its virility.

However, when Yeats imagines an Anglo-Irish alternative to the radical nationalism of 1916 he uncannily repeats the haggard Cathleen Ni Houlihan's transformation into the 'young girl' with 'the walk of a queen'. In his other lyric from *Michael Robartes and the*

Dancer about the revolutionary period of 1917–19, Yeats transforms through the power of memory Constance Markievicz, in Holloway Gaol for sedition, 'her mind/ . . . a bitter, an abstract thing', into the young aristocrat riding 'Under Ben Bulben to the meet'.[50] The 'quiet' and 'tired' Old Woman of *Cathleen Ni Houlihan* with 'all the *stir* . . . gone out of'[51] her is now the patient political prisoner, fifty years old at the time of her arrest, who is transfigured into the woman whose 'lonely wildness' is '*stirred*', not with rebellion, but with 'The beauty of her country-side' (my emphasis).[52] Yeats confessed to writing the poem 'to avoid writing one on Maud'[53] but the images of Markievicz patiently feeding the grey gull and then becoming a 'sea-borne bird' herself is reminiscent of his association of Gonne with birds and his observation of her patience with them in the Autobiography.[54]

Of course the reversal of time through memory in 'On a Political Prisoner' is not the same thing as the miraculous reversal of its effects in *Cathleen Ni Houlihan*. Since the revolutionary nationalists desire to supplant the English their consummation will be real whereas Yeats's Anglo-Irish consummation only occurs within the mind. Nevertheless neither consummation issues any life. In the later elegy for Markievicz and her sister, Eva Gore-Booth, the transformation of the women – one 'lonely' and '[c]onspiring among the ignorant', the other 'withered old', 'skeleton-gaunt' and dreaming of '[s]ome vague Utopia' – into the 'two girls in silk kimonos' whom he remembers gracing their family home, Lissadell, issues in the same kind of cataclysm awaiting Michael after he leaves home to join the 1798 Rebellion:

> The innocent and the beautiful
> Have no enemy but time;
> Arise and bid me strike a match
> And strike another till time catch;[55]

The rival now is time rather than the English and the act of armed insurrection has been replaced by something more metaphysically incendiary but in both cases the repossession of the beloved is also, paradoxically, a defeat.

All elegies, obviously, are about the impossibility of reversing time but even when Yeats looks to the future his Anglo-Irish consummation is no more successful. Like 'On a Political Prisoner' and 'In Memory of Eva Gore-Booth and Con Markievicz', the central action of 'A Prayer for my Daughter' is the transformation of a radical nationalist woman into a symbol of Anglo-Irish 'custom' and 'ceremony'. The 'loveliest woman born' who has become an 'old bellows full of angry wind' and the daughter for whom he prays are not, of course, literally the same woman, but by the end of the poem the child 'half hid/Under this cradle-hood and coverlid' has grown to a young bride of about the same age, presumably, as Gonne when she and Yeats first met.[56] In the final stanza he prays that his daughter's 'bridegroom bring her to a house/Where all's accustomed, ceremonious', the crucial substitution being the word 'bring' for 'take' since from the father's point of view a bridegroom *takes* his daughter to her new home.[57] As Harold Bloom notes,

the poem's actual subject is not the new-born Anne Butler Yeats but Maud Gonne, and the bridegroom who ends the poem in so movingly archaic fashion is Yeats himself, making in a phantasmagoria the marriage he was denied in life, yet ironically marrying his own soul.[58]

The 'old bellows' may turn into his bride but – since his bride is also the daughter he has given to himself – this transformation is no more exogamous than the Old Woman's metamorphosis in *Cathleen Ni Houlihan* into the young girl.

Nor is this the only instance in the poetry where Yeats infantilises his beloved. In 'Against Unworthy Praise' she is 'Half lion, half child' while Helen of Troy in 'Long-legged Fly', the mythological figure to whom Gonne is most often compared, 'thinks, part woman, three parts a child'.[59] But Yeats is able to turn this potentially patronising trope to his poetic advantage. In 'Among School Children' the 'sixty-year-old smiling' father figure in the classroom is suddenly 'driven wild' as he sees Gonne standing before him as a 'living child'.[60] This vision is immediately contrasted to Gonne's 'present image', something 'Hollow of cheek as though it drank the wind/And took a mess of shadow for its meat' but the tone is certainly not one of bitter regret.[61] The first three stanzas explore the father–child relationship, the fourth allows the girl to become a mother, and the next three describe how both 'nuns and mothers worship images'. But this intricately symmetrical poem does not privilege the father–daughter relationship over that of the mother–son. The poet recognises that the images worshipped by nuns reflect not the worshipper but some 'heavenly glory' just as the son so beloved by his mother must leave home and grow old. These are not devouring mothers. The direction of the poem runs counter to Yeats's political instincts, the order of its stanzas preparing for the final eighth demanded by its symmetry, in which the images of an endlessly consummated and renewed desire, the dancer and the chestnut tree, are unaffiliated with those of the preceding family romance.

There is, however, no *political* correlative to the dancer and the chestnut tree. Elsewhere Yeats simply replaces one politically endogamous relationship with another. Mother Ireland is transformed into an Anglo-Irish daughter, the poet matures from rebellious son to Anglo-Irish father, and John Bull is supplanted by middle-class Irish nationalist children. Every point of the triangle is changed utterly but none of its axes lie outside the possible permutations of the family romance. Thus the virility which Yeats increasingly attributes to the Anglo-Irish during the 1920s is no more politically convincing than the impotence and sterility he projects on to their victorious Catholic adversaries. The exemplary modern-day Anglo-Irishman, Parnell, 'loved his country/And . . . loved his lass' while his rival, Captain O'Shea, the husband of his 'lass', 'had sold his wife/And after that betrayed'[62] but what most characterises Parnell, like all those of his class, is his 'solitude'. While in 'Parnell's Funeral' the great man's successors – De Valera, Cosgrave, 'even O'Duffy' – are depicted as having failed, like emasculated sons, to have 'eaten Parnell's heart',[63] such rhetoric sounds strained, even hysterical, when transplanted, as in the following transcription of Yeats's famous 'speech' on the divorce bill, into the political arena of the Irish Senate:

We against whom you have done this thing are no petty people. We are one of the great stocks of Europe. We are the people of Burke; we are the people of Grattan; we are the people of Swift, the people of Emmet, the people of Parnell. We have created the most of the modern literature of this country. We have created the most of the best of its political intelligence. Yet I do not altogether regret what has happened. I shall be able to find out, if not I, my children will be able to find out whether we have lost our stamina or not. You have defined our position and given us a popular following. If we have not lost our stamina then your victory will be brief, and your defeat final, and when it comes this nation may be transformed.[64]

But as Deane notes, the 'Anglo-Irish were held in contempt by the Irish-speaking masses as people of no blood, without lineage and with nothing to recommend them other than the success of their Hanoverian cause over that of the Jacobites.'[65] Thus while the paternal lineage cited by Yeats is undeniably impressive, the extension of its prestige to a *class* or 'stock' must have raised some eyebrows in the senate. Critics usually describe this often quoted extract as a passage from one of Yeats's 'speeches' but it is in fact part of a senate debate. 'I have been looking through this report [on divorce]', begins Yeats's immediate respondent, Lord Glenavy, who was, according to Yeats's po-faced editor, 'reading the Report for the first time while Yeats was speaking'.[66] Returned to its original context, Yeats's rhetoric sounds somewhat less heroic.

This Anglo-Irish lineage was also less than ancient. Yeats laments that the 'one Irish century that escaped from darkness and confusion', the century of his Anglo-Irish triumvirate of Berkeley, Swift and Burke, had not been 'our fifteenth, sixteenth, or even our seventeenth century'.[67] However, although this Irish Renaissance was rather more modern than Yeats would have liked, it was also in his view essentially an anti-Enlightenment which ensured that Ireland would be less swamped by the 'filthy modern tide'[68] than most of the rest of Europe, primarily the England of Locke and Newton. As the Cambridge student in *The Words Upon the Window-Pane* says, 'everything great in Ireland and in our character, in what remains of our architecture, comes from that day . . . we have kept its seal longer than England'.[69] Thus while the England of Locke and Newton is quintessentially modern, Yeats's Anglo-Irish eighteenth century is both anti-modern and modern. This explains many of its ambiguities: the Battle of the Boyne might have brought 'intelligible laws . . . attitudes of mind that could be multiplied like an expanding bookcase . . . [and] an instinct for Roman rhetoric, Roman elegance' but it also 'overwhelmed a civilisation full of religions and myth'; Swift might have 'found his nationality through the *Drapier Letters*' but as 'a boy of eighteen or nineteen he called the Irish people "natives" as though he were in some foreign land'; and the aristocracy might have built the new Parliament and great houses but they were 'masters of a country demoralised by generations of war and famine and shared in its demoralisation'.[70] Although critics such as Frank Kermode detect in Yeats's writing a secularised myth of the Fall,[71] his beloved eighteenth century is not represented as a prelapsarian age since it represents both that moment before Europe became overwhelmed by the Enlightenment or bourgeois modernity and the period during which Ireland became a modern nation. If Celtic Ireland is pre-modern and mercantile England is quintessentially modern, then Anglo-Ireland is not only modern and anti-modern but, it could be argued, an embodiment of aesthetic modernity.

In the terms of *A Vision*, Yeats's eighteenth century is an antithetical age. As one passes from a primary phase to an antithetical, there is a 'Discovery of Strength' culminating in 'Unity of Being', a state which Yeats always compares 'to a perfectly proportioned human body'.[72] No human life is possible at the height of the antithetical gyre, phase 15, but 'many beautiful women',[73] including Helen, belong to the phase immediately preceding it and 'some beautiful women'[74] to the one succeeding it. However, since both the antithetical and primary phases are the two halves of the Great Wheel, the dreams which '[e]nd in a beautiful man's or woman's body' have no final consummation.[75] Significantly, the women at phase 14 – including presumably Gonne, the woman who married the 'drunken, vainglorious lout'[76] and 'taught to ignorant men most violent ways'[77] – are 'subject to violence. . . [and] carried off by robbers and ravished by clowns'.[78]

Of course Yeats favours the antithetical over the primary and the suddenness and violence of their transition often suggests an apocalyptic rather than cyclical view of history. In his note to 'Leda and the Swan,' he describes how – what I have been describing as bourgeois modernity – or

[a]ll our scientific, democratic, fact-accumulating, heterogenous civilization belongs to the outward [primary] gyre and prepares not the continuance of itself but the revelation as in a lightning flash, though in a flash that will not strike only in one place, and will for a time be constantly repeated, of the civilization that must slowly take its place.[79]

Yeats is straining here towards the apocalyptic, as though he desires that this antithetical civilization not just 'slowly' replace its opposite but in a 'revelation' or 'lightning flash' prepare for some transcendence of the antinomies or the two modernities. But Yeats always resists some final consummation: 'I had . . . never thought with Hegel that the two ends of the see-saw are one another's negation, nor that the spring vegetables were refuted when over'.[80] Yeats's gyres are rivals, each 'dying the other's life living the other's death',[81] neither able to triumph over the other. Kiberd believes that the antithetical gyre is Celtic[82] but if we think of the antithetical as Anglo-Irish (*A Vision* was after all written during his Anglo-Irish phase), then we can see how it is both something which strains towards a transcendence of the antinomies or towards a conflation of the two modernities, and yet, since the *new* English or Catholic nationalists are well and truly in power, is something which remains locked in permanent opposition to the primary gyre of bourgeois modernity.

But the gyres do not necessarily correspond in any fixed way to the dominant *non*-Irish ideologies of the period. Many readers associate the 'rough beast' of 'The Second Coming' with fascism, an interpretation possibly supported by one of Yeats's own letters,[83] but the beast's birth marks both the culmination of a primary gyre and the beginning of an antithetical age. Is fascism, then, the end product of Locke's and Newton's 'filthy modern tide' or its antithetical negation? Similarly, while in a letter of early 1933 Yeats compares De Valera to Mussolini and Hitler and finds that '[a]ll three have exactly the same aim' not much more than a year later he writes enthusiastically of forming a 'Fascist opposition' to De Valera.[84] Although O'Brien finds these two statements 'hard to reconcile',[85] there is nevertheless some kind of logic to the apparently contradictory way in which Yeats situates fascism within both the primary gyre of bourgeois modernity and the antithetical gyre of aesthetic modernity.

Usually, Yeats's anti-fascist references are accompanied by assertions of poetic autonomy:

> I never bade you go
> To Moscow or to Rome,
> Renounce that drudgery,
> Call the Muses home.[86]

And in the final verse of *The Poems*:

> How can I, that girl standing there,
> My attention fix
> On Roman or on Russian
> Or on Spanish politics?[87]

Since the opposition of the Muses to politics or ideology (or the Romantic Imagination to Reason), is a consequence of the rift between aesthetic and bourgeois modernity it can never be without its political implications. For example during the 1900s, as we have seen, it is politically inflected by his defence of both the Abbey Theatre against one kind of nationalist ideology and, more speciously, of the 'well born' against the mercantile middle class.

However, when Yeats became briefly enthusiastic in 1933 about the fascist opposition to the new De Valera government, it was not to compromise his commitment to aesthetic autonomy:

Politics are growing heroic. De Valera has forced political thought to face the most fundamental issues. A fascist opposition is forming behind the scenes to be ready should some tragic situation develop. I find myself constantly urging the despotic rule of the educated classes as the only end to our troubles . . . I know half a dozen men any one of whom may be Caesar – or Cataline. It is amusing to live in a country where men will always act. Where nobody is satisfied with thought. There is so little in our stocking that we are ready at any moment to turn it inside out and how can we not feel emulous when we see Hitler juggling with his sausage of stocking. Our chosen colour is blue, and blue shirts are marching about all over the country, and their organiser tells me that it was my suggestion – a suggestion I have entirely forgotten – that made them select for their flag a red St Patrick's cross on a blue ground – all I can remember is that I have always denounced green and commended blue (the colour of my early book covers). The chance of being shot is raising everybody's spirits enormously.[88]

As many commentators have observed, this notorious letter (and a few others) to Olivia Shakespear exemplifies Benjamin's proposition that fascism aestheticises politics. Yeats goes on to inform Shakespear that '[t]here is some politics for you of which your [English] newspapers know nothing'[89] and yet, in this letter at least, he is as much concerned with the colour of the Blueshirt uniform and flag as anything explicitly ideological. But Yeats's attempt to render politics 'tragic' and 'heroic' is not so much a conflation or collapse of aesthetics into politics as an attempt to transcend the opposition between them: the aesthetic becomes integrated into the political but only insofar as the latter becomes itself an aesthetic object. The ensuing scene is both political and an aesthetic spectacle. '[M]en will' indeed 'always act' in the drama of Irish politics. As his joke about being shot indicates, the obvious thrill Yeats feels at the recent turn of events derives partly from the fact that he views them from an appropriate distance. Men 'act' both as participants in political affairs and as theatrical players. Thus Yeats is anti-fascist to the extent that he resists any transcendence of the antinomies and remains committed to 'modernist' aesthetic autonomy and yet fascist to the extent to which he desires an avant-gardist resolution of the oppositions between aesthetics and politics or the two modernities.

The obvious irony is that this brief attempt to transcend the politics/aesthetics opposition occurs at precisely the time that Yeats's old nationalist rivals – the losers of the Civil War and the more radical of the men and women of 1916 – had, following the 1932 General Election, won their final victory. In an April 1933 letter Yeats interprets De Valera's actions as being motivated by 'the cult of sacrifice planted in the nation by the executions of 1916' but since in the same letter he also favourably mentions his hero O'Higgins saying that 'Nobody can expect to live who has done what I have' it is clear that the sacrifices of the fascists and nationalists mirror each other.[90] In 'Three Songs to the Same Tune' – which Yeats maintained were sung by the Blueshirts[91] – the Grandfather who fought, according to one version, 'in the great Rebellion',[92] sings

> 'Money is good and a girl might be better,
> No matter what happens and who takes the fall,
> But a good strong cause' – the rope gave a jerk there,
> No more sang he, for his throat was too small;
> But he kicked before he died,
> He did it out of pride.[93]

At the end of *Cathleen Ni Houlihan*, Michael has left his dowry and fiancée for the 'good strong cause' of 1798. This verse simply concludes his story.

Because they are marching songs, 'Three Songs to the Same Tune' do not explicitly eroticise death. But in the two plays conceived during this period, the nature of the sacrifice demanded by Cathleen Ni Houlihan becomes quite evident. In the culminating scene of both *The King of the Great Clock Tower* and *A Full Moon in March* a queen dances about the severed and singing head of a lowly suitor but in the earlier play, *A Full Moon*, according to Yeats 'there are three characters, King, Queen and Stroller, and that is a character too many; reduced to essentials, to Queen and Stroller, the fable should have greater intensity'.[94] As in *Cathleen Ni Houlihan*, Yeats chooses to concentrate on only one axis of the triangle in *A Full Moon in March*:

> Child and darling [sings the Queen], hear my song,
> Never cry I did you wrong;
> Cry that wrong came not from me
> But my virgin cruelty.
> Great my love before you came,
> Greater when I loved in shame,
> Greatest when there broke from me
> Storm of virgin cruelty.[95]

The son and lover of *Cathleen Ni Houlihan* is now a 'child and darling' and the repression of erotic instinct demanded of Michael in the nationalist play is symbolised in these later plays by the grotesquely literal image of a head without a body. The deathly consummation of the two later plays – 'Dance! Dance! If you are nothing to him but an image, a body in his head, he is nothing to you but a head without a body'[96] – is a kind of macabre parody of the dance at the end of 'Among School Children'. 'Love is all/Unsatisfied/That cannot take the whole/Body and soul', says Crazy Jane,[97] but Yeats's women seem so often to be either, like the women in these plays, capable of only 'virgin cruelty' or, like Crazy Jane herself, whores. Crazy Jane might protest that the soul and the body are 'near of kin' but her own body is old and 'foul'.[98] Desire is neither exogamous nor undivided.

Yeats was quickly disillusioned with O'Duffy and his Blueshirts, observing after a few months that his movement had descended into a 'political comedy' and that he was longing 'for conversation on something else but politics'.[99] On the evidence of *On the Boiler* (1938), however, there is reason to suppose that his interest in fascism revived just before his death in 1939. In this political tract Yeats argues that because 'mother wit' increases as one ascends the social hierarchy and the upper classes have not been 'replacing their numbers', the European races have degenerated.[100] Although he asserts that this is the case for 'all Western Europe, Catholic and Protestant alike', it is clear from his contrast of the Anglo-Irish patricians nominated for the Irish Senate to the 'typical elected man, emotional as a youthful chimpanzee'[101] – the nineteenth-century representation of Fenians as ape-like resurfacing – how he imagines such eugenic theory might be applied in Ireland. As to why the Catholic urban classes, whom he has often represented since the 1900s as sterile and dead from the waist down, have succeeded in replacing their 'stock' where the virile Anglo-Irish have failed, Yeats does not explain.

Yeats chose to publish *On the Boiler* with his play *Purgatory* because of their shared preoccupation with eugenics. In an interview for the *Irish Independent*, he said that

I know of old houses, old pictures, old furniture that have been sold without apparent regret. In some few cases a house has been destroyed by a *mésaillance*. I have founded my play on this exceptional case, partly because of my interest in certain problems of eugenics, partly because it enables me to depict more vividly than would otherwise be possible the tragedy of the house.

In Germany there is special legislation to enable old families to go on living where their fathers lived. The problem is not Irish, but European, though it is perhaps more acute here than elsewhere.[102]

The *mésalliance* in the play is between an Anglo-Irish lady and a stable groom. Both are dead when the Old Man, their son, returns with his son, the Boy, to the ruins of the Big House. The Old Man tells the Boy that he had murdered his father and, after witnessing the ghosts of his parents on the wedding night in which he was conceived, he then murders the Boy 'because had he grown up/He would have struck a woman's fancy,/Begot, and passed pollution on'.[103] As the Old Man stabs the Boy he cries 'My father and my son on the same jack-knife',[104] as though past and present were occurring simultaneously.

Apart from this dual murder, the most curious aspect of the play is its protagonists' ages. We would expect the son of an Irish Catholic father and Anglo-Irish mother to belong to what could be called a 'postcolonial' generation, that is the generation which comes after the Irish Catholics have seized the reins of government from the English and the Anglo-Irish have been forced to occupy the dominated and therefore feminine position previously occupied by the Irish during the colonial period. The Old Man has such parents but as his name suggests he was hardly born in 1923 when the Irish Free State was created and the Anglo-Irish were (to some extent) forcibly wed to their new Catholic masters. Similarly, although we would expect the Old Man's father, the stable hand, to belong to that revolutionary generation which expelled the English and dominated the Anglo-Irish, to have been born sometime before the turn of the century like all the 1916 rebels, he belongs to a past so distant as to be almost mythological or pre-colonial. And we would expect the grandson of a successful revolutionary and son of a postcolonial father to belong (for a play written and staged in 1939) to a future generation. In the play, however, the Boy is sixteen years old, the same age as independent Ireland. In other words, the main protagonists are all two generations older than we would expect. It is as though Yeats were attempting like the Old Man to abolish or reverse the generational process, a process which is also one of decolonisation.

The grandfather and his grandson are identified in the play. Both are loutish and avaricious; both are murdered at the same symbolic moment. Thus the Old Man's murder of his son, the Boy, is a parody of parricide, closely resembling the act of parricide while nevertheless reversing its outcome. By murdering the sixteen-year-old boy, the Old Man ends sixteen years of Irish revolutionary government, not for a post-revolutionary or postcolonial cause but in the name of his Anglo-Irish mother, a symbol of the colonial period. The murder is therefore also a parody of revolution, an action which resembles the revolutions which have preceded it while also being their antithesis. Similarly, just as the revolutionary process can never end, every rebellious son in turn becoming a father and thus victim of parricide, so the Old Man's murder of his son, an action intended to end genetic 'pollution', only ensures that his mother will remain for ever in purgatory:

> Twice a murderer and all for nothing,
> And she must animate that dead night
> Not once but many times!
>   O God,
> Release my mother's soul from its dream!
> Mankind can do no more. Appease
> The misery of the living and the remorse of the dead.[105]

Some readers detect an ironic distance between the Old Man and Yeats but the Old Man's action is mirrored by Yeats's generational shifts. As Bloom argues 'the old wanderer acts for Yeats' and '[w]hether or not Yeats fully intended it, the closing prayer is simply inaccurate and becomes an irony, for the actual repetition in the play is not one of remorse, but of fierce pleasure, of lust fulfilled and yet again fulfilled'.[106]

I began this discussion by citing O'Brien's verdict that 'at the bottom of it all was the Anglo-Irish predicament'.[107] Because of his Anglo-Irishness, Yeats distanced himself from the oedipal fantasy of revolutionary nationalism to be in turn rejected by the revolutionaries of 1916. After Irish independence Yeats could have identified himself with an exiled or politically disenfranchised and therefore feminised Anglo-Irish class but instead he chose to assert his Anglo-Irish male virility against the new Catholic ruling class. This second phase could be described as conservative because it envisioned a perpetual state of rivalry between these two classes for the beauty of the Anglo-Irish inheritance. In his final fascist phase, Yeats sees an opportunity to emerge from his Anglo-Irish solitude, vanquish the modern-day nationalists and repossess an Anglo-Irish

Romantic Ireland. Since this means occupying the position previously held not just by the nationalists but the English, it repeats
with a difference the original revolutionary phase. Although there
are obvious disturbing aspects to the oedipal revolution, it is a
revolution which every generation repeats as part of the inevitable
historical process of decolonisation. Yeats's final attempt to marry
the modern state to the nation's mythic past was, however, an
attempt to reverse not just the process of decolonisation but also
modernity.

CHAPTER 2

Ezra Pound and the poetics of literalism

I

In one of his early, Imagist manifestoes Pound warns the aspiring poet to '[g]o in fear of abstractions' and to '[u]se either no ornament or good ornament'.[1] Several years later in 1917 such admonitions would culminate in his famous prediction that

[a]s to Twentieth century poetry, and the poetry which I expect to see written during the next decade or so, it will, I think, move against poppy-cock, it will be harder and saner, it will be what Mr Hewlett calls 'nearer the bone'. It will be as much like granite as it can be, its force will lie in its truth, its interpretative power (of course, poetic force does always rest there): I mean it will not try to seem forcible by rhetorical din, and luxurious riot. We will have fewer painted adjectives impeding the shock and stroke of it. At least for myself, I want it so, austere, direct, free from emotional slither.[2]

With its repeated references to 'force' or 'power' of one kind or another this reads like a kind of riot act. However if forcefulness is to be a distinguishing feature of the new poetry, its opposition to the use of decorative figures is hardly new. In the Preface to the *Lyrical Ballads 1805*, Wordsworth tells us that he has also taken 'pains' to avoid 'poetic diction' and a 'large portion of phrases and figures of speech which from father to son have long been regarded as the common inheritance of poets'.[3] As Wordsworth maintains that he has avoided 'personifications of abstract ideas' so a little more than a century later Pound admonishes us not to 'use such an expression as "dim lands *of peace*"' because '[i]t mixes an abstraction with the concrete'.[4] Similarly, Wordworth's claim that 'some of the most interesting parts of the best poems will be found to be strictly the language of prose'[5] and his conception of the poet as someone who walks in step with 'the man of science'[6] are later echoed by Pound's

43

attention to 'The Prose Tradition in Verse' (the shorter title of an essay written in 1914) and his repeated assertions that the 'borders' of poetry or the arts and science 'overlap'.[7] Although Pound's references to Wordsworth are nearly always dismissive, his various Imagist manifestoes and essays are in many ways re-writings of the latter's prefaces.

Since at least the Romantics it has been 'the primary function of . . . poetry', Northrop Frye reminds us, 'to keep re-creating the first or metaphorical phase of language during the domination of the later phases'.[8] However, Frye also points out that it is only during the later phases of language that a distinction between figurative language and 'prose' can be made:

Homer's language is metaphorical to us, if not necessarily to him. In his poetry the distinction between figured and literal language hardly exists . . . With the second phase, metaphor becomes one of the recognized figures of speech; but it is not until the coming of a different conception of language that a tension arises between figurative and what is called 'literal' meaning, and poetry begins to become a conscious and deliberate use of figures. In the third phase this tension is often very sharp. A demotic descriptive writer will tend to avoid as many figures of speech as he can, on the ground that they are 'merely verbal' and interfere with the transparency of description.[9]

Of course Pound's view of figurative language is not that of Frye's 'demotic descriptive writer'. Although he frequently repeats Ford Madox Ford's dictum 'that poetry should be written at least as well as prose', he also expresses nothing but contempt for Mr Nixon's advice in *Hugh Selwyn Mauberley* to 'give up verse, my boy,/There's nothing in it'.[10] Pound's Imagist poetics could be described as an attempt to repair the rift apparent in modern languages between poetry and prose, the figurative and the literal. His hostility towards figurative language and 'abstractions' is, like Wordsworth's, primarily motivated by a desire to 'make it new' by a return to a more primitive form of 'poetry'.[11]

However what might be loosely described as the poststructuralist critique of Pound has drawn attention to an animus which is more than just an attack on the figures of modern languages. Richard Sieburth, for example, describes Imagism as a

poetics of 'im-mediacy' which seeks to close the gap between word and object, poet and reader, poem and 'the real', and it does this by postulating the possibility of a language so pellucid, so unencumbered by rhetoric or figure as to become the virtually transparent medium for the direct and radiant revelation of the 'thing.'[12]

Similarly this critique has also alerted us to the ways in which Pound's animosity towards the 'abstractions' of modern languages extends even towards 'history'. For example Robert Casillo argues that Pound 'stands as the major example in modern literature of fascist nostalgia for prehistoric society, for myth, ritual, sacrifice'.[13] Thus while Pound intended to write 'a poem including history' what he actually ended up writing was a text whose figures and abstractions duplicated the very 'rhetoric' he repeatedly attacked in his prose.

This poststructuralist critique usually describes Pound's animus towards 'metaphor' and 'history' as some form of 'closure'.[14] However such 'closure' can also be described in more historical terms. The debased language attacked by Wordsworth in his prefaces is usually thought to be that of the late eighteenth century and Frye argues that the 'third phase of language', in which the tension between the figurative and the literal is at its greatest, 'begins roughly in the sixteenth century, where it accompanies certain tendencies in the Renaissance and Reformation, and attains cultural ascendancy in the eighteenth.'[15] If we think, then, of such 'rhetoric' as the consequence of a rift which produces on the one side the figurative language of a marginalised aesthetic modernity and on the other the abstractions of the instrumental reason of bourgeois modernity, then Pound's attempt to write a 'poem including history'[16] by abolishing 'rhetoric' can also be described as avant-gardist in intent. However since, as Andrew Parker first pointed out, Pound equates 'rhetoric' with Judaism,[17] his 'poem including history' commits a form of violence towards the inventors of modernity and therefore parodies the avant-garde.

II

Although analogies in Pound's criticism between poetry and science can be found as early as *The Spirit of Romance* (1910),[18] the ideogrammatic method as a 'science' dates from when Pound received Fenollosa's manuscripts in October of 1913. According to Fenollosa's 'Essay on the Chinese Written Character as a Medium for Poetry'

Chinese notation is something much more than arbitrary symbols. It is based upon a vivid shorthand picture of the operations of nature. In the algebraic figure and in the spoken word there is no natural connection between thing and sign: all depends upon sheer convention. But the Chinese method follows natural suggestion.[19]

In part the Chinese language can 'provide' such a picture of nature because the transitive structure of its sentences is the same as the basic agent–act–object structure of 'nature itself'[20] and because its 'chief device', metaphor, is the very 'substance of nature'.[21] Yet while such 'primitive' languages as Chinese are opposed to 'logic' (or the shuffling of what Pound calls 'abstractions'), they are nevertheless in agreement with 'science'.[22] For Pound what this means is that the ideogram also presents us with facts that are like scientific data. When a Chinese writer wants to define the colour red, for example, he puts together the ideograms for rose, cherry, iron rust and flamingo from which we infer the 'general idea' of redness.[23] The ideogram is both primitive poetry and modern science.[24]

Furthermore, there is also a sense in which the ideogram heals the rift between subject and object which, according to Frye, is characteristic of the 'third phase of language'.[25] In *The Spirit of Romance* Pound asserts that Dante uses 'no abstraction, no figure of speech'.[26] Both abstractions and figures of speech could be said to occur when the 'general idea[s]' referred to by Pound no longer have any natural correlatives. Thus Robert Burns's comparison of his 'luve' to a 'red rose' would become what is sometimes referred to as a 'dead' metaphor when a red rose becomes merely a decorative figure of speech ceasing to evoke any meaningful emotion or when a 'general idea' such as love becomes an abstraction lacking any correspondence to natural phenomena such as red roses. However as both metaphor and data, the ideogram provides a 'picture' of both 'nature' and Locke's 'secondary characteristics' or 'general idea[s]' such as redness. The ideogram spans both the poetry/science and object/subject divides. In fact we know that very few Chinese characters can be traced to some pictorial origin.[27] Thus the relationship between signifier and referent is as arbitrary in Chinese as in any other natural language. Nevertheless, Pound made the extraordinary claim that

Gaudier Brzeska, who was accustomed to looking at the real shape of things, could read a certain amount of Chinese Writing without ANY STUDY. He said, 'Of course, you can *see* it's a horse' (or a wing or whatever).[28]

As Ken Ruthven has shown, although Pound's 'Romantic mystification of individual genius' and championing of a non-academic linguist such as Fenollosa was primarily motivated by his hostility towards the professionalisation of criticism, particularly by the nineteenth-century German tradition of 'philology',[29] his admiration for *clerici vagantes* like Fenollosa was extended after the war to such non-literary authorities as Major Douglas and Silvio Gesell, the latter according to Pound being 'right in thanking his destiny that he had begun his study of money unclogged by university training'.[30] Pound's belief in Brzeska's genius might also be seen as an anticipation of the 'act of faith' required to understand Mussolini.[31]

However after the war when he turned his attention to the economic causes of war, there is, as Nicholls points out, a 'striking absence of . . . [any] analogy between money and discourse in most of Pound's own writings'.[32] As several critics have observed, Pound's ideogram oscillates somewhere between an 'icon' (which resembles its referent) and an 'index' (which has a causal relationship to its referent).[33] By contrast the monetary sign for Pound is essentially arbitrary. Money is created, according to the dictum of Aristotle which he often cites, '[n]ot by nature, but by custom, whence the name NOMISMA'.[34] Thus Pound believes that its cost should be 'reduced almost to nothing, to something like the mere cost of postage'.[35] Such worthlessness, he believes, will also ensure that money circulates more rapidly and in greater quantity. Although Pound does not in practise always differentiate between the velocity and quantity of money, we might say that his advocacy of Gesell's 'stamp script' is designed to increase the former while his advocacy of Major Douglas's 'A + B Theorem' is largely intended to remedy the insufficiency of the latter. Gesell, for example,

saw the danger of money being hoarded and proposed to deal with it by the issue of 'stamp scrip'. This should be a government note requiring the bearer to affix a stamp worth up to 1 per cent of its face value on the first day of every month. Unless the note carries its proper complement of monthly stamps it is not valid.[36]

Because of the cost of retaining or hoarding them, such notes would therefore circulate at an 'increased velocity'.[37]

By contrast Major Douglas recognised that what a factory

> pays in wages and dividends
> stays fluid, as power to buy, and this power is less,
> per forza, damn blast your intellex, is less
> than the total payments made by the factory
> (As wages, dividends AND payments for raw material
> bank charges, etcetera)

> and all, that is the whole, that is the total of these is
> added into the total of prices
> caused by that factory, any damn factory
> and there is and must be therefore a clog
> and the power to purchase can never
> (Under the present system) catch up with
> prices at large.[38]

In other words, there is simply not enough money in circulation to buy all the available commodities.[39] Pound's economic cure is simple: make money inherently different from what it refers to or worthless and it will circulate more quickly and in greater quantity and therefore realise what he calls here its full 'power to buy'. We might say that for Pound, Quantity × Velocity = Power to Buy.

The scatological imagery frequently used by Pound in his references to rhetoric and usury reflect this fundamental difference between the two kinds of sign. '[M]oney is like muck', according to the dictum of Francis Bacon's approvingly quoted by Pound, '"no good except it be spread"'.[40] Thus in the *ABC of Economics* Pound twice refers to unhealthy economies as 'constipated'.[41] However in the Hell Cantos, it is rhetoric rather than healthy language which is compared to 'muck' or excrement. Certainly in these Cantos both rhetoricians and usurers, the 'obstructors of knowledge' and the 'obstructors of distribution', wallow in excrement. Nevertheless it is largely the rhetoricians – politicians like Lloyd George and Wilson, 'vice-crusaders', preachers and the 'british weeklies'[42] – who produce such excrement whereas those whom Pound associates with usury – the '[p]rofiteers drinking blood sweetened with sh-t', Calvin and St. Clement of Alexandria who are 'like black-beetles, burrowing into the sh-t', and the 'fabians crying . . . for a new dung-flow cut in lozenges' – consume it.[43] In a sense the unhealthy body politic produces too much language and too little money. An unhealthy body politic suffers both from linguistic diarrhea and economic constipation.

Yet despite these fundamental differences language and money both refer to analogous referents. 'All value comes from labour and nature',[44] Pound informs us. Thus as the ideogram provides a 'picture' of 'nature' and 'general idea[s]' so the healthy monetary signifier can be exchanged for the bounty of nature and the products of labour. As the ideogram closes the gap between object and subject so money bridges the nature/culture divide.

Another striking similarity between the ideogram and Pound's healthy monetary signifier is what Sieburth calls their 'immediacy'.[45] Pound argues that

Marxian economics deal with goods for sale, goods in the shop. The minute I cook my own dinner or nail four boards together into a chair, I escape from the whole cycle of Marxian economics.[46]

Other kinds of work are also independent of exchange value:

The new economics bases value on the cultural heritage, that is to say on labour PLUS the complex of inventions which make it possible to get results, which *used* to be exclusively the results of labour, with very little labour, and with a quantity of labour that tends steadily to diminish.[47]

Pound tends to divide work into two kinds: mechanical 'labour' of the sort done for money by men and women in offices and factories and the kind of work done either in the private sphere or by creative people such as artists, scientists or engineers which, although financially rewardable, cannot be reduced to an exchange value. The 'quantity' of mechanical 'labour' 'tends steadily to diminish' because industrial production is increasingly being done by machines or the 'inventions' of creative labour. Indeed Pound even argues that there should be an equitable 'distribution' of mechanical 'labour' of about four hours' work a day to every individual between the ages of twenty and forty.[48] Thus not only do certain kinds of work escape the mediation of exchange value altogether but what mediation there is must or should be 'steadily' diminishing. Perhaps in some utopian future there will be no mechanical labour and therefore no such thing as exchange value. Paradoxically although the monetary signifier is purely conventional it must be exchanged directly for the 'cultural heritage' just as the ideogram refers directly to 'general idea[s]'.

Furthermore, not only do the ideogram and healthy money resemble each other despite the fact that one is motivated and the other conventional, but rhetoric and usury are fundamentally alike. Pound defines usury as a 'charge for the use of purchasing power, levied without regard to production; often without regard to the possibilities of production' and on several occasions attributes to the founder of the Bank of England (on the authority of Christopher Hollis), the economic principle that the bank '*[h]ath benefit of interest on all the moneys which it the bank, creates out of nothing*'.[49] Whereas a rhetorical abstraction refers to nothing but an artificial mental construct, so usury refers to nothing but the bank's own financial transactions. An abstraction or artificial mental construct is as different from the 'general idea[s]' evoked by ideogrammatic data as usurious profit is from 'production'.

Furthermore if by Pound's account such creation *ex nihilo* parodies the Judaeo-Christian God (or for that matter Yeats's often cited claim to have 'made it out of a mouthful of air') it also parodies His Creation, Nature. Usury is not just, as Pound was fond of saying, 'contra naturum' but something which perversely imitates natural fecundity. 'By great wisdom', Pound decares, 'sodomy and usury were seen coupled together'.[50] As Sieburth explains, this 'wisdom' is Aristotle's:

[The] creation of money out of money, [the] incestuous propagation of like out of like, underlies Aristotle's condemnation of usury as an unnatural form of generation in which money bears interest that resembles it as offspring resembles parent. Since the Greek term *tokos* signifies both monetary interest and biological offspring, usury thus tends to be conceived as an inanimate or perverse copy of animate or natural generation.[51]

Thus as Pound chants all the forms of natural and human productivity destroyed by usury in Canto 45, the figure of 'usura' slowly but surely acquires an extraordinary if perverse power and energy. Just as the figures of rhetoric are a perversion of what Fenollosa claims is the inherent metaphoricity of nature, so usury parodies natural generation.

Pound favours paper currency over metal currency, then, because it is less likely to be confused with nature:

Money is not a product of nature but an invention of man. And man has made it into a pernicious instrument through lack of foresight. The nations have forgotten the differences between animal, vegetable, and mineral; or, rather, finance has chosen to represent all three of the natural categories by a single means of exchange, and failed to take account of the consequences. Metal is durable, but it does not reproduce itself. If you sow gold you will not be able to reap a harvest many times greater than the gold you sowed. The vegetable leads a more or less autonomous existence, but its natural reproductiveness can be increased by cultivation. The animal gives to and takes from the vegetable world: manure in exchange for food.

Fascinated by the lustre of a metal, man made it into chains. Then he invented something against nature, a false representation in the mineral world of laws which apply only to animals and vegetables. The nineteenth century, the infamous century of usury, went even further, creating a species of monetary Black Mass. Marx and Mill, in spite of their superficial differences, agreed in endowing money with properties of a quasi-religious nature. There was even the concept of energy being 'concentrated in money', as if one were speaking of the divine quality of consecrated bread.[52]

There is a significant shift in the first of these paragraphs from the category of 'money' (which includes paper currency as well as coins) to the category of metal coinage and then to gold. Irrespective of the particular debates after the war about the gold standard,[53] what bothers Pound about gold is that it is a form of conventional currency which refers to objects of value and yet as something which comes from nature it also appears to have an inherent value. As consecrated bread is both a symbol and what is symbolised, so gold confuses the relationship between sign and object. Indeed Pound is so concerned to distinguish gold from the rest of nature that he is even prepared to invest gold coins with an inherent aesthetic value so as to de-invest them of any inherent natural value. Elsewhere, for example, he praises the 'design' and manufacture of gold coins during the time of Demosthenes and maintains that

early and avid merchants carried money as we still see an occasional amateur with a couple of double eagles (20 dollar gold pieces) hung on his watch chain, as ornament and as sort of insurance that he won't be completely broke if someone pinches his pocket book.[54]

Yet even when Pound deals with paper currency rather than gold he fetishes the very currency which he frequently insists is of no inherent value. In one of his discussions of Gesell's stamp script, for example, he claims that

[i]t is unjust that money should enjoy privileges denied to goods. It would be better, too, if money perished at the same rate as goods perish, instead of being of lasting durability while goods get consumed and food gets eaten.[55]

Stamp script, then, oddly behaves like the very vegetable realm which Pound insists elsewhere should never be confused with currency.

Although he is careful to distinguish between the conventionality of money and the motivated characteristics of the ideogram, Pound seems to believe that both share a similar unmediated relationship to their respective referents. In his 1939 essay 'What is money for?', for example, he makes an extended analogy between money and theatre tickets and repeats Orage's question ' "Would you call it inflation, if there were a ticket for every seat in the house?" '.[56] But money is *not* analogous to theatre tickets because it can be exchanged for any good or service whereas a theatre ticket can be exchanged for only one performance. In a sense theatre tickets are more like words than money. Because the latter is 'abstract' any increase or decrease in its quantity would result respectively in inflation or deflation. Significantly, although Pound never opposes the charging of interest for legitimate loans he never exactly specifies how such transactions are to be distinguished from usury. It is one thing to define usury as a 'charge . . . levied without regard to production' and quite another to determine – at least in a complex modern economy – when this has occurred.

Thus while Pound insists that '[w]e will have defined money properly when we have stated what it is in words that can NOT be applied to anything else',[57] there is a sense in which his poetics and economics are fundamentally alike. Pound maintains that since '[n]ature habitually overproduces' and the 'world's producing plant can produce everything the world needs' then '[p]robably the only economic problem needing emergency solution in our time is the problem of distribution'.[58] '[W]e are to be saved', he argues, 'by a few hundred chartered, but honest accountants working in a plate-glass room under communal supervision'.[59] Just as the abolition of rhetoric enables a form of writing which is both primitive poetry and modern science so the total transformation of the sphere of finance capital will ensure the equitable distribution of nature's bounty and the products of the modern industrial state.

The fundamental flaw in such logic is that linguistic and economic signs are not alike in the way that Pound assumes. Whereas the split between the figures of aesthetic modernity and the abstractions of instrumental reason is a feature of the 'modern' era, money as a conventional sign has always had the abstract and self-generating functions which Pound thinks it shares with rhetoric. Homer would have been familiar with what Pound calls 'usury' but not with 'rhetoric'. Furthermore whereas Pound is right to think of 'rhetoric' as an 'evil', the characteristic of abstraction which he attributes to 'usury' is what is 'good' about money. Because of its ability to 'refer' to any commodity, money mediates between its users thereby facilitating not only the circulation of commodities but the generation of wealth. However, as Murray points out, Pound

talks of money as certificate of work done, or certificate of goods available, but the real problem – and it is at the heart of Pound's ambivalence about money – is that money as he wants it to operate is an abstraction, a sign referring to a *relation* between things of value, not to something concrete.[60]

One side of Pound's economics recognises this aspect of money in its insistence on the worthlessness of money while the other resists it by representing the mediatory aspects of money as an 'evil'. Thus whereas Pound's desire to sweep away the figures and abstractions of rhetoric accords with just about every radical poetics since the Romantics, his economics attacks not just the useful aspects of money but the wealth-generating capacity of financial capital while at the same time leaving the realm of industrial capital and its labour divisions intact.

Perhaps it is not surprising, then, that Pound should associate Judaism with 'usury'. Just as his economics mistake what is useful about money for the evil of 'usury', so he mistakes the inventors of a modernity he would seek to renew for the original purveyors of 'rhetoric' and 'usury'. As early as *The Spirit of Romance* (1910), Pound claimed that there are 'only two kinds of religion':

There is the Mosaic or Roman or British Empire type, where someone, having to keep a troublesome rabble in order, invents and scares them with a disagreeable bogie, which he calls god.

Christianity and other forms of ecstatic religion, on the other hand, are not in inception dogma or propaganda of something called the *one truth* or the *universal truth*; they *seem* little concerned with ethics; their general object appears to be to stimulate a sort of confidence in the life-force.[61]

Pound conflates the Mosaic invention of a universal and therefore abstract God not just with the later imperialisms of Rome and Britain but with the kind of 'dogma or propaganda' which characterises only 'modern' languages. Hyam Maccoby observes that Pound believes that the Jews are 'the chief exponents of discursive rational thinking'[62] but, as a lifelong advocate for science, Pound actually believes that the Jews are responsible for only such debased forms of reason as 'dogma or propaganda'. Similarly the inevitable consequence for Pound of removing God from Nature is that 'myth' is reduced to merely figurative language. As he later argued in 1918:

It was only when men began to mistrust the myths and to tell nasty lies about the Gods for a moral purpose that . . . matters became hopelessly confused. Then some unpleasing Semite or Parsee or Syrian began to use myths for social propaganda, when the myth was degraded into an allegory or a fable, and that was the beginning of the end. And the Gods no longer walked in men's gardens.[63]

Just as 'rhetoric' includes figures and abstractions, so Judaism's jealousy of other gods produces a form of discourse which is both indirect and dogmatic.

The social corollaries of 'allegory' and 'propaganda' or, respectively, the figures of aesthetic modernity and the abstractions of bourgeois modernity, are a private sphere characterised by cloying sentimentality and a public sphere dominated by cold calculation. In Canto 35 Pound, on the authority of someone called Tsievitz, describes

> the warmth of affections,
> the intra mural, the almost intravaginal warmth of
> hebrew affections, in the family, and nearly everything else.[64]

And yet most instances of such affection are motivated by calculation of some kind or another: the conductor Nataanovitch requests that his 'audience come in black clothes'[65] to a performance of the Mattias Passion, presumably for theatrical effect; the family of 'the young lady' who says she is a '"product"' '"of Mitteleurope"' do not 'wire about papa's death for fear of disturbing the concert',[66] Mr Elias claims he gets 'inspiration . . . occasionally' from 'looking at a pretty girl' and then specifies that it is 'an I-de-a, I-mean-a biz-nis I-de-a?';[67] and the 'peautiful chewisch poy . . . wit a likeing for to make arht-voiks . . . orderet a magnificent funeral [for his 'brudder'] and tden zent dh pill to dh vife'.[68] Just as sentimentality and calculation are the twin aspects of 'Mitteleuropa' so the artistic activities of many of the Jews in this canto are inseparable from 'biz-nis'.

For while Pound desires a return to the mythic or pagan as a way of closing the rift between the two modernities, he does not desire to compromise the autonomy of art or the various kinds of science he regularly champions. Indeed 'Mitteleuropa' represents not just a realm in which the worst aspects of the divisions between the private and public spheres, art and commerce are exaggerated but also the place where such divisions are eroded altogether. '[T]he general indefinite wobble'[69] characterises not only both sides of such divisions but also the relationship between them. As Casillo has exhaustively documented, Pound represents the Jews as 'figures of confusion, indeterminacy, undifferentiation, and monstrosity',[70] habitually comparing them to parthenogenic life forms which, like the figures of rhetoric, endlessly reproduce only themselves, or holding them responsible for the sterility and abstractness of modern historical life. Pound's antisemitism is, therefore, less a case of 'heterophobia' than 'proteophobia' or what Zygmunt Baumann describes as

the apprehension and vexation related not to something or someone disquieting through otherness and unfamiliarity, but to something or someone that does not fit the structure of the orderly world, does not fall easily into any of the established categories, emits therefore contradictory signals as to the proper conduct – and in the result blurs the borderlines which ought to be kept watertight and undermines the reassuringly monotonous, repetitive and predictable nature of the life-world.[71]

According to Baumann such 'ambivalence', which the Jews 'incarnate' in antisemitic discourse, is not only what the 'ordering bustle' of modernity seeks to eliminate but a product of such 'ordering'. 'Ambivalence', he argues, 'is the one enemy without which order cannot live'.[72]

Baumann's analysis could, I think, be described as philosemitic because Judaism is excluded from his entirely secular concept of modernity. However Steiner's observation that the Holocaust was '*Hell made immanent*' seems to me irrefutable.[73] The 'monotheistic idea' also creates a 'demonic' realm which has all the characteristics of what Baumann calls 'ambivalence'. Pound's 'argument' seems to be that monotheistic transcendence is always false because it creates *only* 'ambivalence', *only* the figures and abstractions of 'rhetoric'. However the problem with such an argument, aside of course from its antisemitism, is that it may well be impossible to reject monotheism in the name of the 'pagan' gods without replicating the very modernity which is being negated. For as Daniel Pearlman and Casillo observe, Pound has his own New Jerusalem ('the city of Dioce'), a messianic leader or prophet (Mussolini, 'the Boss') his Chosen People (such 'avant-gardes' as Imagism and Vorticism), his sacred texts (compiled, for example, in his *ABC of Reading*) and his idolaters (the usurers).[74] A non-parodic modernity might well resist, as Pound does, the negative aspects of 'the monotheistic idea' in the name of some kind of instinctual, polymorphous 'paganism' but only as a way of renewing such an 'idea'. By contrast Pound's attempt to expunge all traces of Jewish influence from his 'pagan' tradition casts 'the Jews' out of Heaven and into Hell and thereby not only parodies the 'monotheistic idea' but reproduces, I would now like to argue, the kind of 'rhetoric' which he would otherwise eliminate.

III

In an interview after the war, Pound maintained that in *The Cantos* 'there is a turning point . . . toward the middle; up to that point it is a sort of detective story, and one is looking for the CRIME'.[75] The 'crime' of usury is also referred to as a 'disease' throughout *The Cantos*.[76] Just as the ideogram presents data from which we can infer such 'general idea[s]' as redness, so the 'phalanx of particulars' presented in the poem are clues and symptoms from which the reader as detective and doctor can, by a process of inductive reasoning, arrive at the 'crime' or 'disease' of usury. Usury acts like a signifier throughout *The Cantos* but, just as a symptom signifies a disease or clues a crime, so it is also the signified of the poem.

The rhetorical substitution of effect for cause is usually regarded as a form of metonymy and indeed some critics argue that Pound's poetry is fundamentally driven by this figure. According to Herbert Schneidau, for example, Pound's 'literalism' constitutes a revolutionary 'break-away from metaphorical habits in composing poems' in favour of metonymy.[77] Roman Jacobson – from whom this metonymy/metaphor distinction derives – defines metonymy as substitution on the basis of spatial and temporal contiguity. Prose he argues tends towards the metonymic pole of language, poetry towards the metaphoric pole.[78] As such it is difficult to see how the metonymic pole of language could adequately accommodate the medical and forensic discourses of *The Cantos* since Pound's primary intention is to show how, because of various historical processes, the signified of usury has become separated from the symptoms and forensic evidence which signify it. According to Pound, for example, the usurious principles on which the Bank of England was founded still affect the contemporary economy more than two hundred years later. Stephen Ullmann points out that '[I]t is an essential feature of a metaphor that there must be a certain distance between tenor and vehicle. Their similarity must be accompanied by a feeling of disparity; they must belong to different spheres of thought'.[79] Technically, then, Pound's 'particulars' are metonymies since they do not belong to different spheres from their tenors or the signified of usury but their temporal and spatial distance from these tenors – initially for the reader if not the author – makes them not dissimilar to metaphors.

Nor does the category of metonymy adequately label the most

obtrusive technical device of *The Cantos* – quotation. Certainly, a typical quotation in *The Cantos* functions like a synecdoche, a trope included under the category of metonymy by Jakobson and often defined as the substitution of part for whole.[80] For example when Pound quotes the founder of the Bank of England, William P. Paterson, as saying that the bank '*Hath benefit of interest on all the moneys which it the bank, creates out of nothing*' he is referring to a larger text which is itself embedded in an even larger historical context. The quotation is a part which stands for the whole, in this instance according to Pound one of the most notorious institutionalisations of usury in history. Significantly, the reader is not expected to be familiar with all the facts concerning the founding of this bank. Pound uses allusion far less than any of the major modernist poets because allusion requires precisely the kind of shared knowledge between poet and reader which *The Cantos* denies. However, while the poem's lack of allusiveness or 'flatness' suggests a mode of writing which tends towards discursive prose, reference to events such as the founding of the Bank of England are not entirely of the most direct and literal kind. Sometimes Pound quotes from con- versations for which there are no written records. For example Canto 19 has, according to Carroll F. Terrell, 'no published sources' and consists of 'a pastiche of memories of café talk, news-making events, and gossip drawn from pre-World War I years through the early 1920s'.[81] The first four reported conversations of the canto were with an unnamed businessman who sold a patent for an invention which remained in the 'desk' of a 'big company', another businessman called Spinder living in Paris on the proceeds of 'rent' from a business in America, a 'slender diplomatdentist' who '"never finished the book"', and Arthur Griffith, the leader of Sinn Fein, who told Pound that you '"Can't move 'em with a cold thing, like economics"'.[82] In some way or another these conversations, like all the others in this canto, are related to economic conspiracies of some kind. The first word of the canto is the interrogative 'Sabotage?' but while what follows answers in the affirmative it leaves the nature of the 'sabotage' or conspiracies deliberately vague. Why wasn't the invention ever manufactured? What was the book which the 'slender diplomatdentist/Qui se faisait si beau' 'never finished'?[83] Pound believed that during his conversation with Arthur Griffith they were being spied on by a 'slick guy in the other corner reading The Tatler,/Not upside down, but never turning the pages' and that after

their conversation 'the telephone didn't work for a week'.[84] This
cartoonish spy is Pound's double, someone (if he existed) who knew
that Griffith was up to something but who did not know exactly
what. Pound knows that all these incidents point ultimately towards
some kind of blockage of 'credit, or distribution' but he is not sure
exactly how. He is both very direct and indirect at the same time.
While the canto is about various conspiracies its method is itself
conspiratorial.

Thus while Pound wants us to read both inductively like a scientist
and intuitively like a poet, the cantos actually require us to read with
both the pedantry and paranoia of a conspiracy theorist. Consider
for example the following passage from the middle of Canto 46:

> 17 years on this case, and we not the first lot!
> Said Paterson:
> > Hath benefit of interest on all
> the moneys which it, the bank, creates out of nothing.
> > Semi-private inducement
> Said Mr RothSchild, hell knows which Roth-schild
> 1861, '64 or there sometime, "Very few people
> "will understand this. Those who do will be occupied
> "getting profits. The general public will probably not
> "see it's against their interest."
> > Seventeen years on the case; here
> Gents, is/are the confession.
> > "Can we take this into court?
> > "Will any jury convict on this evidence?
> 1694 anno domini, on through the ages of usury
> On, right on, into hair-cloth, right on into rotten building,
> Right on into London houses, ground rents, foetid brick work,
> Will any jury convict 'um? The Foundation of Regius Professors
> Was made to spread lies and teach Whiggery, will any
> > JURY convict 'um?
> The Macmillan Commission about two hundred and forty years LATE
> with great difficulty got back to Paterson's
> The bank makes it *ex nihil*
> Denied by five thousand professors, will any
> Jury convict 'um? This case, and with it
> the first part, draws to a conclusion.[85]

The forensic evidence referred to is (in order): the founding of the
Bank of England; a Rothschild Bros. letter from the early 1860s;
Pound's first meeting with Major Douglas seventeen years earlier in
the offices of the *New Age* (or possibly nineteen years, according to

other references in the canto); the endowment of Whig professors at Oxford and Cambridge universities by George I; and the 1929 Macmillan Commission on finance and industry which recommended that the gold standard be replaced.[86] We know that what connects the Bank of England, the Rothschilds and the Foundation of Regius Professors is usury both because Pound tells us this directly when he says that he is taking us 'through the ages of usury' and because of outside information we can bring to the poem such as his source (Christopher Hollis's *The Two Nations*) or his own essays (e.g. 'A Visiting Card'). There is no way, however, that we could – purely from the evidence provided and by only the method of inductive reasoning – conclude that these three institutions all have the same usurious principles in common. They are, after all, separated by more than one and a half centuries of history! Thus Pound arraigns these individuals in his imaginary court and keeps asking 'will any jury convict 'um?' The answer of course is 'no' but the lack of evidence for a conviction is itself evidence of a conspiracy to 'spread lies' and ensure that the '"general public"' not see what is '"against their interest"'. Merely stating the question ensures a verdict of guilty in this imaginary court. Thus while Pound meticulously compiles evidence for the prosecution he can also be deliberately careless about the facts. '[H]ell knows which Roth-schild/1861, '64 or there sometime' he tells us in this canto while in his later war-time essay, 'A Visiting Card' the same letter is dated 25 June 1863.[87] It does not much matter which Rothschild wrote the letter nor when since merely mentioning the family name is sufficiently damning. Earlier in the canto Pound refers to Max Beerbohm's drawings 'an'/ one w'ich fer oBviOus reasons has/never been published'[88] but he never tells us these reasons. Innuendo supplies, in other words, what inductive reason fails to provide.

The evidence presented by Pound in this and other cantos has a dual status. Towards the end of the canto he refers to

> 1527. Thereafter art thickened. Thereafter design went to hell,
> Thereafter barocco, thereafter stone-cutting desisted.
> 'Hic nefas' (narrator) 'commune sepulchrum.'
>
> 19 years on this case/first case. I have set down part of
> The Evidence.[89]

Pound never informs us of the precise significance of 1527 although we know from his reference to Martin Luther immediately before this passage that it has something to do with the Reformation. Thus Protestantism – which he speculates elsewhere 'may have sprung from nothing but pro-usury politics'[90] – was both Pound's 'first case' and the 'first case' of usury in European history. However, just prior to this passage Pound has located 'usura' during the reign of Antoninus in the second century AD. In fact the 'first case' of usury could have been during Antoninus' reign, the Reformation, or any of the other historical periods analysed in the canto. The 'first case' of usury is something which can be known both historically since it is a cause which produces knowable effects, and imaginatively since it is an endlessly repeatable myth. When we inductively trace the economic ills of contemporary society back to an original cause such as 1527 or 1694 we end up receding into a kind of debased mythopoeisis or innuendo. After all, what *did* happen in 1527? Where are the documents which support Pound's claim that the founders of the Bank of England were involved in a massive economic conspiracy? The dates 1527 and 1694 are historically precise and yet also empty of empirical content. Alternatively, however, what would otherwise be an unbelievable myth – that our current woes are the result of some original sin of usury committed long ago – becomes more credible when bolstered by an enormous and heterogeneous 'phalanx of particulars'. Myth and empiricism are entangled and mutually supportive.

It is appropriate, then, that the canto finishes both with a flurry of new evidence and the insistent repetition of courtroom rhetoric:

> FIVE million youths without jobs
> four million adult illiterates
> 15 million 'vocational misfits', that is with small chance for jobs
> NINE million persons annual, injured in preventable industrial accidents
> One hundred thousand violent crimes. The Eunited States ov America
> 3rd year of the reign of F. Roosevelt, signed F. Delano, his uncle.
> CASE for the prosecution. That is one case, minor case
> in the series/Eunited States of America, a.d. 1935
> England a worse case, France under a foetor of regents.
> 'Mr Cummings wants Farley's job' headline in current paper.[91]

The main 'poetic' device of *The Cantos*, juxtaposition, is, as Frye observes, a form of implicit metaphor that does without the word 'is'.[92] However Pound's juxtaposition or collage often degenerates into a form of repetition which resembles the rhetoric of propaganda. Very little new meaning is created, at least as far as I can see, either by the juxtaposition of Paterson's dictum, Rothchild's letter, and the references to the Foundation of Regius Professors and the Macmillan Commission or by this barrage of evidence which concludes the canto. Significantly, Pound seems unable to terminate. The third last line would be a natural place to end but then it is as though more evidence springs to his mind, and evidence of such a weighty kind that it can only be referred to in the most general terms. The tone becomes more urgent, even frantic. If you think these crime and unemployment figures are bad, Pound says, then what about England? what about France? And then as though realising that he has moved away from the particular, Pound concludes with a reference that manages to be both obsessively specific and grandly conspiratorial. Mr Cummings was the US Attorney General and Farley the Postmaster General. Does Pound simply mean that the political aspirations of a man like Cummings are irrelevant, even immorally so, in such an economic climate as Terrell suggests?[93] Or is he hinting at something darker? For the paranoid imagination, everything is the product of both a simple cause and mysterious influences. Thus there must always be more and more evidence even while the necessarily limited evidence presented is always conclusive. The case for the prosecution has been made after the first page or so of the canto and yet Pound continues to amass evidence during the rest of this canto and in those which succeed it. In one of his radio broadcasts, he asks his listeners

just WHICH of you are free from Jew influence? Just which political and business groups are free from JEW influence, or, bujayzus, from JEW control? Who holds the mortgage? Who is the dominating director? Just which Jew has asked what Jew to nominate which assemblyman who is in debt to WHOM? And which whom is indebted to Jewry, or dependent on credits which he can not get without the connivance of Jewry? Just which college or university will distinguish itself by adding to its history courses a course in the study of chewisch history, and the Fuggers, and the effects of Jewsury and of usury on the history of Europe during the past thousand years?[94]

The questions could go on for ever because 'Jewsury' is everywhere and yet invisible at the same time, a direct cause of all ills and a nebulous influence. Like many paranoids, Pound sees the world as both a system of simple causal relations and unfathomably dark forces.

This dual aspect of 'usura' as both signified and signifier has not always been recognised by Pound's critics. For example while Hugh Kenner describes 'usura' as a 'synecdoche' for 'the separation of wealth from living processes',[95] Chace replies that this ignores

the truly radical and mechanical nature of his beliefs. It is to mitigate his unqualified and unmistakable contention that the charging of excessive interest is at the very root of all cultural collapse. Pound's poetry does not gain its power through the manipulation of connotative elements. It is entirely of the surface; it speaks and does not suggest.[96]

But Kenner and Chace are in a sense both right: 'usura' is both a metaphor and a literal first cause. In Canto 51, Usura is figured as Geryone, the monster on whose back Dante and Virgil descend down to the Eight Circle where are the shades of Usurers:

> circling in eddying air; in a hurry;
> the 12: close eyed in the oily wind
> these were the regents; and a sour song from the folds of his belly
> sang Geryone; I am the help of the aged;
> I pay men to talk peace;
> Mistress of many tongues; merchant of chalcedony
> I am Geryone twin with usura.[97]

Suitably, Geryone does not speak honestly and directly but in 'many tongues'. The antithesis of such language is Pound's description just before this passage of how to make and use the two trout fishing flies, the Blue Dun and Granham. Lifted from *The Cantos*, these eighteen lines of 'poetry' could presumably be used by an angler who had never otherwise read a line of poetry. The companion to this canto, Canto 45, combines poetry and prose, the figurative and literal, in an equally striking way. Canto 45 concludes:

> Usura rusteth the chisel
> It rusteth the craft and the craftsman
> It gnaweth the thread in the loom
> None learneth to weave gold in her pattern;
> Azure hath a canker by usura; cramoisi is unbroidered
> Emerald findeth no Memling
> Usura slayeth the child in the womb
> It stayeth the child in the womb
> It stayeth the young man's courting
> It hath brought palsey to bed, lyeth
> between the young bride and her bridegroom
>   CONTRA NATURAM
> They have brought whores for Eleusis

Corpses are set to banquet
at behest of usura.

N.B. Usury: A charge for the use of purchasing power, levied without regard to production; often without regard to the possibilities of production. (Hence the failure of the Medici bank.)[98]

With its archaisms, biblical parallelisms, euphonious repetitions, and lack of fragmentation, this is the most 'poetic' of the cantos. However its analytical listing of the effects of usury also resembles the discursive prose of a medieval sermon and the definition of usury with which it concludes is one of the most prosaic passages of *The Cantos*. Indeed, the distinctively Poundian *frisson* of this ending is the result of its startling juxtaposition of poetry with prose, of the medieval banquet of death with the definition of a modern economics textbook. The final surprise of the canto is its addendum about the failure of the Medici bank, or its abrupt transition from a transhistorical abstract definition to an historical particular. Suddenly, the gap between universal and particular, cause and effect, is telescoped. 'A charge for the use of purchasing power, levied without regard to production' is what caused an Italian bank during the mid-eighteenth century to fail![99] It is also, according to the rest of the canto, what prevents houses, paintings and bread to be well made; it is what keeps the stonecutter from his stone, the weaver from his loom, wool from coming to market; and it is what keeps young men from courting and children from being born. As Pound's list grows we become aware that while usury directly affects specific people and specific practices its malevolent influence also seems to be everywhere. The canto could potentially go on for ever since there is no end to the effects of usury. Usura is both distant from its effects, as the vehicle of a metaphor is distant from its tenor, and therefore applicable to an enormous array of circumstances, and the direct, immediate cause of specific cultural and social practices. Indeed much of the material and many of the phrases of this canto are repeated with only slight differences somewhat later in Canto 51 and then again in 'Addendum for C'. The canto summarises what has come before and yet the repetition which lies at its heart keeps sounding for the rest of the cantos. Thus with its repetitions of economic and political doxa and poetic juxtapositions of particulars,

Pound's poetry comes to resemble what it is meant to oppose, the abstractions and endlessly proliferating figures of rhetoric. His attempt to bridge the great divides between prose and poetry, reason and the imagination, lapses into paranoia, or the creation of a world which is both one of extremely mechanistic causal connections and one which is controlled by malevolent influences of a virtually magical kind.

IV

While Pound is never reluctant to name usury as the cause of both economic and political decay, he is often evasive when it comes to naming the Jews. Usury is partly an abstract economic principle which can be held accountable for any kind of malady whereas the influence of the Jews is of a more nebulous kind. Although his use of neologisms such as 'Jewsury' assert a direct connection between the Jews and usury he is also deliberately vague about the nature of this connection. In Canto 52, for example, he writes:

> Stinkschuld's sin drawing vengeance, poor yits paying for Stinkschuld paying for a few big jews' vendetta on goyim.[100]

Although it is probably impossible to unravel this tortuous chain of victimisation, it would seem that if 'Stinkschuld' pays for the 'few big jews' vendetta on goyim' then it must be the 'goyim' who victimise him. Like the Jews, the Gentiles are both the perpetrators and victims of usury.

Similarly in one of his often quoted radio broadcasts he disingenuously pleads:

> Don't start a pogrom, that is not an old style killing of small Jews. That system is no good whatever. Of course, if some man had a stroke of genius, and could start a pogrom up at the top . . . there might be something to say for it.[101]

Such 'a stroke of genius' would turn the world upside down, the powerful or those at the top becoming the victims of those at the bottom.

Another version of this 'small Jew'/'big Jew' opposition is Pound's distinction between orthodox and secular Jews:

> Usurers have no race. How long the whole Jewish people is to be sacrificial goat for the usurer, I know not . . . It cannot be too clearly known that no man can take usury and observe the law of the Hebrews. No orthodox Jew

can take usury without sin, as defined in his own scriptures. The Jew usurer being an outlaw runs against his own people, and uses them as his whipping boy . . . But the Jew is the usurer's goat. Whenever a usurer is spotted he scuttles down under the ghetto and leaves the plain man Jew to take the bullets and beatings.[102]

Presumably it would not be a Gentile usurer who 'scuttles down under the ghetto' when 'spotted' since only Jews live in the ghetto. 'Usurers have no race', therefore, only to the extent to which they have ceased to observe their own scriptures.

As these few examples indicate, Pound's antisemitism is frequently inseparable from his philosemitism. While the latter might seem to contradict the former (as well as my previous assertion that he demonises the Jews), Pound's figure of the 'small' Jew is an entirely passive victim and therefore one as antithetical to his 'pagan' tradition of heroic artists and patrons as his 'big' Jew. Yet what this split figure does indicate is that 'the Jews' are not only figures *of* ambivalence but figures who occasion ambivalence in the antisemitic writer. Much as misogynist discourse frequently divides the feminine into the 'good' and the 'bad', the pure and the polluted, so by splitting the Jews into the 'small' and the 'big' Pound is able to express the kind of ambivalence which Baumann argues is character-istic of Judaeophobia in general. Indeed it could be argued that most forms of prejudice, at least to the extent that they involve symbolic scapegoating of one kind or another, should be classified under the generic phenomenon of 'proteophobia'. As Derrida notes, the *pharmakos* or scapegoat was originally chosen from amongst the citizens of the city and was therefore not just a 'representative of an external threat or aggression' but also something '*constituted*, regu-larly granted its place by the community, chosen, kept, fed, etc., in the very heart of the inside'.[103]

Thus just as the Jews for Pound are both the main practitioners of usury and its victims, so they are both representatives of an evil which must be named and types of the innocent and anonymous masses who must always remain unnameable. From the Hell Cantos onwards, he frequently refers to individuals he wants to vilify using initials, ellipses and pseudonyms, partly because, as he writes in Canto 35, certain names must be 'respect[ed] because of the/law of libel'.[104] However Pound also uses such initials and ellipses in 'Addendum for C' (for Sassoon and Rothschild), a canto written after the outbreak of war and before his arrest and therefore at a moment when he presumably had nothing to fear from 'the law of libel'. By feigning self-censorship in this way, Pound is able to suggest that certain individuals have a power and influence so great that they can effectively resist naming or any process of casting-out. Alternatively his insistent habit of making references and allusions, often by means of nicknames, to valorised figures whom the reader is unlikely to know suggests that they possess not only an undeserved obscurity but some kind of mysterious power. Pound's heroes and villains double each other.

Of course such doubling could be attributed to Pound's 'paganism' or his attempt to renew the kinds of cultural values which are grounded in the ancient Greek scapegoat rituals described by Derrida. However while Satan might be a fallen angel (at least within certain Christian traditions), his banishment is irreversible and therefore represents a division of the sacred from the demonic which is more radical than the ancient Greeks' boundary between the inside and outside of the city. Pound's often noted habit of dividing the world into a series of manichean oppositions (such as industry/usury, polytheism/monotheism, Confucianism/Buddhism, Mussolini/Roosevelt or Churchill) is ethically absolutist and therefore more a parody of the ethical impluse which he attributes to 'the Jews' than a form of pagan renewal.

On the other hand the ambivalent relationship between these manichean oppositions is sufficiently strong, paradoxically, to allow Pound to accommodate the defeat of Mussolini to his economic and cultural 'system'. Mussolini as fascist 'hero' before his death becomes Mussolini the tragic scapegoat not just after his death but after the war. Thus during his confinement in St Elizabeth's Hospital after the war, Pound maintained or established new relationships with various racist and antisemitic organisations and individuals. When he arrived back from Italy in 1958 he gave the fascist salute to assembled reporters; three years later he was photographed at the head of a neo-Fascist parade.[105] The cantos written after the defeat of Italian fascism reflect these commitments. It is true that there are, as Pound's defenders point out, confessions of failure and attempts at contrition, notably in the Pisan Cantos, but these are also always evasions of moral responsibility and denials of symbolic violence. Typically, Pound either diminishes the extent of his errors or projects them on to others. One of the most astounding of these was his confession to Allen Ginsberg in 1967 that 'the worst mistake I made was that stupid, suburban prejudice of anti-Semitism',[106] a confession which not only raises the issue of what real or 'urban' prejudice would be but one which implicitly diminishes the antisemite's target. More than two decades earlier he had written in Canto 76

> L.   P.   gli onesti
>   J'ai eu pitié des autres
> probablement pas assez, and at moments that suited my own
> convenience'[107]

Carpenter observes that '[i]f "des autres" were taken to mean those who were *not* "gli onesti" ("the honest ones") – that is, the rest of humanity, he would be accusing himself simply of a failure of charity towards the great mass of flawed and somewhat *dis*honest humanity'.[108] It might be added, however, that if Pound includes the Jews amongst such flawed humanity then he has labelled them as dishonest but if he does not include them then they are beneath what little pity he has. Then again his pity might be only for 'gli onesti', or L. and P., the arrested leaders of the Vichy government, Pierre Laval and Henri Petain.[109] If so then Pound would only be sympathising with and excusing those in a similar predicament to himself.

Pound also and famously admonishes himself in Canto 81 to 'Pull down thy vanity' but this consists only in what was 'not done,/ . . . in the diffidence that faltered'.[110] But as Peter D'Epiro argues, Pound might also be addressing others as well as himself in this rather Old Testament style sermon. His plea much later at the end of his writing career is more moving:

> Let the Gods forgive what I
>   have made
> Let those I love try to forgive
>   what I have made.[111]

But at the risk of being moralistic and therefore repeating Pound, it might be observed that it is not from the Gods or those he loves that he should be asking forgiveness.

Nor does Pound, at least in *The Cantos*, renounce Mussolini. The Pisan Cantos begin defiantly:

> The enormous tragedy of the dream in the peasant's bent
> shoulders
> Manes! Manes was tanned and stuffed,
> Thus Ben and la Clara *a Milano*
>   by the heels at Milano
> That maggots shd/eat the dead bullock

DIOGONOS, Δ_γονος, but the twice crucified
    where in history will you find it?
Yet say this to the Possum: a bang, not a whimper,
    with a bang not with a whimper,
To build the city of Dioce whose terraces are the colour of stars.[112]

Pound is extraordinarily insistent about the sacrificial nature of
Mussolini's death. Mussolini ('Ben') is Dionysus, a sacrificed God,
who is 'twice crucified' because he was first shot by the Partisans and
then hung by his feet; he is Manes, the Persian philosopher whose
crucified body was stuffed with hay; he is in the opening line a figure
of 'tragedy', possibly the victim of those sacrificial rites out of which
Greek tragedy developed; and his life ended with 'a bang, not a
whimper', not like 'Possum'['s] or Eliot's 'hollow men' but possibly
like the 'Mistah Kurtz' referred to in Eliot's epigraph to *The Hollow
Men*, a figure whose death at the end of *Heart of Darkness* represents
both the end of barbarism and civilisation. Those who sacrificed
Mussolini are called 'maggots', a fascist name for the Partisans[113]
but one which might also refer to the Jews since they are elsewhere
obsessively associated with parasites.[114] This is supported by the fact
that the reference to Mussolini as a 'dead bullock' anticipates
Pound's references later in the canto to the 'goyim' as 'cattle' who
'go to saleable slaughter' because of the 'stimulant' of the 'yidd'.[115]
Thus as Casillo observes, 'the participants in violence are doubles
and hence potentially interchangeable as conquerors or victims'.[116]
Of course the interchangeable nature of the sacrificer/victim couple
was present even before the defeat of fascism: the Jews were
scapegoats and yet almost omnipotent; Mussolini was 'the Boss' and
yet vulnerable to their influence. However if the participants in this
violence are always interchangeable then the fall of 'the city of
Dioce' or Mussolini's fascist empire must also be reversible. 'To
build the city of Dioce' is an ambiguous line on which not just this
passage but the whole of the Pisan and later cantos hinge. The line
and sentence lacks a subject and primary verb. *Was* it Mussolini's
(and Pound's) ambition '[T]o build the city of Dioce' or *is* it Pound's
ambition to build this city? Was Mussolini hung by his heels because
he built, or attempted to build, 'the city of Dioce' in Italy or will his
sacrifice allow the creation of a new fascist empire? This passage and
the rest of the Pisan Cantos are certainly elegiac but they are also
defiant. 'I surrender neither the empire nor the temples plural/nor
the constitution nor yet the city of Dioce',[117] Pound asserts later in

the canto. The Pisan Cantos lament the death of Mussolini but like all or most elegies they also offer consolation. Mussolini's sacrificial death will also enable a new city of Dioce to be built.

The other sacrifice in the Pisan Cantos is, of course, Pound himself. In Canto 74, he refers on two occasions to three of his other inmates as 'Barabbas and two thieves', implicitly identifying himself with Christ.[118] (Nearly twenty years later he was still describing himself as 'being "crucified for an idea"' in an interview with Donald Hall.)[119] These thieves are excused since 'if theft be the main motive in government/in a large way/there will certainly be minor purloinments'.[120] The crimes of some of the other inmates, however, are more serious:

> and Till was hung yesterday
> for murder and rape with trimmings   plus Cholkis
> plus mythology, thought he was Zeus ram or another one[121]

And a few lines later Till is associated with Odysseus or 'No Man' just as the sacrificial victim of the scapegoating rituals described by Girard is 'a person who comes from elsewhere'.[122]

Of course after the death of Mussolini, the city of Dioce can only be rebuilt 'in the mind indestructible'[123] and Pound can only 'dream the Republic'.[124] In *Drafts and Fragments* he confesses

> that I lost my center
> fighting the world.
> The dreams clash
> And are shattered –
> and that I tried to make a paradiso
> terrestre.[125]

Bernstein writes that '[i]t is Pound's most cherished dream of all, the historical reinstatement of an earthly paradise that is here labelled the seed of all his errors'[126] but in fact Pound does not actually renounce the idea of a *paradiso terrestre;* he only admits that the attempt to create one failed. 'Muss.[olini], wrecked for an error', he says in Canto 116 without specifying what this 'error' was.[127] In the Pisan Cantos he had written that some of Mussolini's

> words still stand uncancelled
> 'Presente!'
> And merrda for the monopolists
>   The bastardly lot of 'em
> Put down the slave trade, made the desert to yield
> and menaced the loan swine.[128]

H. Finer's *Mussolini's Italy*, published in 1935, explains the significance of 'Presente':

For members who have died in great exploits . . . When the roll is called, and the unbreathing lips remain silent, his circle of Fascist comrades reply, 'Presente!'[129]

Dead but still 'presente', Mussolini's sacrificial death keeps the 'dream [of] the Republic' alive. Since the roles of conqueror and victim are always reversible, the fascist cycle of violence can never end. Except in silence, which Pound chose for the last years of his life.

CHAPTER 3

'Neither Living nor Dead': T. S. Eliot and the uncanny

I

In his conclusion to *The Use of Poetry and the Use of Criticism*, T. S. Eliot asks

Why, for all of us, out of all that we have heard, seen, felt, in a lifetime, do certain images recur, charged with emotion, rather than others? The song of one bird, the leap of one fish, at a particular place and time, the scent of one flower, an old woman on a German mountain path, six ruffians seen through an open window playing cards at night at a small French railway junction where there was a water-mill . . .[1]

This list proceeds from the familiar, from images we have all seen, towards the unfamiliar, an image which we know, because of its specificity, only Eliot has. Yet while Eliot tantalises us with a personal confession he does not tell us that these ruffians were men he actually saw once at a small French railway junction. As personal as this image clearly is it also seems to be one *we* have all seen. These mysterious ruffians, as though in a dream, seem vaguely familiar.

Such charged images occur often in Eliot's writing: a man asks another whether the corpse he planted last year in a suburban garden has begun to sprout; another keeps seeing two people walking ahead up a white road when he can count only one; a speaker recites what is a familiar nursery rhyme but for its substitution of a prickly pear for a mulberry bush. With all these images, something unsettling or even menacing seems also somehow familiar. Such images 'may have symbolic value', Eliot tells us after mentioning the six ruffians, 'but of what we cannot tell, for they come to represent the depths of feeling into which we cannot peer'.[2]

According to Freud, 'the uncanny [*unheimlich*] is something which is secretly familiar [*heimlich*], which has undergone repression and

71

then returned from it'.[3] The canny, familiar, or *heimlich* is, Freud argues, the 'animistic stage' in both individuals and cultures, and, once repressed, it can only recur as something frightening.[4] Thus the corpse in the suburban garden might be a god from a primitive fertility rite, buried by bourgeois modernity but resurfacing after the violence of the Great War; or the apparition walking up the road could be read as some kind of double, a product according to Freud of the 'primary narcissism which dominates the mind of the child and of primitive man', something which was once 'an assurance of immortality' but has reversed itself into 'the uncanny harbinger of death';[5] or the song about the prickly pear might once have been an ancient fertility dance but is now, after the repression of centuries of secular culture, something bleak and arid. Indeed, as I shall argue, these uncanny images or moments when the repressed returns are not just, as James Longenbach has ably demonstrated, one of the main themes of Eliot's writing but the central experience to which all his poetry reacts.[6] In part what makes Eliot's poetry so powerful is its ability to register both the *anomie* consequent upon personal and cultural repression as well as that moment 'after the collapse of religion' when, as Freud says paraphrasing Heine, 'the gods turned into demons'.[7] Or, in more historical terms, Eliot's poetry is a reaction to that moment when the gap between an aesthetic modernity which in part harbours the archaic and pre-modern and the other modernity becomes so great that they collapse into each other. The return of the repressed or that moment when id and ego, primitive and modern become conflated is also therefore the moment of what might be described (at least from Eliot's point of view) as a kind of diabolical avant-garde.

This uncanniness is expressed in Eliot's earliest original poems as a '*dédoublement* of personality'.[8] In the most powerful and original of these poems – 'The Love Song of J. Alfred Prufrock', 'Portrait of a Lady', 'Rhapsody on a Windy Night' – we can discern the same basic structure: a male speaker in the presence of a woman becomes split between an active social self who resists the attractions of the woman and a passive observer consumed with romantic longing. A similar structure is discernible in the other poems from Eliot's first book, *Prufrock*, but it is only partially realised. In 'Cousin Nancy' the figure of the Suffragist and proto-flapper, 'Miss Nancy Ellicott', is tentatively approved by her aunts and presumably frowned upon by 'Matthew and Waldo, guardians of the faith'[9] but of course there is no male speaker to interact with this modern woman. 'Hysteria' and 'Conversation Galante' are dramatic monologues of sorts but both of the male speakers are so overwhelmed, and in the case of 'Hysteria' virtually consumed, by their respective female interlocutors that they are unable to assume the role of a detached observer. 'La Figlia Che Piange' does dramatise this psychological doubling in the form of a self who turns away from a beloved and another troubled self who observes himself doing so but this poem, which is placed at the end of the collection, is Eliot's most conventionally lyrical because there is no further split, or at least a very underdeveloped one, between the male speaker and author. The rest of the minor poems from *Prufrock* combine both these attributes, that is they are partial dramatic monologues in which the doubling of the speaker's personality is not fully developed. 'Morning at the Window' and 'Preludes' are, of course, conventional lyrics in which the authorial presence is only partially divided, in the former between the 'I' who is 'aware of the damp souls of housemaids' and the self who observes the more violent apparition of the disembodied 'aimless smile' and 'Twisted faces'[10] and in the latter between the speaker who says 'I' and the speaker who refers to himself as 'you'. (The use of the second person itself dramatises this division since it can be regarded as combining the first and third persons.) The remaining poems are all partial dramatic monologues in which there is either no detached romantic self ('The Boston Evening Transcript') or it is projected on to a separate character, the footman 'Holding the second housemaid on his knees' in 'Aunt Helen'[11] or the priapic and eponymous Mr Apollinax.

The three long major poems of *Prufrock*, however, all extend this doubling of the self to its logical culmination. Confronted by a woman who is both threatening and desirable, the male speakers of these poems split into a defensive and repressed social self and a desiring asocial self, a split which in part accounts for their ambivalent tone, one which is both 'classical' and 'romantic' at the same time. In 'Prufrock' there are 'you and I', a 'you' who meets the women in the room and an 'I' who either remembers or anticipates himself doing so. In contrast, the man who visits the woman in 'Portrait' speaks in the first person like the self who loses self-possession when he hears a street piano or suddenly desires to metamorphose into a series of animals. 'Rhapsody' is different again since the self who observes the menacing woman in the 'light of the door'[12] or imagines the moon as some kind of prostitute has been projected on to the muttering street-lamp although the other self, the one possessed by memory and desire speaks, like the romantic selves of the other poems, in the first person.

There are other similarities between these poems. When these men interact socially with women, they are defensive to the point of paranoia. The women are all perceived as threatening and yet nothing they do or say is menacing in any objective sense. The lady in 'Portrait' who regrets that they have 'not developed into friends'[13] might just as plausibly be confessing her vulnerability as making an accusation; the women in 'Prufrock' might be kindly trying to ease an awkward young man into some degree of social comfort rather than attempting an interrogation; and a woman hesitating in the light of a door could be regarding the stranger passing with harmless curiosity rather than hostility. Nevertheless, these men seem to fear something which borders almost on castration. The speakers of 'Rhapsody' and 'Prufrock' are fixated on the eyes of women, in the former on an eye which 'Twists like a crooked pin' and in the latter on the eyes which leave the speaker 'formulated, sprawling on a pin',[14] a reversal of Freud's somewhat literal claim that 'anxiety about one's eyes, the fear of going blind, is often enough a substitute for the dread of being castrated'.[15] The woman in 'Portrait' says 'you do not know/What life is, you who hold it in your hands' while, the speaker observes, 'Slowly twisting the lilac stalks'[16] as though she were appropriating some kind of phallic life force. Indeed, the women in these poems are all rather masculinized and Prufrock is the only speaker to meet any men and then, apart from the 'lonely men' he views from a distance, it is 'the eternal Footman',[17] a personification of omnipotent death, certainly, but also at the literal level a social inferior. There is also, incidentally, a footman in 'Aunt Helen', but he only dares to hold 'the second housemaid on his knees'[18] after the impressive Aunt who employs him has died and the 'elderly', trembling waiter in 'Hysteria' cannot rescue the man from the woman's cavernous throat.

In contrast to these defensive egos, the asocial selves either welcome being embraced by their fluid, feminised surroundings, like the Prufrock who feels muzzled by the yellow fog and smoke as though it were an affectionate cat, or desire to be polymorphous like the speaker in 'Portrait'. Furthermore, the socialised selves tend to perceive women as complete physical beings even when fixating on their eyes while the romantic selves attach themselves to partial objects, to arms, hair, voices and smells.

All this might suggest that these buried selves are unfamiliar and the social selves conventionally familiar but this is not the case. When Prufrock refers to himself in the second person, he has already defamiliarised the self which is otherwise extremely prim and predictable. The voice which expresses such distaste for women in 'Rhapsody' does not even emanate from the speaker's skull and the man in 'Portrait' who can be seen 'any morning in the park/ Reading the comics and the sporting page' relishes the sensational and lurid – aristocrats, actresses, foreigners, murders, and bank defaulters.[19] Furthermore this last hears a 'tom-tom' hammering in his head as though he were Marlowe up the Congo and he feels 'like one who smiles, and turning shall remark/Suddenly, his expression in a glass' as though he had suddenly met his doppelgänger while taking tea.[20]

In contrast, the romantic self, when not daydreaming during the afternoon's banalities, believes it

> must borrow every changing shape
> To find expression . . . dance, dance
> Like a dancing bear,
> Cry like a parrot, chatter like an ape.[21]

But the bear has been trained to dance, the parrot might be crying some phrase it has been taught and the ape sounds like someone at an afternoon tea. Similarly, Prufrock's sudden regret that he 'should have been a pair of ragged claws/Scuttling across the floors of silent seas',[22] or a primitive creature in a world prior to human occupation, nevertheless seizes on those parts of the crab which are used for nothing other than defence against other creatures. In other words, the familiar self is strange and consumed with violent or asocial fantasies whereas the primitive self which metamorphoses into various totemic animals can be also, paradoxically, socialised and even familiar. If the unfamiliar or *unheimlich* was once familiar or *heimlich* then it would also follow that the familiar or *heimlich* may once have been repressed or *unheimlich*.

A similar reversal characterises the speakers' sense of time. The Prufrock who has 'measured out . . . [his] life with coffee spoons'[23] is not the active Prufrock whose temporal dimension is the clock-time of social existence but the passive, meditative self. Alternatively, the time occupied by Prufrock in the room with the women is discontinuous, swollen by anticipation, climactic. This Prufrock might have 'wept and fasted, wept and prayed'[24] as though he were some kind of ascetic, but these activities – mourning, fasting and prayer – are all located within sacred time. And while many readers have been puzzled by Prufrock's age, the man who meets the older women behaves like a quite young man, possibly of about the same age as Eliot when he wrote the poem, someone still growing out of the awkwardness and prudery of adolescence, while the other Prufrock is presumably much older because he is not far from needing to roll the bottoms of his trousers, one of the necessities of getting smaller in old age.[25] Of course the ego or social self is only formed at a later stage of psychological development and can therefore be described as young but this nevertheless reverses the romantic association of childhood with innocence and desire.

Despite Eliot's confession many years later to a 'temporary conversion to Bergsonism',[26] it is impossible to read these early poems in any straightforward Bergsonian fashion. The street-lamp in 'Rhapsody' does intone the divisions of clock-time while the male streetwalker feels 'the floors of memory/And all its clear relations,/ Its divisions and precisions'[27] dissolve as though the mechanical time of *la durée* were being dissolved by the creative, continuous time of *l'étendu* but what 'The memory throws up high and dry' is

> A crowd of twisted things;
> A twisted branch upon the beach
> Eaten smooth, and polished
> As if the world gave up
> The secret of its skeleton,
> Stiff and white.
> A broken spring in a factory yard,
> Rust that clings to the form that the strength has left
> Hard and curled and ready to snap.[28]

These are partial objects, separate from each other and, unlike the interpenetrating totalities of *l'étendu*, commonplace, familiar, and, above all, dead. Unlike Bergson, Eliot does not prefer one kind of temporality over the other since the selves which occupy the temporal realm of *l'étendu* are routinised, dead and empty while the selves which are constituted and trapped by *la durée* have a peculiar energy and life. Indeed while a doubling of the psyche suggests a differentiation between two levels of subjectivity, these selves are also oddly similar. Which self tells us that 'In the room the women come and go/Talking of Michelangelo'?[29] Since this is spoken in the present tense it could be the Prufrock who actively engages with the women but the languid droning of the rhyme seems more appropriate for the man who remembers and anticipates the time measured by coffee spoons. Significantly, the two occasions when these lines are spoken are both moments of transition, the first occurring as Prufrock moves into the fog and the second when he steps out of the fog into a social world. If the fogbound Prufrock seems somehow familiar and the tea-sipping Prufrock strange then these two selves, like mirror images, are both alike and dissimilar.

Such psychological doubling cannot be restricted to just the monologists although not all of the major early poems are equally uncanny in this respect. 'Portrait' is often described as Jamesian, in part because of its attention to the nuances of polite society whereas 'Rhapsody', with its exploration of involuntary memory, is Eliot's most Bergsonian poem. In Prufrock, however, the women combine the characteristics of the *salonnière* in 'Portrait' and the street women of 'Rhapsody', being both society women and women who are met after a journey through streets of 'one-night cheap hotels'.[30] The cityscape is partly genteel Harvard and partly the seedier suburbs of Boston overlayed with the Montparnasse of Charles-Louis Philippe. However, in combining these kinds of women, the poem is able to suggest that they are both in part projections of Prufrock's imagination. The women in 'Prufrock' are just as present, just as threatening and alluring but they barely speak, unlike the lady from 'Portrait', and, unlike the street women in 'Rhapsody', they are barely described. They are like ghosts, beings who are strange and other and yet as emanations of the mind also familiar.

Because there is no sense of a reality against which to measure the extent of Prufrock's paranoia (or even to judge for that matter whether he is paranoid), the distance between speaker and implied author is similarly indeterminate. Is Prufrock simply absurd as his name might suggest or is he one of the young 'men of 1914', to use Wyndham Lewis's phrase, who would forge a masculinist modernism? The answer of course is that he is both these people, both an abject being and the image of his implied author. From what position could the implied author judge his character? To play ego to his character's id, censoring Prufrock's asocial and violent desires is a role Prufrock has already adopted towards himself just as he has also played id to his own repressed and prudish ego. The doubling of the character's personality cannot be contained but must spread to its relationships with others, including other characters, the implied author and even the reader. Of course such doubleness is the basis of any dramatic monologue since the relationship between implied author and speaker is much like that between a ventriloquist and his dummy. However while there is always something uncanny about any act of ventriloquy, about the animation of something dead and the silence of someone who is alive, Eliot refuses to mount any resistance to this in 'Prufrock'. The poem is, therefore, the logical culmination of the nineteenth dramatic monologue, a poem which fully utilises this form's uncanny potential while, by dissolving the distinction between speaker and implied author which is its structural basis, terminating it as a literary form.

Of course Eliot was to write another substantial dramatic monologue, 'Gerontion', but this poem is considered by some critics to be aesthetically problematic and even, because of its antisemitism, morally reprehensible.[31] The poem's somewhat unsatisfactory formal characteristics and its general tone of unresolved animus are, I think, related. Unlike the speakers of the previous dramatic monologues, Gerontion is not primarily engaged by one or more women. It is true that history is personified as a woman with 'many cunning passages, contrived corridors/And issues' whose 'giving famishes the craving'.[32] The figure of history in this passage is like the woman in 'Hysteria', a kind of memory of the mother's body which has returned as something uncanny not because, as with the *vagina dentata*-like woman in 'Hysteria', it desires rather than is desirable, but because it refuses desire.[33] However this is only one of several passages and for the rest of the poem Gerontion is primarily occupied with the boy who reads to him, 'the Jew' who owns his house, the ghosts which haunt it, and others. Like the selves of the earlier dramatic monologues, all these figures have ambivalent characteristics: the boy distracts the old and feeble Gerontion by reading to him but this is an activity often done by a parent or older pedagogue; 'the Jew' owns Gerontion's house and yet he does not live in it, he is a cosmopolitan figure associated with several major European cities and yet he 'squats on the window sill', on a place which is neither inside nor outside the house, neither above nor below, in a characteristically 'primitive' or non-Western posture; Mr Silvero has 'caressing hands' and yet his walking 'all night in the next room' suggests a troubled person; Hakagawa, 'bowing among the Titians' could be according respect or making a mockery of European art; Madame de Tornquist moves or 'shifts' candles but in a 'dark room'; and Fräulein von Kulp, 'Who turned in the hall, one hand on the door' might have been leaving or entering the room.[34] With the exception of 'the Jew', these characters are all moving or doing something, and even 'the Jew['s]' cosmopolitanism suggests restlessness and his squatting posture an interim position or the activity of excretion. Gerontion, by contrast, does nothing and barely desires.

If we think of the house as Gerontion's mind, then he is its ego and those ghostly presences who conduct what appears to be a black mass in its rooms, and the primitive, possibly infantile Jew, are those who usurp the ego's sovereignty. Thus the main difference between 'Gerontion' and the previous dramatic monologues is that the speaker's ambivalence towards the feminine object of desire has shifted towards the masculine non-social self. In the earlier poems, there is a balanced or even *dédoublement* of personality, neither self being inherently more ridiculous than the other. However, in 'Gerontion' the asocial self is now so alien that it is played by *other* characters and the social self, no matter how feeble and risible, is the only locus of speech. Thus the ghostly figures who return to haunt the self are all in some way culturally 'other': Jewish, Eastern, eastern European, or southern European but not Greek like Gerontion. The one exception is the boy but then he is a figure so clearly benign or neutral in a cast of quite dubious, even malign, characters as to provide almost a form of psychological relief.

All the other poems from Eliot's second collection have a similar triangular structure to 'Gerontion' and the dramatic monologues from *Prufrock* except that most dispense with the first-person speaker. Like the women from the earlier poems, nearly all have female figures who possess ambivalent characteristics. Some, such as Griskin and Princess Volupine, are *femmes fatales* while others, such as the heartbroken Aspatia in 'Sweeney Erect' or the nightingales who sing when Agamemnon is murdered in 'Sweeney Among the Nightingales', are paired with women who possess opposite characteristics, in the former Doris, Sweeney's good-time girl, and in the latter Rachel and the woman in the Spanish cape, nightingales in the sense of prostitutes. The one apparent exception amongst the poems in English is 'Mr Eliot's Sunday Morning Service', but here none of the protagonists are conventionally male, the bees carrying the pollen from the male stamen to the female pistil as the self-castrated Origen and Mr Eliot pass on the word of God the Father to the feminised masses, and even Sweeney, usually considered to be a quintessentially manly fellow, is shifting in his bath from 'ham to ham' as one of his girlfriends might do.[35]

What distinguishes the poems which have troubled readers with their prejudice from the others in this collection is not, then, their female characters but the relationships between their male protagonists.[36] Like 'Gerontion', there is a disequilibrium in these poems – 'Burbank with a Baedeker: Bleistein with a Cigar', 'A Cooking Egg', and 'Sweeney Among the Nightingales' – between the male protagonists. By contrast authorial sympathy is evenly balanced in the other poems: the eponymous hippopotamus is absurd and yet ascends to heaven while 'the True Church remains below/Wrapt in the old miasmal mist'; some men are compelled by Griskin's vulgar 'promise of pneumatic bliss' and yet 'our lot', those who resist her charms, 'crawls between dry ribs/To keep our metaphysics warm'; the bees and Origin are equally 'philoprogenitive', Sweeney and Mr Eliot equally absurd.[37] A possible exception might be 'Sweeney Erect' and yet Sweeney and Doris are quite likeable and Aspatia is rather melodramatic. Aspatia's lost lover is of course absent from the poem, but might we not read the poem's obscure allusions as something of a scholarly parody and therefore a parody of the reader who identifies with this woman and takes her grief too seriously?

However in the other poems not only is there more authorial sympathy for the social selves than for the asocial or alien selves – for Burbank rather than Bleistein, the 'I' of 'A Cooking Egg' rather than '[t]he red-eyed scavengers', Agamemnon rather than Sweeney and his friends, Gerontion rather than the aliens who occupy his house – but the former are always passive and lacking the violent desires which characterised the social selves of the other poems from both *Prufrock* and *Poems* whereas the latter are threatening and without the passivity which characterised the romantic, asocial selves of the other poems. The social selves are never unfamiliar whereas the various alien figures of these four poems are both unfamiliar and familiar. Whereas in the other poems both selves are uncanny, or we cannot distinguish between them, or the social self seems to be more uncanny, in these poems only the alien selves possess any uncanny characteristics.

There is a double movement in these poems. In 'Burbank with a

Baedeker: Bleistein with a Cigar' the 'lustreless protrusive eye' which '[s]tares from the protozoic slime/At a perspective of Canaletto' belongs to a primitive and therefore undifferentiated animal but it also confuses or conflates the primitive and civilised. Possibly as a consequence, these lines are soon followed by what must be the most vicious lines of Eliot's published *oeuvre*: 'The rats are underneath the piles./The Jew is underneath the lot'.[38] Prejudice issues from confusion but prejudice in turn produces anxiety: '[t]he Jew' may have been cast safely 'underneath the lot' but it is the mere thickness of a floor which separates the merchants trading in the Rialto from the rats 'underneath the piles'. Similarly when the speaker in 'A Cooking Egg' who has previously said 'I shall not want' four times confesses to having wanted 'To eat with Pipit behind the screen', this self who desires familiar earthly pleasures is suddenly renounced with the lines which come immediately after, about the '[t]he red-eyed scavengers'. However these 'scavengers' are creeping/*From Kentish town and Golder's Green*'[39] (my emphasis) *to* somewhere, presumably towards 'us'. Just as the speaker's ambiguous renunciations of earthly pleasures are succeeded by a capitulation to nostalgic desire, so the speaker's symbolic casting of the residents of Kentish Town and Golder's Green into the realm of scavengers is inseparable from his anxiety that they are moving towards and therefore possibly into his own neighbourhood. A few lines into 'Gerontion' 'the Jew' is identified as the 'owner' of Gerontion's 'decayed house' to be never mentioned again but he is succeeded by a series of considerably more ambiguous characters whose existence in turn can only raise further suspicions about the house's owner. In 'Sweeney Among the Nightingales' 'Rachel *née* Rabinovitch' is reduced to a feeding animal but '[s]he and the lady in the cape', although 'suspect' are only '*thought* to be in league' (my emphasis) and the man who '[t]herefore . . . [d]eclines the gambit' and leaves 'room' then 'reappears/Outside the window, leaning in'.[40] The revelation that Rachel's maiden name is Jewish does not reveal anything specific about the nature of her suspicious relationship to the mysterious 'lady in the cape' and the sinister 'man with heavy eyes[']' exit from the house only increases anxiety since by 'leaning in' the window he is now neither inside nor outside the house.

Thus if the naming of these Jews casts them into the realm of the 'other', it also results in them returning as frighteningly familiar figures who confuse the boundaries between self and 'other'. Alternatively, it is precisely their ambiguous characteristics which incite naming. Prejudice is succeeded by the uncanny, and the uncanny provokes further prejudice. As Anthony Julius argues, not only can antisemitism be a 'poet's inspiration', even 'muse', but it is possible that a poet such as Eliot can actually enliven the 'fatigued topoi' of antisemitic discourse.[41] The repressions of prejudice lead inevitably to ambiguity and the ambiguities of poetic language can in turn demand the certainties of prejudice.

Nevertheless Christopher Ricks's apparently contrary insight that Eliot's poetry undertakes 'the challenging double enterprise of inciting both shrewd suspicion and a suspicion of such shrewd suspicions' is no less elucidatory.[42] The lines which provoke the most prejudice – 'The rats are underneath the piles./The Jew is underneath the lot.'; 'The red-eyed scavengers are creeping/From Kentish Town and Golder's Green'; and 'Rachel *née* Rabinovitch/Tears at the grapes with murderous paws' – are not only different from the lines which surround them but also different from themselves. These lines quite clearly imply that Jews are not human and yet they also just as clearly imply that the boundary between the Gentile and Jewish is uncertain: the preposition 'underneath' implies that the Gentile might be supported by the Jewish, 'the Jews' of Golder's Green are moving towards 'us' and Rachel might be married to a gentile. Such uncertainty produces two apparently quite contradictory responses: either 'the Jews' are human or at least not inhuman or 'they' are, respectively, undermining, invading or infiltrating (by marriage) 'us'. The uncanniness of these lines both relieves their prejudice and inflames further prejudice while their prejudice both ruins and inspires their poetry. Thus Eliot's poetry or uncanniness can be at the same time both different from his prejudice, as Ricks implies, or, as Julius argues, indistinguishable from it.

In terms of structure, these Jews are both the named 'contents' of the poems and yet at the same time part of neither the poems' contents nor form. According to Pound's well-known account of the genesis of the quatrain poems

> At a particular date in a particular room, two authors . . . decided that the dilution of *vers libre* . . . had gone too far . . . Remedy prescribed 'Emaux et Camées' (or the Bay State Hymn Book). Rhyme and regular strophes.[43]

Thus there is an obvious discrepancy between the poems' form and content, between the austerity of their 'classical' and traditional quatrains and their disreputable, seedy contents. Indeed Pound's reference to the *Bay State Hymn Book* makes something of a joke of this discrepancy. No doubt it is also inflected by considerations of gender since the poet most responsible for this dilution according to Pound was a woman (and a lesbian at that), Amy Lowell. Nevertheless, it is precisely the austerity and concision of such stanzas which not only distinguishes them from their contents but which also allows them to be so promiscuously allusive. To consider only the matter of rhyme, the arrangement of words according to their sounds makes the reader aware of the discrepancy between form and content, of the way in which words which sound the same nevertheless have quite different signifieds and yet the spatial contiguity of these signifiers gives us permission to find and invent connections between their signifieds. 'Burbank with a Baedeker', for example, rhymes 'hotel' with 'fell', Bleistein's 'knees' with 'Viennese', 'protozoic slime' with the 'End of time', 'Piles' with the 'smiles' of the boatman, Princess Volupine's 'phthisic hand' with 'Sir Ferdinand', the 'pared' 'claws' of Venice with the 'seven laws'.[44] Doubtless pages could be spent teasing out the associations compelled by these rhymes. As is often observed, the constraints of a traditional verse form are also enabling. In these poems, the quatrain form allows Eliot to distance himself from the 'other' as 'content' but it is also what allows the 'other' as something which cannot be named, something which is both more and less than 'content' to invade the entire structure. Indeed with the exception of Ricks, what seems to worry most readers of these poems is not their rigid structure nor their exploitation of antisemitic stereotypes but precisely what Ricks calls their 'compulsive allusiveness',[45] lack of structure and political slipperiness. But both these aspects are related. Just as repression creates the uncanny, so the austerity of these poems' formal structure generates the menace of their uncertain allusions. Jews are the despised content of these poems but they are also what returns as the uncanny and the literary.

For whatever reason, this identification of Jews with the uncanny is found only in the poems from this second collection. There are antisemitic verses in the original drafts of Eliot's next book of poetry, *The Waste Land*, but these were not only discarded but among the least uncanny of his poetry. Unlike Pope's affectionate satire of Belinda in *The Rape of the Lock*, Eliot feels nothing but disgust for Fresca, her toilette the morning after Lady Kleinwarm's party consisting of labouring at the 'needful stool' while reading Samuel Richardson and disguising her 'hearty female stench' with French concoctions.[46] From the same section he also discarded the lines about the 'swarming life' or 'pavement toys' of London and those which, by specifying the Thames-daughter's lower-middle-class background, limit our potential identification with her.[47] As for the other deleted poems or lines, the most lamentable is 'Dirge' in which Bleistein reappears, unlike his namesake in 'Burbank with a Baedeker', 'Lower than the wharf rats dive',[48] beneath even the piles of the earlier poem and as a consequence almost entirely unrecognisable as a human being. There can be no uncanny return for Fresca and Bleistein from the depths into which Eliot has cast them.

The Waste Land, however, surpasses even Eliot's first collection because it exploits not just the potential uncanniness of one literary form, the dramatic monologue, but the uncanniness of literature in general, its simultaneous difference from and similarity to reality. This uncanniness is quite different from the kind of relationship which much Eliot criticism sees as pertaining in the poem between the literature of the past and the reality of the present. For example F. O. Matthiessen, in one of the earliest and most influential studies of Eliot, argues that towards the end of 'The Fire Sermon'

[a]lthough mention of Elizabeth and Leicester brings an illusion of glamour, closer thought reveals that the stale pretence of their relationship left it essentially as empty as that between the typist and the clerk.[49]

Similarly, Cleanth Brooks maintains that at the end of 'The Burial of the Dead'

Eliot in having the protagonist address the friend in a London street as one who was with him in the Punic War rather than as one who was with him in the World War is making the point that all the wars are one war; all experience, one experience.[50]

But Brooks's reading ignores the weirdness of this simultaneity of past and present in the passage:

> There I saw one I knew, and stopped him, crying: 'Stetson!
> 'You who were with me in the ships at Mylae!
> 'That corpse you planted last year in your garden,
> 'Has it begun to sprout? Will it bloom this year?
> 'Or has the sudden frost disturbed its bed?
> 'O keep the Dog far hence, that's friend to men,
> 'Or with his nails he'll dig it up again![51]

One thing these lines do *not* say is that the fertility rituals of the past have simply declined into trivial gardening practises. Stetson's gardening and the ancient fertility rituals alluded to involve, respectively, real and symbolic corpses. However stoic consolation cannot be derived from any belief that the burying of corpses at the bottom of the garden is as suburban as the throwing of images of the gods into the water in these rituals was commonplace, or that the just concluded Great War was as sordid as the trade war of Mylae. For if this reduces the mythic past by making it imitate the ordinariness of the present, it is also the case that the present repeats the mythic past. Suburban murders have a mythic dimension, the Great War an aspect of tragedy. The Dog does not just dig up the usual kinds of buried bones but something rather more terrifying. The past is made familiar, the mythic ordinary, and our own apparently sordid violence has a mythic aspect.

There is the same recognition in the preceding passage recounting the speaker's meeting with Madame Sosostris, 'famous clairvoyante'. The passage does, it is true, represent 'the ancient mysteries of the Tarot now reduced to the comic banality of fortune-telling'[52] but Madame Sosostris is like the grasping clairvoyante of Yeats's play, *The Words Upon the Window-Pane*, a medium, someone who knows nothing about the ancient mysteries but through whom the past speaks. Indeed, just as our forgetting of the past guarantees its return, so the ordinariness of a medium in Yeats's play is a guarantee of her authenticity. Thus the cards dealt by Madame Sosostris do have significance and not just for her client, the speaker, but for us, the readers of the poem, who will later encounter, as Eliot's note points out, figures like the Phoenician Sailor, 'the one-eyed merchant', and the Hanged Man.[53] However while the cards dealt by Madame Sosostris do have a significance, it is somewhat different from that of the ancient mysteries. The Phoenician sailor might once have been the image of a fertility god thrown into and then recovered from the sea but there is no indication in 'Death by Water' that Phlebas the Phoenician will ever resurface. As Madame Sosostris says later, 'Fear death by water'.[54] Belladonna is presumably like Eliot's previous *femmes fatales*, a woman who takes but never gives life and Eliot tells us in his note to this section that he associates the Man with Three Staves 'quite arbitrarily, with the Fisher King'[55] leaving us free to associate this card with a figure in the poem of a less redemptive kind. Similarly, the 'one-eyed merchant' might once have been a Syrian merchant responsible for the export of various mystery religions but in the poem he is Mr Eugenides, an unshaven merchant who invites the speaker in 'demotic French' for a weekend at an hotel in Brighton.[56] The card he carries on his back is 'blank'.[57] The Hanged Man is Frazer's Hanged God according to Eliot, but he is also the 'hooded' figure who walks beside 'the speaker and his companion' in the final section, an apparition like the 'crowds of people, walking round in a ring' of an altogether more menacing kind.[58] We might have forgotten the ancient mysteries but they have not forgotten us.

Yet if the stoic consolation that the past is depressingly like the present is largely unavailable, then neither can we cheer ourselves up by looking for ways in which the present might have its own glories not dissimilar to those of the past. In a recent and influential article, David Chinitz takes issue with those who believe that Eliot is simply expressing some kind of nostalgia for the high culture of the past. For example

the 'Shakespearian Rag,' the second-rate 1912 send-up that Eliot quotes in 'A Game of Chess' . . . is usually taken to indicate ironically how far culture has fallen since Shakespeare's time, yet from a reader's perspective, its appearance in the middle of one of the most painful sections of *The Waste Land* comes, I think, as something of a relief.[59]

Eliot is not, Chinitz argues, the elitist he has been customarily taken for, but someone who is attempting to heal the rift between high and popular art, past and present. Whereas Matthiessen, Brooks and others argue that Eliot makes the past like the present by deflating our nostalgia for the former, Chinitz argues that Eliot heals the great cultural divide between the high culture of the past and the popular culture of the present by finding vitality in the latter. But while the previous generation of critics lowers the past to the level of the present and Chinitz elevates the present to the level of the past, both produce consolatory readings of the poem, albeit of quite different kinds. The reality of the text is somewhat different.

'O O O O that Shakespeherian Rag – /It's so elegant/So intelligent' are 'spoken' during a kind of dialogue between a middle- or upper-middle-class woman and a man, presumably her husband. Husband and wife bear strong resemblances, respectively, to the asocial and social selves of Eliot's earlier poetry. Like the asocial Prufrock, the husband is preoccupied with other worlds – 'rats' alley', the 'infinit vexation' of 'man's own thoughts' in Webster's *The*

White Devil, Alonso's apparent 'sea change' in *The Tempest* – and yet his words have a kind of quiet, even monotonal quality. Alternatively, although the wife's speech is highly repetitious it has a staccato forcefulness and is charged with an hysterical energy. In other words, the woman who is trapped in a continuous present is paradoxically more alive than the man who can remember Ariel's song. This should support Chinitz's contention that the culture of the present can invigorate that of the past except for the fact that the words 'O O O O that Shakespeherian rag – /It's so elegant/So intelligent' are spoken not by the woman but by the man. Furthermore the man actually *improves* on the words of the original 1912 rag-time song, 'Shakesperian Rag', by syncopating Shakespeare's name and by adding the 'O O O O', so like what we might hear in any popular song but also the dying Hamlet's last sounds, at least in the Folio text.[60] Chinitz has elsewhere pointed out that the words of the original song are a kind of camp put-down of Shakespeare, mockingly suggesting that the trials, tribulations and loves of the Bard's characters are just like our own.[61] However the man's song and by implication Eliot's (since there are no quotation marks around the man's 'speech') not only beat the original at its own rag-time game but remind us that even the frivolity of the Jazz Age cannot outpace Hamlet's fate. The Jazz Age might forget or dismiss Shakespeare but Shakespeare will not forget it.

The past haunts the poem's other fragments of popular culture: the barman's repeated final call at the end of 'A Game of Chess', 'HURRY UP PLEASE ITS TIME', becomes towards the end a reminder that our own lives are ending;[62] the popular song of the Australian troops in 'The Fire Sermon' about Mrs Porter and her daughter washing their feet in soda water is in its surrounding context of slimy rats, '[w]hite bodies naked on the low damp ground' and rattling bones in a garret, more than just a humorous warning about what kind of disease can be caught at Mrs Porter's Cairo establishment;[63] and the London Bridge which 'is falling down falling down falling down' at the end of the poem symbolises all the poem's other ruins.[64]

However, the past which returns is never the same as the past which was forgotten or repressed:

> April is the cruellest month, breeding
> Lilacs out of the dead land, mixing
> Memory and desire, stirring
> Dull roots with spring rain.[65]

makes an ironic contrast between the Aprils of yesteryear and our own cruel Aprils, Chaucer's tale about the beginning of a pilgrimage in spring and our own miserable attempts at rebirth, Whitman's elegy for the time when lilacs last bloomed in the door-yard and our bestial and unlamented deaths. However the barren month in which we live seems to have its own morbid vitality, as the series of hanging participles – 'breeding', 'mixing', 'stirring', 'covering', and 'feeding' – which terminate five of the seven opening lines indicate. If that is so then it must also be the case that the vitality of past has something of the present's morbidity. These cruel Aprils are not just a recent phenomenon.

Nearly all of Eliot's allusions in *The Waste Land* work in this way. 'By the waters of Leman I sat down and wept' establishes an ironic contrast between the Israelites' lament in Babylon and the poet's lament both by the side of his mistress or 'leman' and by the waters of Lake Leman or Lake Geneva where Eliot received treatment for his mental breakdown.[66] The lament of the poet, however, has an elegiac quality not dissimilar to that of the original song and so it is possible that we might hear a hint of the lustful and the mentally unbalanced in the lamentation of the Israelites. A few lines later the poet hears at his 'back in a cold blast . . ./The rattle of the bones, and chuckle spread from ear to ear', lines which ironically recall Marvell's 'winged chariot' but which also distort his *carpe diem* into something fearful and panic-struck.[67] And later again, '[w]hen lovely woman stoops to folly', we are not without some sympathy for the typist since Eliot largely reserves his disgust for her seducer, 'the young man carbuncular', and as a consequence Goldsmith's heroine loses some of her tragic loveliness.[68] Maud Ellmann argues that the poem 'uses nostalgia in order to conceal its vandalism'[69] of tradition but the truth is, I think, that the poem shows us how *we*, both poet and reader, desecrate the past by forgetting it. Eliot's allusions help us to remember both what the tradition once was and what it has become.

Because the past when forgotten can never be revived in any benign form, the tradition can never be a source of imaginative vitality for the chaos of contemporary reality. Freud points out that 'an uncanny effect is often and easily produced when the distinction between imagination and reality is effaced, as when something that we have hitherto regarded as imaginary appears before us in reality'.[70] Thus in the opening section of 'A Game of Chess' we see that

> Above the antique mantel was displayed
> As though a window gave upon the sylvan scene
> The change of Philomel, by the barbarous king
> So rudely forced; yet there the nightingale
> Filled all the desert with inviolable voice
> And still she cried, and still the world pursues,
> 'Jug Jug' to dirty ears.
> And other withered stumps of time
> Were told upon the walls; staring forms
> Leaned out, leaning, hushing the room enclosed.
> Footsteps shuffled on the stair.
> Under the firelight, under the brush, her hair
> Spread out in fiery points
> Glowed into words, then would be savagely still.[71]

The picture of the rape of Philomela becomes a window, not a representation of reality like a picture, but something which is and is not a border between inside and outside. Although we are taken into the world of this picture – which is also partly Milton's 'sylvan scene' just as Satan arrives, our first but nevertheless estranged home – we are also outside, the nightingale's cry of 'Jug Jug' both the cry of springtime and a smutty Elizabethan reference to sexual intercourse, innocent like Philomela, and yet heard by the 'dirty ears' of fallen men. These 'withered stumps of time/Were told upon the wall' as though consolatory mirrors to our own depravity, and yet the forms within them are 'leaning' out of their frames as '[t]he silent man in mocha brown' of 'Sweeney Among the Nightingales' is '[o]utside the window, leaning in'.[72] The sounds of the nightingale silence the room so that we hear footsteps shuffling on the stair. As silent viewers we are outside the pictures and yet inside the silent room just as the cry of a woman raped long ago becomes the words of an hysterical modern woman combing her hair, someone outside now but within her bedroom, a figure who is in turn to be silenced a few lines later by a noise outside, maybe the wind.

Such conflation of inside with outside, past with present, and imagination with reality is only heightened by the Notes. Eliot famously tells us that '[n]ot only the title, but the plan and a good deal of the incidental symbolism of the poem were suggested by Miss Jessie L. Weston's . . . *From Ritual to Romance*' and that '[w]hat Tiresias *sees*, in fact, is the substance of the poem'.[73] However the fact that Eliot feels compelled to point out the ordering principles of the poem can only raise suspicions that the poem might not have

any. If Tiresias 'sees' the 'substance' of the poem then surely a
perceptive reader will see it eventually as well. Such notes tend to
undermine their own assertions. Alternatively we can often detect
significance in certain lines only to find that Eliot's note pulls the rug
from underneath us, such as when he tells us that the 'dead sound on
the final stroke of nine' – the sound whose hour suggests both the
time at which City workers begin work and the time of Christ's
death – is '[a] phenomenon which I have often noticed'.[74] If such a
note refuses to ascribe anything other than an arbitrary and personal
significance it also, paradoxically, stimulates our desire for meaning.
By frustrating our need for meaning such notes also suggest that it is
to be found in the poem rather than in any authorial commentary.
Thus the apparent authority of one kind of note actually undermines
its own assertions while the apparently self-deprecating modesty of
another kind tends to reassert the poem's authority.

Just as the Notes assert that the poem gives 'a shape and a
significance to the immense panorama of futility and anarchy which
is contemporary history' (to use Eliot's own description of *Ulysses*[75])
while at the same time suggesting that the poem is as anarchic as
'contemporary history', so they are both an essential part of the
poem and an unnecessary supplement. Like the Cretan Liar's
dictum, the notes which point out the poem's underlying structure
are unnecessary if what they say about the poem is true whereas the
scholarly spoofs or the most superfluous notes are necessary remin-
ders that the poem has its own truth. The history of the Notes
reproduce these paradoxes. When the poem was first published in
The Criterion and *The Dial* it was without the Notes which were only
added to the later book edition to satisfy the publisher's desire for a
larger volume. Pound thought them superfluous, Eliot later regretted
their 'bogus scholarship', and every generation of scholars since has
contained its sceptics and yet they refuse to go away, enticing every
new reader as though they were a key to unlock the poem's secrets
and enjoying, as Eliot himself pointed out, 'almost greater popularity
than the poem itself'.[76]

If the boundaries of the poem are uncertain then so too is its
authorship. In 'Sage Homme', a poem included in one of his letters
to Eliot, Pound writes

> These are the Poems of Eliot
> By the Uranian Muse begot;

A Man their Mother was,
A Muse their Sire.

How did the printed Infancies result
From Nuptuals [*sic*] thus doubly difficult?

If you must needs enquire
Know diligent Reader
That on each Occasion
Ezra performed the caesarean Operation.[77]

About a month after receiving this poem, Eliot told Pound that he wished to place it '[i]n italics in front' of the poem.[78] Of course the poem was never used as a kind of epigraph or even published elsewhere by Pound but who is to say that its exclusion was any less arbitrary than the eventual inclusion of the Notes? After all, like any mother, Eliot was both passive and active, suffering at the time of most of its gestation from what he himself diagnosed as 'aboulie',[79] an inability to act, and yet he wrote more lines of poetry at Margate and Lausanne, and of a more haunting kind, than at any time before or after his breakdown. Without contributing a single line to the poem, Pound, unlike Vivienne, Eliot's wife at the time, certainly did give it its final form; and the Muse of the past although passive nevertheless dictated, like the spirits of some kind of Yeatsian automatic writing session, much that was written. Like any child the poem had more than one parent but unlike other children, *The Waste Land* was, at least according to Pound's later claim in 'Sage Homme' to provide 'Cauls and Grave clothes',[80] like Marie, 'neither [l]iving nor dead'.[81]

The Waste Land was to be the last uncanny text Eliot would finish writing. The year after its publication, he began work on a verse play, later to be called *Sweeney Agonistes*, but, possibly because it evokes a kind of daemonic possession even more horrifying than that of *The Waste Land*, it was never completed. Eliot intended the play to address two different kinds of audience, one which would be entertained by its jaunty music hall and jazz rhythms and subject matter, and another much smaller audience which would perceive its sense of an underlying horror.[82] Accordingly, the action of the play takes place at two levels. At the most superficial, Dusty and Doris entertain four ex-servicemen, Wauchope, Horsfall, Klipstein and Krumpacker. Like the female couple of Eliot's earlier poems, one of these women, Dusty, is the voice of social propriety, the other, Doris, like her namesake from 'Sweeney Erect', a woman of easier virtue.

The men are also representative of complementary or antithetical characteristics: they find London's nightlife both 'Perfectly slick' and 'a little too gay'; one of them is 'a real live Britisher' and the others North American;[83] they sing about life on a primitive South Sea Island yet in the most up-to-date fashion. Sweeney is much like these men, indulging Doris in her fantasy of a 'cannibal isle', her as the missionary and himself as the cannibal, but the 'sound of the surf' he hears tells only of 'Birth, and copulation and death'.[84] In the typescript scenario for the play, Sweeney was to murder Mrs Porter[85] but in the published fragments he tells the others only of a man he knew who 'once did a girl in'.[86] The person who might have murdered the girl in the published version is the mysterious Pereira, The King of Clubs drawn by Doris just before she draws The Two of Spades or the coffin. In any case, Doris has Dusty tell Pereira that she is ill rather than speak to him over the telephone, even though he pays her rent. Pereira seems to belong to their Jazz Age set and yet his name suggests someone from the Old World; he is the subject of their conversation and yet he never appears in the published fragments – in short he is, like the murderer whom Sweeney once knew, a ghostly figure, neither alive nor dead.

However, the two levels of action do more than just mirror each other. Doris's refusal to talk to Pereira and her decision to enjoy herself only with the returned soldiers will presumably rile the man who pays her rent and eventually ensure his return to her flat in person. Similarly, the ex-servicemen's refusal to talk about their experiences together in the war as anything other than the jolliest of larks only raises our suspicions as to what it was really like. It is not just that Sweeney's horror story interrupts Doris's fantasy of a Gauguinesque tropical isle but that her inanities provoke his night-marish vision. It is as though the Jazz Age's forgetting of what preceded it only ensures that it will return to haunt the present's somewhat hysterical gaiety.

The sounds of the play are equally haunting. In his poetry up to and including *Sweeney Agonistes*, Eliot often uses simple, almost childish rhymes, usually to create the weird sense of something desirable or threatening lurking within that which is banal and affectless. One thinks here of the women who 'come and go/Talking of Michelangelo', Mrs Porter, her daughter and the soda water, the 'elegant' and 'intelligent' Shakespeherian Rag and, in *Sweeney Agonistes*, Sweeney's boast that 'I'll convert *you*!/Into a stew'.[87] Some-

times the final words of two contiguous lines are the same: 'A crowd
flowed over London Bridge, so many,/I had not thought death had
undone so many' or 'Your shadow at morning striding behind you/
Or your shadow at evening rising to meet you'[88] a technique which
creates an odd sense of flatness. There is also the simple imitation of
bird song, such as the 'Jug jug jug jug jug jug' of 'The Fire Sermon'
or, a little later, the human song of the Rhine Maiden, 'Weialala
leia/Wallah leialala' and in *Sweeney Agonistes* the 'Ting a ling ling' of
Dusty's telephone and the 'KNOCK KNOCK KNOCK' which finishes
the second fragment.[89] In all these instances the sound of the poetry,
even though it imitates something in the 'real' world, has almost
completely drowned what the words signify. In *Sweeney Agonistes* we
could have actually heard a telephone or the sound of knocking or
have had a character tell us that they are hearing these sounds but
instead someone speaks certain onomatopoeic words. Significantly,
Dusty quite rightly fears that it will be Pereira, and the knocking on
the door comes from the hangman. There is much sound in Eliot's
poetry, emitted by speakers barely alive, signifying almost nothing
which nevertheless manages to communicate something, albeit that
which is terrifyingly blank.

If we exempt the fragments of 'eastern and western asceticism'
which surface in *The Waste Land*,[90] Eliot's next major poem, 'The
Hollow Men', marks the beginning of his escape from the uncanny.
The hollow men of the poem are the living dead, Julius Caesar's
assassins, the Gunpowder Plot conspirators, the lost souls of Dante's
Hell and Purgatory, Conrad's colonial apparitions, all of them like
animated effigies and decrepit children. Yet these automatons and
zombies have, like Conrad's Kurtz, not so much lost their youthful
vitality, innocence and idealism as transformed it into something
with a kind of perverse or demonic energy. Nevertheless since the
hollow men are imprisoned in 'death's dream kingdom' there must
be by implication something outside their kingdom, what Eliot calls
'death's other kingdom'.[91]

Since 'The Hollow Men' ends with 'a whimper', the last gasp of a
dying world and the cry of a newborn child, we are given only a
glimpse of this 'other kingdom' but in Eliot's next major and first
post-conversion poem the pathway is more clearly visible. Ricks
describes both 'The Hollow Men' and 'Ash-Wednesday' as 'between-
poems', utilising as they do the word 'between' for its, uniquely for a
preposition, 'antithetical nature', its capacity to signify 'at once a

joining and a separation, disconcertingly accommodating itself to acts of mediation or meeting and to acts of obstruction or disjuncture'.[92] But what Ricks does not observe is that it is only in the later poem that 'between' signifies both these antithetical actions and even in this poem the preposition is also used in a restricted sense, for example in section v when Eliot refers to 'Those who are torn on the hour between season and season, time and time, between/Hour and hour' where the word signifies only an action of disjuncture or splitting[93]. In 'The Hollow Men' the word occurs only in the final section and here it designates an indeterminate zone, neither one thing nor another, where 'Falls the Shadow'.[94] This is also the sense in which it is used in the 'Fire Sermon' where Tiresias is described as 'throbbing between two lives',[95] as living in a ghastly modern limbo without identity although of course there is also a positive sense in which Tiresias *combines* both sexes, a characteristic which allows him the gift of prophecy.

The word 'between' is significant in 'Ash-Wednesday' but perhaps the most important words of the poems which precede it are 'and' and 'neither'. Gerontion 'was neither at the hot gates/Nor fought in the warm rain/Nor knee deep', the fear we are shown 'in a handful of dust' is 'different from either/Your shadow at morning striding behind you/Or your shadow at evening rising to meet you' and Marie is 'neither/Living nor dead'.[96] In these three instances the word 'neither' or its equivalent means much the same as one of the meanings of 'between', that is it refers to something which, like de Saussure's ghostly signifiers, has no positive identity. Yet at least for Marie, the word is closely associated with the conjunction 'and': 'we stopped in the colonnade,/*And* drank coffee, *and* talked for an hour . . . *And* when we were children . . . *And* I was frightened . . . *And* down we went . . . I read, much of the night, *and* go south in winter' (my emphasis).[97] And twenty-odd lines later she remembers

> I could not
> Speak, *and* my eyes failed, I was neither
> Living nor dead, *and* I knew nothing,
> Looking into the heart of light, the silence [my emphasis].[98]

Here the conjunction helps to establish that affectless or monotonal quality of Marie's experience noticed by many readers. If the word 'neither' signifies a lack of identity then the overuse of 'and' can signify a lack of difference or differentiation.

Both these qualities characterise the uncanny. Prufrock, Gerontion, Marie and others are neither living nor dead, neither in the
present nor the past and yet they are, like the ghosts which haunt
them, alive and dead, present and absent. They are possessed by
something which either lacks identity and difference or which has
too much identity and difference. This kind of semiotic breakdown
can be contrasted to Eliot's use of the preposition 'between' in 'Ash-
Wednesday', his first poem to turn its back successfully on the
uncanny. In part IV of 'Ash-Wednesday', Beatrice walks 'between the
violet and the violet . . . between/Various ranks of varied green' and
'Between the yews' while in the final section the poet is in a world, if
not exactly the same as Beatrice's, then not far from it, 'Wavering
between the profit and the loss' in 'The dreamcrossed twilight
between birth and dying'.[99] Beatrice exists in a third world, a world
which is neither living nor dead and yet which combines those two
worlds. Beatrice is a dialectical being, someone who both unifies the
contraries between which mortals are torn and yet someone who
also exists in another, different realm. The uncanny and the sacred
are alike in that both are third worlds, unlike in the sense that the
former is meaningless and the latter meaningful.

In the four major poems which were written after this vision of
Beatrice, *Four Quartets*, Eliot turns his back on the uncanny, dis-
missing 'it' as a kind of popular superstition:

> To communicate with Mars, converse with spirits,
> To report the behaviour of the sea monster,
> Describe the horoscope, haruspicate or scry,
> Observe disease in signatures, evoke
> Biograph from the wrinkles of the palm
> And tragedy from fingers; release omens
> By sortilege, or tea leaves, riddle pentagrams
> Or barbituric acids, or dissect
> The recurrent image into pre-conscious terrors –
> To explore the womb, or tomb, or dreams; all these are usual
> Pastimes and drugs, and features of the press.[100]

Curiously, the alternative to these superstitions (the most recent of
which is psychoanalysis), is named only once in the *Four Quartets*:

> The hint half guessed, the gift half understood, is Incarnation.
> Here the impossible union
> Of spheres of existence is actual,
> Here the past and future
> Are conquered, and reconciled,

Where action were otherwise movement
Of that which is only moved
And has in it no source of movement –
Driven by dæmonic, chthonic
Powers.[101]

The uncanny represents that moment when the past returns to the present and yet it is neither the past nor the present. Similarly the Incarnation or '[t]he point of intersection of the timeless/With time'[102] is both our beginning and our end and yet it is neither a beginning nor an end. However if this turn away from superstition towards religion, from the uncanny towards the Incarnation, re-leased Eliot from 'dæmonic, chthonic/[p]owers' it was also, at least for many readers, a turn away from a genuinely powerful and haunting poetry.

II

In July of 1919 Richard Aldington wrote to Eliot in a state of 'pious terror' expressing his 'admiration' for Eliot's critical articles and his 'dislike' of his 'over-intellectual' poetry.[103] Eliot's reply does not survive but fourteen years later in his lectures at the University of Virginia, he defended the 'apparent incoherence' between his poetry and criticism with the observation that 'in one's prose reflexions one may be legitimately occupied with ideals, whereas in the writing of verse one can only deal with actuality'.[104] Since 'ideals' tend to change more slowly than 'actuality', we might reasonably expect a greater consistency in Eliot's prose than his poetry. Indeed, the widely held assumption that Eliot's writing changed sometime around the time of his conversion is correct, as I have just argued, but by and large only for his poetry; and the more recent minority view of those such as Ronald Schuchard and Lyndall Gordon that certain political and religious beliefs can be traced back to at least 1914 is also true, but generally only in his prose.[105] Whereas Eliot's poetry largely ceased to be uncanny after 1927, his prose always presented certain 'ideals' as alternatives to the uncanny.

With the exception of Irving Babbitt, the earliest and most abiding influence on Eliot's political views was Charles Maurras, a Virgil according to his 1948 'Hommage à Charles Maurras' who led him to the gates of the temple.[106] In his 1924 review of T. E. Hulme's *Speculations*, Eliot associated Maurras with Sorel and Lasserre in

France and the 'solitary figure' of Hulme in England. The latter he describes as 'the forerunner of a new attitude of mind', someone who is 'classical, reactionary, and revolutionary', and the very 'antipodes of the eclectic, tolerant, and democratic mind of the end of the last century'.[107] A few years earlier in his war-time extension lectures, Eliot had explained to his audience that the new classicism in France was 'partly a return to the ideals of the seventeenth century', ideals which 'may roughly be characterized as *form* and *restraint* in art, *discipline* and *authority* in religion, *centralization* in government (either as socialism or monarchy)'.[108] Thus the French classicists – like most revolutionary movements since the Renaissance – called for a return to a distant past by means of a radical break with the present and the immediate past. For those such as Maurras and Lasserre, this immediate past is called romanticism, something Eliot defines as '*excess*' in 'two directions: escape from the world of fact, and devotion to brute fact'.[109] As is often observed this definition might easily be applied to Prufrock, a 'character' as we have seen who is split between a self which is lost in various submarine and fogbound fantasy worlds and a self whose 'devotion to brute fact' is a defence against the encroachments of the feminine. Thus whereas Prufrock and the romantics are divided between fantasy and fact, the new classicism could be interpreted as a movement which transcends this opposition since it allows for both a revolutionary release of desire and the necessities of order and authority. Much later, for example, Eliot nostalgically remembers the *camelots* of Maurras's *Action Française* in Paris in 1910 'cheering the *cuirassiers* who were sent to disperse them, because they represented the Army, all the time that they were trying to stampede their horses'.[110]

However in his 1916 review of *Reflections on Violence*, Eliot also makes it clear that there is no utopian or emancipatory aspect to the forms of political action advocated by the *Action Française*'s most important political ally, Sorel. The latter's myth of the general strike is merely, Eliot argues, the 'instrument with which he hopes to destroy . . . [the] abominations' of 'middle-class democracy and middle-class socialism' rather than a 'weapon by which the lower classes are to obtain political and economic advantages'.[111] Sorel's myth is, he explains, 'not a Utopia but "an expression of a determination to act"'.[112] This is, I think, an accurate description of the way in which Sorel severs action from belief and the affective

qualities of myth from its emancipatory potential since, as we have
seen, he does in fact argue that the general strike will 'restore' not
some classless, golden age but the hierarchical societies of a pre-
democratic era. Eliot does concede that Sorel's scepticism 'is a
torturing vacuity which has developed the craving for belief'[113] but
he allows him no belief as such, only the capacity to hate and to act.

As it turned out, Eliot's review of *Reflections on Violence* was rather
prescient since in 1926 the Vatican condemned the *Action Française*
for making religion merely the 'servant' of political interests and
placed its newspaper and seven of Maurras's books on the Index.[114]
Eliot came to Maurras's support in 1928, conceding that while he
was an agnostic or atheist his intention was not

to pervert his disciples and students away from Christianity. I have been a
reader of the work of Maurras for eighteen years [and] upon me he has had
exactly the opposite effect . . . I should myself consider it preposterous to
suppose that the study of the work of Maurras or of the files of the *Action
Française* could by itself make a Christian of anybody. But where genuinely
religious influences are at work also, or where there is any religious potency
in the individual soul, they will be powerfully advanced.[115]

Furthermore, Eliot's support of Maurras and the *Action Française*
was qualified in important ways. As early as the Extension Lectures,
Eliot had regretted the 'extreme violence and intolerance' of
Maurras[116] and in 1955 he reflected that

I have sometimes thought that if Charles Maurras had confined himself to
literature, and to the literature of political theory, and had never attempted
to found a political party, a *movement* – engaging in, and increasing the
acrimony of the political struggle – if he had not given his support to the
restoration of the Monarchy in such a way as to strengthen instead of
reducing animosities – then those of his ideas which were sound and strong
might have spread more widely, and penetrated more deeply, and affected
more sensibly the contemporary mind.[117]

This accords with the sentiments expressed in 'The Literature of
Fascism', a 1928 article which in part deals with the differences
between the *Action Française* and Italian fascism, where Eliot concludes that Russian communism and Italian fascism 'have died as
political ideas, in becoming political facts' and regrets the tendency
of contemporary ideologies to substitute political for religious
belief.[118]

Even if we agree with C. K. Stead that 'in every respect the *Action
Française* . . . was more illiberal, more "reactionary", than Mussoli-

ni's party' it is still not necessarily the case that their influence on Eliot was of a fascistic kind and that he was therefore 'with Hitler, and . . . there is no point in pretending otherwise'.[119] In the review of *Reflections on Violence*, Eliot certainly admires Sorel's almost nihilistic capacity to act without belief, but by the next decade he is advocating rather the reverse, the importance of keeping religious belief relatively sequested from political action. If we are to take Eliot at his word, then he followed Maurras, as Dante did the pagan Virgil, to the gates of Christian belief but was unwilling to follow him back into the realm of political action. Eliot favoured the modernist side of Maurras, as it were, but not his avant-gardism. One side of Eliot, possibly the most timid, was thrilled by Sorel's and Hulme's violent yoking of reaction and revolution, the distant past and the utopian future, but the more sceptical and conservative side was never far from asserting itself.

Thus while Eliot in 1928 famously declared that he was a 'classicist in literature' (as well as a 'royalist in politics, and anglo-catholic in religion'),[120] he had nevertheless previously displayed considerable scepticism towards the 'classic'/'romantic' distinction. In a letter of 1920 to *The Times Literary Supplement*, Eliot observes that most theories of Romanticism – including those of Lasserre and Babbitt – erroneously apply 'the same term "romantic" to epochs and to individual artists' or assume that 'the terms "romantic" and "classic" are mutually exclusive and even antithetical without actually enforcing this exclusiveness in the examination of particular works of art'. In other words, empirical observation rather diffuses any revolutionary urge to divide the world into those with us and those against us. Thus Eliot concludes with the sensible scholarly suggestion that it might be for the best 'if we even forgot these terms altogether'.[121]

But the other problem with such terms was their utility for creative writers. In his review of Hulme's *Speculations*, Eliot points out that '[t]he weakness from which the classical movement in France has suffered is that it has been a critique rather than a creation'.[122] It is one thing, it could be observed, then, for a critic to want to return to an epoch of order and authority and quite another for a creative writer. The past was for Eliot the poet something rather more potent and disturbing than it was for a group of French royalists. Thus Eliot's break, whether conscious or not, with the *Action Française* occurs when he ceases to demonise the romantics and

instead recognises his own buried romanticism.[123] The crucial texts
in this respect are the essays first delivered as the Norton Lectures at
Harvard University during the winter of 1932–33, at a moment
rather late in some respects but nevertheless before Hitler's accession
to power, the Spanish Civil War and the invasion of Abyssinia. None
of these lectures mention the *Action Française* and indeed as Eliot says
they have 'no concern with politics'[124] but they do make the crucial
assumption that the romantics belong not to the recent past but to
the distant past of the poet's own personal history. They belong, that
is, to Eliot's childhood and that is another country rather different
from the *ancien régime* of the *Action Française*.

Eliot's first lecture is worth quoting at length:

I may be generalising my own history unwarrantably . . . when I put
forward the conjecture that the majority of children, up to say twelve or
fourteen, are capable of a certain enjoyment of poetry; that at or about
puberty the majority of these find little further use for it, but that a small
minority then find themselves possessed for a craving for poetry which is
wholly different from any enjoyment experienced before . . . Recognising
the frequent deceptions of memory, I seem to remember that my early
liking for the sort of verse that small boys do like vanished at about the age
of twelve, leaving me for a couple of years with no sort of interest in poetry
at all. I can recall clearly enough the moment when, at the age of fourteen
or so, I happened to pick up a copy of Fitzgerald's *Omar* which was lying
about, and the almost overwhelming introduction to a new world of feeling
which this poem was the occasion of giving me. It was like a sudden
conversion; the world appeared anew, painted with bright, delicious and
painful colours. Thereupon I took the usual adolescent course with Byron,
Shelley, Keats, Rossetti, Swinburne.[125]

From Eliot's reference a little later to a 'third' stage, it is clear that he
believes that this 'period', which in his case 'persisted until about my
twenty-second year', consists of two stages and yet the 'craving for
poetry' which possesses a 'small minority' at puberty occurred in his
case only after a 'couple of years' during which he had 'no sort of
interest in poetry at all'. This period seems more properly to consist,
therefore, of three stages: childhood, a period, sometimes called
'latency', during which poetry is forgotten (or repressed?), and then
a third stage when what was forgotten returns and

Invades the youthful consciousness and assumes complete possession for a
time. We do not really see it as something with an existence outside
ourselves; much as in our youthful experiences of love, we do not so much
see the person as infer the existence of some outside object which sets in

motion these new and delightful feelings in which we are absorbed. The frequent result is an outburst of scribbling which we may call imitation, so long as we are aware of the meaning of the word 'imitation' which we employ. It is not the deliberate choice of a poet to mimic, but writing under a kind of *daemonic possession* by one poet (my emphasis).[126]

Yet the analogy between this form of romantic possession and 'our youthful experiences of love' is only approximate because the former is neither 'new' nor 'delightful'. Nor is it something experienced only during adolescence, as Eliot's comments in his final lecture make clear:

I know, for instance, that some forms of ill-health, debility or anaemia, may (if other circumstances are favourable) produce an efflux of poetry in a way approaching the condition of automatic writing – though, in contrast to the claims sometimes made for the latter, the material has obviously been incubating within the poet, and cannot be suspected of being a present from a friendly or impertinent demon . . . To me it seems that at these moments, which are characterised by the sudden lifting of the burden of anxiety and fear which presses upon our daily life so steadily that we are unaware of it, what happens is something *negative*: that is to say, not 'inspiration' as we commonly think of it, but the breaking down of strong habitual barriers – which tend to re-form very quickly. Some obstruction is momentarily whisked away. The accompanying feeling is less like what we know as positive pleasure, than a sudden relief from an intolerable burden.[127]

As is well known, parts of *The Waste Land* were written during such a period of ill-health and those that were not are hardly characterised by their canny good health. When he is writing prose, however, Eliot attempts to quarantine such uncanniness by means of a series of dismissive gestures: it is probably not 'responsible for the creation of all the most profound poetry written, or even always of the best of a single poet's work'; '[o]rganisation is necessary as well as "inspiration"'; and, superficial appearances to the contrary, it 'is a very different thing from mystical illumination'.[128] What is really required, Eliot affirms, is that the aspiring poet leave it behind him and enter the 'third, or mature stage' when

We cease to identify ourselves with the poet we happen to be reading; when our critical faculties remain awake; when we are aware of what one poet can be expected to give and what he cannot. The poem has its own existence, apart from us; it was there before us and will endure after us. It is only at this stage that the reader is prepared to distinguish between degrees of greatness in poetry.[129]

Subject/object boundaries are re-established, the object is placed within a hierarchy and the subject acquires what Eliot then calls 'taste', a faculty which is embedded in a social context and is therefore 'limited as one's self is limited'.[130] Significantly, 'taste' is not something which has been lost like the order and authority of some *ancien régime*, but that which is slowly and arduously acquired.

While taste is presumably determined by factors of class and social status, Eliot gives no indication that it is in any way the product of gender. By contrast, he often describes its antithesis, 'inspiration' or 'demonic possession', as feminine. The French classicists habitually feminised (and infantilised) the romantics and of course inspiration has always been described as a form of feminine possession. Eliot, for example, describes Coleridge in another of his Norton Lectures as a poet who 'for a few years . . . had been visited by the Muse (I know of no poet to whom this hackneyed metaphor is better applicable) and thenceforth was a haunted man; for anyone who has ever been visited by the Muse is thenceforth haunted'.[131] Indeed even in 'Tradition and the Individual Talent' (1917) – Eliot's earliest major literary essay and therefore one of his most polemically anti-romantic – the progress of the poet is described as 'a continual surrender . . . to something which is more valuable . . . a continual self-sacrifice, a continual extinction of personality',[132] as though he were some kind of courtly or romantic lover debasing himself before the feminine ideal.[133] Certainly, Eliot's primary target is the romantic cult of personality but his argument that 'the most individual parts' of a poet's work 'may be those in which the dead poets, his ancestors, assert their immortality most vigorously' sounds much like the 'romantic' theories of haunting inspiration which he elsewhere attacks.[134]

The alternative to this 'extinction' of the subject is the extinction or loss of the object. In his slightly later essay on *Hamlet*, Eliot argues that the main character of the play

is dominated by an emotion which is inexpressible, because it is in *excess* [the same word used in the Extension Lectures] of the facts as they appear. And the supposed identity of Hamlet with his author is genuine to this point: that Hamlet's bafflement at the absence of objective equivalent to his feelings is a prolongation of the bafflement of his creator in the face of his artistic problem.[135]

Such 'bafflement' is then repeated by 'that most dangerous type of critic', the frustrated creative writer, who projects his own emotions on to the character. This 'excess' which so easily crosses the boundaries separating character from author and author from critic is, at least for the character, 'occasioned by his mother, but his mother is not an adequate equivalent for it':

To have heightened the criminality of Gertrude would have been to provide the formula for a totally different emotion in Hamlet; it is just *because* her character is so negative and insignificant that she arouses in Hamlet the feeling which she is incapable of representing.[136]

Another way of putting this might be that Gertrude is the occasion of certain feelings of disgust in Hamlet because of what she is *not*, maybe the once beloved mother, but that means she cannot be the cause of these emotions.

In any case, this unrepresentable object or 'stuff that the writer could not drag to light'[137] bears comparison with what Eliot elsewhere thinks of as the origin of primitive ritual. Eliot remembers in 1926 that

Some years ago, in a paper on *The Interpretation of Primitive Ritual*, I made an humble attempt to show that in many cases *no* interpretation of a rite could explain its origin. For the meaning of the series of acts is to the performers themselves an interpretation; the same ritual remaining practically unchanged may assume different meanings for different generations of performers; and the rite may even have originated before 'meaning' meant anything at all.[138]

Substitute the unrepresentable 'stuff' of Hamlet's disgust for the origin of primitive ritual and this could be a description of Shakespeare's play since Hamlet also reacts to and performs a 'series of acts' the origin of which neither he, his author, nor any subsequent generation of critics can ever drag to light. This analogy is not made by Eliot, but then these comments come from his Introduction to his mother's poem about a mystic, *Savonarola*!

In his reviews and discussions of various anthropological texts in the decade after 1916, Eliot repeatedly praises writers such as Durkheim and Frazer who simply describe rather than interpret primitive religious phenomena, although in one of his seminar papers for Josiah Royce he concedes that description might itself be a form of interpretation.[139] The literary critic must also avoid interpretation:

Qua work of art, the work of art cannot be interpreted; there is nothing to interpret; we can only criticize it according to standards, in comparison to other works of art; and for 'interpretation' the chief task is the presentation of relevant historical facts which the reader is not assumed to know.[140]

Like primitive ritual, art can only be described. Yet while Eliot maintains that '*all* art emulates the condition of ritual',[141] we can only assume that he does not want it to emulate primitive ritual too closely. After all, that would result not only in a series of meaningless 'actions' but something as 'inexpressibly horrible' as the object of Hamlet's emotions.[142] 'Poetry begins', Eliot speculates in his final Norton lecture, 'with a savage beating a drum in a jungle' but the great 'variety' of uses to which it has been put since then are by no means inferior to its original ritual function.[143]

Eliot's one deliberate attempt to return art to some kind of ritual is *Sweeney Agonistes*. Because that desirable thing 'an audience which could neither read nor write' is unobtainable for the modern theatre, Eliot satisfied himself with writing a play whose different levels would appeal to different sections of the audience.[144] This audience could be related to Durkheim's concept of 'group consciousness' which according to him lay at the origin of religion, an argument favourably reviewed by Eliot in 1916.[145] However the more obvious anthropological influence on the play was, as Carol Smith[146] and Robert Crawford demonstrate, Francis Cornford and in particular his argument in *The Origin of Attic Comedy* – a text recommended by Eliot to the performers of his play[147] – that Attic Comedy and Tragedy derived from 'similar ritual performances' which differed only according to whether 'emphasis were thrown on the conflict and death of the hero, or on the joyful resurrection and marriage that followed'.[148] One can only imagine, however, that the emotions experienced by the participants of these early rituals were of a somewhat more positive and cathartic kind than the comic horror expressed by Eliot's play. *Sweeney Agonistes* may be partly an attempt to return drama to its origins in ritual and therefore heal the great divide between high and popular culture, but it also expresses the horror of such a return. Significantly, while Eliot often laments the dissociation of poetry and drama into separate genres, he also devotes a large part of his essay on Sir Philip Sidney's literary criticism arguing that Sidney's 'Doctrine of *Unity of Sentiment*', that is the doctrine that the genres should be pure and not mixed, 'in fact, happened to be right'.[149] Eliot concedes that '[i]n the end, horror and laughter may be one' but, significantly, 'only when horror and laughter have become as horrible and laughable as they can be'.[150]

A return to the pre-modern is only possible when modernity's potential has been fully exhausted.

Eliot nearly always expresses some sort of ambivalence when he discusses the similarities between modern art and primitive ritual. In his review of *Tarr* where he states his credo that the 'artist . . . is more *primitive*, as well as more civilized, than his contemporaries' he emphasises Lewis's 'frigid' and 'inhuman' intellect and the protective aspects of his humour,[151] neither quality particularly amenable, presumably, to any kind of ecstatic primitivism. Similarly, in another early review, this time of an anthology of Native American songs, Eliot expends so much energy sneering at the 'New York and Chicago *intelligentsia*['s]' 'romantic' love of things primitive that some of his animus extends even to 'the savage, the barbarian and the rustic', all of whom, despite their exemplary status for the artist, can also 'be improved upon'.[152] Even his famous review of Joyce's *Ulysses*, so often taken as an unambiguous celebration of myth, is unnecessarily authoritarian:

In using the myth, in manipulating a continuous parallel between contemporaneity and antiquity, Mr Joyce is pursuing a method which others must pursue after him. They will not be imitators, any more than the scientist who uses the discoveries of an Einstein in pursuing his own, independent, further investigations. It is simply a way of controlling, of ordering, of giving a shape and a significance to the immense panorama of futility and anarchy which is contemporary history . . . Psychology . . . ethnology, and *The Golden Bough* have concurred to make possible what was impossible even a few years ago. Instead of narrative method, we may now use the mythical method.[153]

Despite his references to the physical and human sciences, Joyce has not *discovered* the mythical aspects of contemporaneity nor the contemporaneity of myth but *imposed* the order of one on to the 'anarchy' of the other. And while the opposition of myth to contemporaneity is obviously to the former's advantage, the reduction of myth to an ordering device must indicate some degree of ambivalence towards its primitive powers.

The real issue for Eliot, then, is how close modern art should come to primitive ritual. Reviewing some now forgotten anthropological works in 1924, he points out that

The arts developed incidentally to the search for objects of talismanic properties. The Egyptian who first fashioned gold into a likeness of a cowrie-shell, the Cretan who designed an octopus on his pottery, the Indian who hung a necklace of bear's-teeth about his neck, were not aiming primarily at decoration, but invoking the assistance of life-giving amulets. At what point, we may ask, does the attempt to design and create an object for the sake of beauty become conscious? At what point in civilisation does any conscious distinction between practical or magical utility and æsthetic beauty arise? . . . Is it possible and justifiable for art, the creation of beautiful objects and of literature, to persist indefinitely without its primitive purposes: is it possible for the æsthetic object to be a *direct* object of attention?[154]

Marc Manganaro writes that '[s]urely Eliot's questions here are rhetorical' but this is surely only the case for his last question.[155] While it is true that Eliot does not believe 'it is possible and justifiable for art . . . to persist indefinitely without its primitive purposes' neither does he think it advantageous for art to be indistinguishable from these 'primitive purposes', to possess no 'æsthetic beauty' independently of its 'practical or magical utility'.

Indeed in essay after essay Eliot insists on what might be called the relative autonomy of art or literature, on the dual imperatives of 'considering poetry . . . primarily as poetry and not another thing' and also of recognising that 'poetry as certainly has something to do with morals, and with religion, and even with politics'.[156]   His example of the poet who most successfully treads this *via media* is Dante. While Dante's poetry can be enjoyed 'primarily as poetry', 'the philosophy is essential to the structure and . . . the structure is essential to the poetic beauty of the parts';[157] thus he is as different from the 'early philosophical poets, Permenides and Empedocles', who 'were not interested exclusively in philosophy, or religion, or poetry, but in something which was a mixture of all three'[158] as he is from a modern poet such as Valéry who, 'perhaps owing to the greater specialization of the modern world', exorcises 'philosophy' from poetry in an attempt to 'produce in us a *state*'.[159]

Ultimately, however, Eliot believes that these two extremes must meet. As we have seen, he believed that during the nineteenth century the 'dissolution of thought . . . the isolation of art, philosophy, religion, ethics and literature, is interrupted by various chimerical attempts to effect imperfect syntheses' and that the theory of 'art for art's sake' is, paradoxically, 'a *theory of life*'.[160] Perhaps the best known of these chimerical attempts to repair what he famously calls elsewhere the 'dissociation of sensibility' is Arnold's concept of Culture. In various essays, Eliot repeatedly takes Arnold to task for substituting Culture for Religion, an action which both extends the secularising tendencies of modernity and attempts to repair the damage done by these tendencies through investing Culture with attributes previously only possessed by Religion. Arnold, according to Eliot,

discovered a new formula: poetry is not religion, but it is a capital substitute for religion – not invalid port, which may lend itself to hypocrisy, but coffee without caffeine, and tea without tannin.[161]

In the same spirit, a humanist such as Irving Babbitt,

seems to think also that the 'outer' restraints of an orthodox religion, as they weaken, can be supplied by the inner restraint of the individual over himself. If I have interpreted him correctly, he is thus trying to build a Catholic platform out of Protestant planks.[162]

Again, this humanist doctrine of the 'inner check' is both an '*alternative* to religion' which accelerates the dissociation of sensibility, and a 'substitute' for religion whose purpose is to arrest such dissociation.[163]

For Eliot, then, there must be what he calls 'an easy and natural association between religion and art'.[164] Once art becomes severed from religion it becomes a kind of parody of religion, like coffee without caffeine. In the words of Jacques Rivière quoted by Eliot, ' "[i]t is only with the advent of Romanticism that the literary act came to be conceived as a sort of raid on the absolute and its result as a revelation" '.[165] However the violation of art's 'integrity' or autonomy also leads towards the same end since the collapse of art back into 'life', religion, or any of the other spheres of human activity only results in a 'chimerical' synthesis, a kind of parody of the undifferentiated state of primitive cultures. If the separation of art from religion requires some degree of repression, then it must be neither too much nor too little; err in either direction too greatly and the primitive returns as the uncanny figure of the romantic poet. Poetry is, Eliot maintains, 'a superior amusement',[166] something considerably less intense than primitive ritual and yet more pleasurable than an entirely pure and autonomous art.

These comments are scattered throughout a number of essays and it was not until after the war in *Notes Towards the Definition of Culture* that Eliot analysed the relationship between culture and religion in any systematic way. Towards the beginning of this text he suggests that 'what we call the culture, and what we call the religion, of a people are . . . different aspects of the same thing: the culture being, essentially, the incarnation (so to speak) of the religion of a people'.[167] Religion and culture are both the same and yet, since the '[t]he point of intersection of the timeless/With time'[168] is rarely glimpsed, also different. However, two chapters later, Eliot writes about this identity in somewhat different terms. After asserting that the undifferentiated aspects of primitive culture 'cannot recur except in the New Jerusalem', he argues that this

identity of religion and culture remains on the unconscious level, upon which we have superimposed a conscious structure wherein religion and culture are contrasted and can be opposed . . . To the unconscious level we constantly tend to revert, as we find consciousness an excessive burden; and the tendency towards reversion may explain the powerful attraction which totalitarian philosophy and practice can exert upon humanity. Totalitarianism appeals to the desire to return to the womb. The contrast between religion and culture imposes a strain: we escape from this strain by attempting to revert to an identity of religion and culture which prevailed at a more primitive stage; as when we indulge in alcohol as an anodyne, we consciously seek unconsciousness. It is only by unremitting effort that we can persist in being individuals in a society, instead of merely members of a disciplined crowd.[169]

Reverting to an unconscious level is quite different from being possessed by something from above. George Bornstein argues that Eliot 'locate [s] sources of power downward and within' and that his 'radical contribution to the tradition of the ecstatic moment is fear, resulting in defense'.[170] It might also be added that one of these defences is to relocate these sources upwards and outwards in the form of a tradition or spiritual realm which incarnates itself in the individual.

Most of *Notes Towards the Definition of Culture*, however, is concerned not with any kind of primitive or totalitarian 'reversion' but with the consequences of too much cultural differentiation or the 'strain' imposed by too much repression of the 'unconscious'. The differentiation of culture from religion and the differentiation of culture into various levels is not only irreversible but desirable. Nevertheless it can proceed too quickly or too far and produce a society in which there is no 'social cohesion' within or between the various levels of culture.[171] According to Eliot this tendency towards social atomisation can be arrested or avoided in three main ways: (1) by ensuring that there is *some* hereditary transmission of culture, that is that classes are not replaced by meritocratic elites; (2) by paying attention to 'the ecology of cultures'[172] or the importance of regional and local cultures; (3) by maintaining a balance between a religion and its 'sects', that is between Rome and Canterbury and Canterbury and the various Protestant churches and Chapels.

By the end of the war, Eliot's cultural and political views had mellowed considerably and as a consequence he was reasonably restrained in *Notes Towards the Definition of Culture* when summoning up the spectres of social disintegration. Twenty-five years earlier, however, he had written in 'The Function of Criticism' that

The inner voice, in fact, sounds remarkably like an old principle which has been formulated by an elder critic in the now familiar phrase of 'doing as one likes'. The possessors of the inner voice ride ten in a compartment to a football match at Swansea, listening to the inner voice, which breathes the eternal message of vanity, fear, and lust.[173]

Paradoxically, such extreme individualism leads towards its apparent opposite, the loss of any individuality in the crowd. A social group which suffers from too much differentiation is ultimately indistinguishable from one which suffers from too little. By specifying that these football supporters are travelling to Swansea, Eliot is obviously having a shot at Protestant sectarianism or Welsh dissent. But it is odd that these supporters are travelling to a football match in a region which is far better known for its rugby. Eliot could be making the point that these Welshmen are so alienated from their own cultural traditions that they are not even supporting their traditional game; but coming from an American with no interest in sport addressing a literary readership this seems extremely unlikely. In *After Strange Gods* Eliot questions whether 'human beings are most real when most violently excited; violent physical passions do not in themselves differentiate men from each other, but rather tend to reduce them to same state'.[174] Obviously, Eliot thinks that the passion these football supporters feel for their club has reduced them to an undifferentiated mass, a condition made even worse presumably by their mobility, but his own passions are not a little responsible.

The economic corollary of these disintegrating forces is advanced industrialism. Indeed, Eliot's hostility towards this mode of production is such that in *Notes Towards the Definition of Culture* he often sounds not only like a contemporary socialist but a much later day environmentalist. But the case against advanced industrialism is most succinctly put in *The Idea of a Christian Society*:

the tendency of unlimited industrialism is to create bodies of men and women – of all classes – detached from tradition, alienated from religion, and susceptible to mass suggestion: in other words, a mob.[175]

Again, the 'mob' possesses the apparently contradictory qualities of too much differentiation and too little and prior to its formation its individual members must experience both extreme isolation and the overwhelming urge to belong in some larger collectivity. These passions can even affect some of industrial societies' most virulent critics:

the whole history of Lawrence's life and of Lawrence's writings . . . is the history of his craving for greater intimacy than is possible between human beings, a craving irritated to the point of frenzy by his unusual incapacity for being intimate at all. His struggle against over-intellectualized life is the history of his own over-intellectualized nature. Even in his travels to more primitive lands, he could never take the crude peoples simply for what they are; he must needs always be expecting something of them that they could not give, something peculiarly medicinal for himself.[176]

For others the medicine was radical nationalism.

Although these 'mobs' clearly represent the return of repressed instincts, the craving for intimacy and the 'desire to return to the womb', they are not in the least uncanny. 'Mobs' are always, as Williams notes, formed by *other* people.[177] In the poetry, however, 'crowds' – never 'mobs' – have ambivalent characteristics: they may be like '[t]he readers of The *Boston Evening Transcript*' who '[s]way in the wind like a field of ripe corn' or like the 'red-eyed scavengers . . . creeping/From Kentish Town and Golder's Green' but usually they combine these characteristics like the 'brown waves of fog' in 'Morning at the Window' which, for all its 'Twisted faces' and 'aimless smile[s]', at least represents some kind of life.[178] '[B]rown fog' is again present in 'The Burial of the Dead' when

> A crowd flowed over London Bridge, so many,
> I had not thought death had undone so many.
> Sighs, short and infrequent, were exhaled,
> And each man fixed his eyes before his feet.[179]

Like the 'mob' the members of this crowd are all completely isolated and yet, paradoxically, form something which is fluid; yet unlike any 'mob', an individual appears out of its midst, Stetson, and addresses the speaker in the most familiar of terms. On any other day the speaker might be a part of this crowd. In the final section of the poem, the uncanny crowd returns:

What is that sound high in the air
Murmur of maternal lamentation
Who are those hooded hordes swarming
Over endless plains, stumbling in cracked earth
Ringed by the flat horizon only.[180]

The figures 'swarming' over a featureless terrain are, like the 'hooded' figure walking ahead up the road in the previous section, of indeterminate gender: they might be men who have provoked a 'maternal lamentation' or this 'sound high in the air' might even issue from them, as sounds from afar often seem to come from above. Eliot's note to Hermann Hesse indicates that he had at least partly in mind the revolutionary crowds of 1917, a manifestation of European modernity and yet, as Hesse's references to Dmitri Karamozov's drunkenness and Eliot's use of the anthropological term 'hordes' suggests,[181] also a primitive 'reversion'.

Calling these uncanny crowds 'mobs' is a form of exorcism or a casting outwards of something disturbing into the realm of the 'other'. However, Eliot's more usual strategy is the considerably less violent one of attempting to balance the demands of culture against those of the instincts. This requires in terms of rhetoric a kind of prose 'so nicely/Restricted to What Precisely/And If and Perhaps and But'[182] and in terms of ideological affiliation considerable scepticism.[183] Thus even Eliot's admiration for the *Action Française* was, as we have seen, qualified in important ways and in any case it was not an exportable political movement. A political alliance in Britain similar to that between the *Action Française* and the Syndicalists was forged in the pages of the *New Age* but Eliot found something lacking in all three of its main anti-liberal ideologies. Reviewing a number of books by prominent contributors to the *New Age* in 1927, Eliot concludes that the Toryism of Anthony M. Ludovici (who was better known before the war as a promulgator of Nietzschean doctrine) is wrong to 'discard the Church of England in favour of a better organised and more firmly hieratic Church, the Church of Rome' since 'Toryism is essentially Anglican'; Chesterton's and Belloc's Distributivism is too oriented towards France and its remedy of distributing wealth amongst a series of small landholders would merely concentrate power in the hands of a few large capitalists; and J. A. Hobson's Guild Socialism demonstrates how the '*one* problem' – presumably liberal capitalism – 'is so huge' that we are left 'almost in a state of despair of human ability to solve it'.[184]

Indeed, reading through the pages of *The Criterion* from 1922 to 1939, and in particular his 'Commentaries', one is struck by Eliot's intense curiosity about all things political and his equally strong reluctance to make any kind of political commitment. At different moments, Eliot commends virtually every variety of anti-liberalism *for* its anti-liberalism while always remaining sceptical about its constructive programme. Thus in 1929 he confesses 'to a preference for fascism [over communism] in practice, which I dare say most of my readers share' since 'the fascist form of unreason is less remote from my own than is that of the communists'[185] and yet he prefers a king to a dictator and the *Action Française*'s aim of decentralisation to the centralising ambitions of the Italian fascists.[186] A year later, however, he even praises the Communists for their refusal to compromise while making it clear that they must always remain enemies.[187]

In part Eliot's scepticism towards the radical alternatives to liberal capitalism lay in his conviction that 'political belief' is often 'a substitute for religion'.[188] Thus in 1927 he maintains that '[j]ust as Mr Russell's radicalism in politics is merely a variety of Whiggery, so his Non-Christianity is merely a variety of Low Church senti-ment'.[189] Radical political ideologies are like Arnoldian concepts of Culture since they provide a kind of pseudo-religion which is like 'coffee without caffeine'. However Eliot's stronger objection is that such political belief is not just a weak substitute for religious belief but something which revives a more primitive and powerful form of 'religion'. In *The Idea of a Christian Society*, for example, he argues that the radically secular ideologies of both fascism and communism are 'totalitarian' and 'the tendency of totalitarianism is to re-affirm, on a lower level, the religious–social nature of society'.[190] The radical ideologies of communism and fascism extend the secularising ten-dencies of liberalism and 'Liberalism can prepare the way for that which is its own negation: the artificial, mechanised or brutalised control which is a desperate remedy for its chaos'.[191] However, this 'negation' is not just a modern authoritarian state but also a reversion to the kind of primitive society in which there is no distinction between religion and culture. The totalitarian state is uncanny because it suffers both from too much social differentiation and too little.

Eliot's 'Tory' remedy consists in achieving some kind of balance between Church and State. As he says 'if there is one idea, however vague, by which Toryism may be tried, it is the idea, however vague, represented by the phrase "Church and State" '.[192] By slowing down the differentiating processes of modernity or what Eliot frequently calls the atomising tendencies of liberalism, the moment described by Adorno and Horkheimer in *Dialectic of Enlightenment*, when 'enlightenment reverts to mythology', may be avoided.[193] In terms of art and literature this means upholding some kind of relative aesthetic autonomy in the face of, on the one hand, the avant-gardisms of either the left or the right, and, on the other, the radical aesthetic autonomy of either a reactionary or progressive modernism. However if the 'totalitarian' ideologies of communism and fascism merely extend certain tendancies within liberalism, then conservativism always faces the danger of becoming complicit with the liberalism it merely attempts to check or slow down. Thus while Eliot often refers to himself as a Tory he virtually never has anything favourable to say about the actual British Tory Party. '[W]ithin the memory of no living man under sixty', Eliot writes in 1928, has the Conservative Party 'acknowledged any contact with intelligence'.[194] In fact, he confesses two years later, he is reluctant to use 'the term "Tory", because such public men as Mr Churchill and Lord Birkenhead are called Tories'.[195]

Nevertheless Eliot's attempt during the 1930s to provide a principled Tory alternative to liberalism and its radical pseudo-alternatives is in practice not that different from the capitalist Toryism of those such as Churchill and Birkenhead. During the Abyssinian crisis, for example, he argues that

in the League of Nations, the constitution of which reflects, I think, the British liberal mentality rather than any other, there is room for a confusion of the religious and the secular. The charge brought by the French intellectuals of French intellectuals of the Right, that the League of Nations has put higher and lower civilisations, superior and inferior nations, on the same level, is not without foundation . . . There will probably always remain a real inequality of races, as there is always inequality of individuals.[196]

Apart from its liberal constitution, Eliot's hostility towards the League of Nations may have derived from its association with the Treaty of Versailles, a treaty which in his opinion produced a 'bad peace'.[197] Of course Eliot's views were at odds with those of the coalition Labour–Conservative government since the latter supported not only the Treaty but the League of Nations' economic sanctions against Italy. However while Eliot expresses sympathy for the Right he also maintains, like the French Catholics who opposed the invasion, that '[a]ll men [and races] are equal before God; if they cannot be equal in this world'.[198] He is as it were no further to the 'right' than the British government is to the 'left'. Furthermore, just as the League's opposition to the Italian invasion was ineffectual because it was not accompanied by any military threat, so Eliot's sympathy for the Right does not extend to any support for the Italian government. In fact Eliot never actually says whether or not he supports the invasion. In practical terms, his mildly right-wing views are as inconsequential as the 'liberal mentality' of both the League of Nations and the British government.

Two years later Eliot expresses similar attitudes towards that other, though far greater, political litmus test of the 1930s, the Spanish Civil War. Although '[s]ome people have agitated for the raising of the embargo on the export of arms to the Spanish Government', Eliot expresses the suspicion that those who support such an embargo 'are really asking us to commit ourselves to one side in a conflict between two ideas: that of Berlin and that of Moscow, neither of which seems to have very much to do with "democracy"'.[199] Rejecting the arguments of both sides in what he describes as this 'international civil war of opposed ideas',[200] Eliot attempts to steer a *via media* between the two political armies which between them had mobilised virtually all public and intellectual opinion. Ironically, however, Eliot's neutralism is in practical political terms indistinguishable from the now Conservative British government's policy of non-intervention. Eliot never ceased attacking liberalism but in practice it is not always clear how a conservative *via media* is to be distinguished from a liberal muddle.

In 1938, then, Eliot concludes that '[o]ne sees no hope either in the Labour Party or in the equally unimaginative dominant section of the Conservative Party. There seems no hope in contemporary politics at all.'[201] Of course, his most considered political work, *Notes Towards the Definition of Culture* (1948), was still to be written but this text is almost entirely disengaged from practical politics. In a sense, Eliot's contention in *After Strange Gods* that 'orthodoxy may be upheld by one man against the world'[202] was now applicable to himself. The *via media* between a Godless society and a society which worships strange gods had proven almost impossible to hold.

CHAPTER 4

The homosocial and fascism in D. H. Lawrence

[I]t is this hating homophobic recasting of the male homosocial spectrum [exemplified by D. H. Lawrence] – a recasting that recognizes and names as central the nameless love, only in order to cast it out – that has been most descriptive of the fateful twentieth-century societies, notoriously but by no means exclusively the Fascist.

(Eve Kosofsky Sedgwick, *Between Men: English Literature and Male Homosocial Desire*[1])

It is widely believed that Lawrence's life and writing took a radical turn sometime between the completion of *The Rainbow* and the publication of *Women in Love*. According to Cornelia Nixon, for example, '[a]ll indications suggest that Lawrence suffered a private disaster in 1915, possibly a crisis of sexual identity.'[2] In 1915 his health deteriorated, he experienced difficulties in his marriage, and he met for the first time – and was horrified by – such Cambridge homosexuals as Duncan Grant and John Maynard Keynes. Nixon argues that Lawrence's 'turn against women' during this period involved a rejection of heterosexuality in favour of 'homosexuality' or what she often calls the 'homoerotic'. Lawrence felt considerable ambivalence towards homosexuality, she maintains, because 'he was unable to accept' that his own 'sexual orientation was primarily homoerotic'.[3]

On the contrary, however, I would like to argue that the homosocial communities imagined by Lawrence most fully in his 'leadership novels' are not, as Nixon and others assume, based upon some form of displaced or latent 'homosexuality' but upon a quite explicit and self-conscious rejection of the 'homosexual'.[4] Lawrence's authoritarian male communities conjoin, I will argue, the modern and the primitive by acts of symbolic violence towards a feminised realm which crosses the heterosexual/homosexual divide. As such they exemplify not only the 'fateful societies' referred to by Sedgwick but also a parodic modernity grounded in violence rather than transcendence. Not only was the apparent invention of 'homosexuality' towards the end of the nineteenth century roughly contemporaneous with the emergence of modernism, but for at least one variety of modernism it may well have been a necessary other.

Nevertheless, while this 'crisis' was certainly significant in the development of Lawrence's writing, his 'turn against women' and therefore by implication against 'homosexuals' is present, if only in an embryonic state, from the beginning of his writing career. In his first major novel, *Sons and Lovers*, the mother's claustrophobic and somewhat vampish attachment constitutes for the son precisely the kind of 'crisis' which the 'leadership' novels will later attempt to resolve. In the struggle for possession of the children, Mrs Morel triumphs over her husband because the advantages of her class background (she 'came of a good old burgher family'[5]) outweigh the disadvantages of her gender. However, as many readers have recognised, there is an undercurrent of sympathy in the novel for the drunken, violent and domestically marginalised father.[6] Paul Morel does move into the middle-class world of 'ideas' but he nevertheless retains a love of the 'warmth' of the 'common people'[7] and an appreciation of his father's 'wonderfully young body, muscular, without any fat'[8]. Similarly, while the narrator's opinion that Paul's sleeping with his mother is 'still most perfect, in spite of hygienists'[9] trivialises the incest taboo by reducing it to a kind of faddish prohibition, it also registers, perhaps unconsciously, the full force of this oedipal arrangement by invoking that most fundamental of ontological binaries, the pure/unclean.

According to Lawrence's famous letter to his editor, Paul's close attachment to his mother produces a 'split' in his subjectivity such that his mother and Miriam fight for his 'soul' while his 'mistress' Clara becomes the object of his sexual 'passion'.[10] But Lawrence's statement that 'the mother realises what is the matter, and begins to die' is something of a misreading of his own novel: Mrs Morel does deliberately avoid consulting a doctor about her health but it is Paul and his sister who, like 'two conspiring children',[11] lace their mother's milk with morphia and in the process quite literally kill a woman who has until then obstinately refused to die.

This drift of sympathy away from the mother towards the father is duplicated by Paul's relationships with his lover Clara and Clara's estranged husband Baxter. Miriam comments to Paul that Clara and

Baxter Dawes are 'something like your mother and father' to which Paul replies, 'Yes, but my mother, I believe, got *real* joy and satisfaction out of my father at first'.[12] Clara and Baxter before they meet Paul are what Paul's parents have become: at war with each other, the one violent and drunken and the other somewhat haughty and frigid. The curious thing, however, is that while Clara is, like Paul's mother, an imposing Suffragist when he meets her, she becomes once their relationship begins an entirely sexual being, something of the stock Victorian figure of the older, fallen woman. Similarly, Paul finds Baxter at first a 'bit *too* natural: a bit too near the native beast'[13] yet after they fight – and Paul's 'body, hard and wonderful in itself, [has] cleaved against the struggling body of the other man'[14] – Paul befriends and civilises the initially surly and hostile Baxter, feeling 'an almost painful nearness' to him.[15] Because of their respective relationships with Paul, Clara acquires a body and Baxter a mind. When this process is complete, the now submissive Clara is then 'given back'[16] to a reinvigorated Baxter, much as a father 'gives away' his daughter, while the older man behaves like a dutiful son-in-law and willingly accepts her. Paul has reconciled his own parents by, as it were, fathering them but this is only achieved by empowering the father at the expense of the mother.

In Lawrence's next major novel, *The Rainbow*, there is a similar underlying dual fantasy of parental reconciliation and paternal empowerment, again a kind of imaginary solution to the primal contradiction in Lawrence's life between gender and class. There is in fact an almost mathematical quality to the way in which this novel works out the effect of the single variable of class upon marriage. The first generation marriage of Tom and Lydia is one of a man from a considerably lower class than his wife. The second generation marriage of Will and Anna is one of class equals as is the higher-class, third generation marriage of Anton and Ursula. Thus the only kind of marriage which does not exist in the novel is between a husband who belongs to a higher class than his wife.

What is striking about these three marriages is that their relative harmony does not correspond to that which we would expect considering only the variable of class. Tom and Lydia clearly have the most harmonious marriage despite the fact that Tom is the only man who is socially inferior to his partner. Will and Anna have a less harmonious relationship than Tom and Lydia even though Will's wife is not his social superior and the next couple, Anton and

Ursula, do not even manage to get married even though they are both more middle-class than their predecessors. Finally the marriage which we would expect to be the most patriarchically secure – that between a husband from a higher class than his wife – is, as it were, so unstable that no such characters even meet in the novel. In Lawrence's continuation of the Brangwen saga, *Women in Love*, Gerald and Gudrun approximate very roughly to such a relationship but, significantly, the higher-class character, Gerald, is killed.

In part, the unexpected stability or lack of stability in these marriages is made plausible by the various characters' class mobility. Lydia, for example, has moved an enormous distance down the social hierarchy from being a Polish 'lady well born, a landowner's daughter' to virtually a servant nursing 'an old rector in his rectory'[17] when she meets Tom, a reasonably prosperous farmer. Anna and Will from the next generation are cousins and belong to roughly compatible social classes. However, whereas for the first generation it is the woman who moves socially downwards, for this generation it is the man who moves upwards: Will, who is a 'junior draughtsman, scarcely more than apprentice, in a lace-factory'[18] when he first meets Anna, eventually, and apparently without much effort, becomes a Handwork Instructor for the Nottingham Education Committee, a member of 'the élite of Beldover',[19] and therefore less dominated by 'Anna Victrix'. Ursula is the only woman to move socially upwards and yet her experience of teaching and then of University (where she fails to take her BA) is disillusioning to the point of abject bitterness. Significantly, by attending university (itself a not inconsiderable achievement for a woman at that time), Ursula moves up to the same class level as her lover Skrebensky, a commissioned officer, not above him and when they break up he almost immediately becomes engaged to another women whereas she almost dies of a miscarriage. In short not only does the social mobility of these characters make the success or failure of these relationships more plausible but it favours only the male characters.

As *The Rainbow* progresses from the first to the third generation, from the mid-nineteenth century to a period contemporaneous with Lawrence's own early adulthood, the novel becomes, as many critics have commented, more conventionally 'realist', more concerned with political and social realities outside the family. As Graham Holderness observes, the first generation seem to belong to 'no rural . . . community only a family'.[20] Yet there is no sense in which the success of the marriage of the most historically distant couple, Tom and Lydia, is any more improbable than the absence of a fourth generation (or its failure in Gerald and Gudrun in *Women in Love*). Similarly, the failure of Anton's and Ursula's relationship is no more probable than the relative success of Will's and Anna's. The shift from a kind of mythological to realist style does not bring the lives of the characters any closer to what we would expect their lives to be like if we considered only the two variables of class and gender. The 'realist' part of the novel is no more realistic or probable than the early non-realist chapters. Thus if the class mobility of the characters is the means by which the fantasy of marital harmony between a husband from a lower class than his wife (or alternatively the fantasy of discord between a man from a higher class than his wife) is realised or made more probable, then it is inherently misogynist since it empowers men at the expense of women.

A few months after the outbreak of war, Lawrence divided his ur-novel 'The Wedding Ring' into *The Rainbow* and the material which would become *Women in Love*. In the latter, Lawrence's sympathy for the working-class male and his homoerotic attraction to the working-class male body are even stronger than in the earlier novels and the gender see-saw tilts even further towards the men. As a consequence his earlier fantasies of heterosexual harmony are now replaced by the fantasy of a *Blutbruderschaft*. However while such a fantasy is to some extent a logical extension of his earlier sympathies, it is hard to explain why it became fully expressed only a year or so after the outbreak of the war. After all the war which Lawrence so opposed had, on the one hand, mobilised its own *Blutbrudershafts* and, on the other, more or less quelled the kind of suffragist agitation to which he responded so ambivalently with the creation of characters such as Clara (who loses her feminism as soon as she meets Paul) or Ursula (who is almost destroyed in the process of becoming a New Woman). Perhaps Lawrence felt resentful of the ever-increasing numbers of women entering the previously male-dominated work-force. Although he frequently supported the work of women writers such as HD and Katherine Mansfield, he also wrote to Betrand Russell in July of 1915 that 'as the men elect and govern the industrial side of life, so the women must elect and govern the domestic side'.[21] But since Lawrence was employed neither in the governance of 'the industrial side of life' nor with much economic security, he may have resented this entry of women into the workforce.

However another possible and probably more likely reason is that Lawrence felt uncomfortable in the fact that his anti-war views aligned him with such Bloomsbury and Cambridge homosexual pacifists as Grant and Keynes. A *Blutbrudershaft* is, at least potentially, a more war-like or conventionally virile community than a Bloomsbury salon or Cambridge common room. For whatever reasons, though, Lawrence's vehement moral objections to the war were paradoxically combined with a strong identification with the men fighting on either side.[22] In a poem written in 1915, 'Eloi, Eloi, Lama Sabachthani?', Lawrence imagines the enemy as a virgin bride 'wanting' to be 'planted and fertilized' by his bayonet and yet the speaker also reverses this trope, as the title of the poem would suggest, asking, 'Are the guns and the steel the bridegroom,/Our flesh the bride?'[23] Actual women, rather than 'brides', 'Feed on our wounds like bread'. In the same year, Lawrence maintains in a letter that

Germany is the child of Europe: and senile Europe, with her conventions and arbitrary rules of conduct and life and very being, has provoked Germany into a purely destructive mood. If a mother does this to a child – and it often happens – is she to go on until the child is killed or broken, so that the mother have her way? – Is she not rather, at a certain point, to yield to the paroxysm of the child, which passes away *swiftly* when the opposition is removed? And if Prussia for a time imposes her rule on us, let us bear it, as a mother temporarily bears the ugly tyranny of the child, trusting to the ultimate good. The good will not be long in coming, all over Europe, if we can but trust it within ourselves. (This is not yielding to the child – this is knowing beyond the child's knowledge.)[24]

Presumably, the father is England. Although Lawrence is clearly horrified by the violence between England and Germany, father and son, it has, nevertheless, some fascinating redemptive value, particularly so if it is then redirected against maternal Europe. Lawrence hated the war about as much as he hated his father – which is to say with considerable ambivalence.

But there is nothing ambivalent about his hatred for the Cambridge homosexual 'set'. In a letter to David Garnett, he confesses that he had 'never considered Plato very wrong, or Oscar Wilde' until he had been recently surprised by Maynard Keynes in his rooms at Cambridge suddenly appearing

blinking from sleep, standing in his pyjamas. And as he stood there gradually a knowledge passed into me, which has been like a little madness to me ever since. And it was carried along with the most dreadful sense of repulsiveness – something like carrion – a vulture gives me the same feeling. I begin to feel mad as I think of it – insane.[25]

This Cambridge 'set' makes him dream of 'beetles'. Eleven days later in a letter to Ottoline Morrell, he reports a similar bout of homosexual panic, again associating insects with this 'most dreadful sense of repulsiveness':

Yesterday at Worthing, there were many soldiers. Can I ever tell you how ugly they were: 'to insects – sensual lust.' I like sensual lust – but insectwise, no – it is obscene. I like men to be beasts – but insects – one insect mounted another – oh God! The soldiers at Worthing are like that – they remind me of lice or bugs: – 'to insects – sensual lust'. They will murder their officers one day. They are teeming insects. What massive creeping hell is not let loose nowadays.[26]

Drawing upon the work of Otto Rank, Freud observes that in fairy tales insects and small animals often represent 'the brothers in the primal horde, just as in the same way in dream symbolism insects or vermin signify brothers and sisters (contemptuously, considered as babies)'.[27] If such imagery in fairy tales signifies repressed fraternal rivalry, then in Lawrence's nightmares and daytime fantasies it might signify repressed homosexual desire.

But desire between men in Lawrence is not particularly repressed: in the 'Prologue' to *Women in Love* written soon after these letters, it is 'for men that . . . [Birkin] felt the hot, flushing, roused attraction which a man is supposed to feel for the other sex'.[28] Lawrence then describes at length the kinds of men to whom Birkin has been sexually attracted: 'a policeman who suddenly looked up at him, as he enquired the way . . . a soldier who had sat pressed up close to him on a journey from Charing Cross to Westerham' and in general either 'white-skinned, keen-limbed men with eyes like blue-flashing ice and hair like crystals of winter sunshine' or 'men with dark eyes that one can enter and plunge into, bathe in, as in a liquid darkness, dark-skinned, supple, night-smelling men'.[29] Admittedly, Lawrence excised this 'Prologue' but the wrestling match between Birkin and Gerald remained. And, as Jeffrey Meyers observes, there are similar scenes elsewhere, notably in *The White Peacock, Aaron's Rod* and *The Plumed Serpent*.[30] Given their explicit and celebratory nature it seems rather implausible to interpret such scenes as merely the displaced fantasies of some kind of repressed homosexuality. But what is it, then, which so disturbs Lawrence about homosexuality?

In a poem called 'The Noble Englishman', Lawrence makes the conventional association of homosexuality with narcissism. The speaker in the poem refers to Ronald, the 'Noble Englishman' of the title, as a 'Don Juan' only to be told by Ronald's present 'peaked' lover that

Don Juan was another of them, in love with himself and taking it out on women. –
Even that isn't sodomitical, said I
But if a man is in love with himself, isn't that the meanest form of homosexuality? she said.[31]

In another of his letters of 1915, in this case to Bertrand Russell, Lawrence makes the same associations:

The ordinary Englishman of the educated class goes to a woman now to masterbate [*sic*] himself. Because he is not going for discovery or new connection or progression, but only to repeat upon himself a known reaction.
    When this condition arrives, there is always Sodomy. The man goes to the man to repeat this reaction upon himself. It is a nearer form of masterbation [*sic*]. But still it has some *object* – there are still two bodies instead of one. A man of strong soul has too much honour for the other body – man or woman – to use it as a means of masterbation [*sic*]. So he remains neutral, inactive.[32]

Significantly, Lawrence is not particularly concerned about distinguishing between heterosexual or homosexual sexual practices. We do not know, for example, whether Lawrence is referring at the start of the second paragraph to women or men. Masturbation with a woman and sodomy with a man amount to much the same thing. And in novels such as *The Rainbow*, *Women in Love* and *Lady Chatterley's Lover*, Lawrence's male protagonists show a particular liking for sodomy with women. There is, therefore, a particular zone of sexual activity in Lawrence which does not distinguish between the gender of the object and which therefore crosses the hetero/homo divide.[33]

Later, in *Studies in Classic American Literature*, Lawrence, in fact, is insistent that certain kinds of heterosexual and homosexual love are not all that different. For 'great mergers' such as Walt Whitman,

woman at last becomes inadequate. For those who love to extremes. Woman is inadequate for the last merging. So the next step is the merging of man-for-man love.[34]

Lawrence is far less bothered by the subject's choice of sexual object than he is by his narcissism.

Such an account of the genesis of homosexuality closely resembles Freud's. Three years before the publication of *Studies in Classic American Literature*, Freud explained the relationship between the 'Oedipus complex' and '[t]he genesis of male homosexuality in a large class of cases . . . as follows':

A young man has been unusually long and intensely fixated upon his mother in the sense of the Oedipus complex. But at last, after the end of puberty, the time comes for exchanging his mother for some other sexual object. Things take a sudden turn: the young man does not abandon his mother, but identifies himself with her; he transforms himself into her, and now looks about for objects which can replace his ego for him, and on which he can bestow such love and care as he has experienced from his mother.[35]

Although some have commended Freud's view that homosexuality is not a disease of certain individuals but a stage in the development of all male subjects, this description does imply that homosexuals have become arrested at an immature stage of sexual development. Furthermore, it resembles the definition of homosexuality as a form of 'inversion' advocated by the late nineteenth-century sexologists since it implies that the male homosexual, by identifying with his mother, has adopted the behaviour or characteristics of the opposite gender.[36]

Nevertheless it also closely resembles aspects of Lawrence's almost exactly contemporaneous essay on Whitman. In this essay, Lawrence describes precisely the way in which identification with the 'Female' becomes 'manly love, the love of comrades':

The great merge into the womb. Woman.
And after that, the merge of comrades: man-for-man love.[37]

Thus for Whitman, 'Everything was female . . . even himself'.[38]

Lawrence warns that one cannot love the mother but nor can one identify or 'merge' with the mother and love one's self or other men. The third and no less narcissistic alternative is for the ego which has merged with – or, in Freud's terms, identified with and therefore renounced – the mother to love not other men but the father or the 'ego ideal'. This is in fact what happens, according to Freud, in social groups such as the church or the army: 'A primary group of this kind is a number of individuals who have put one and the same object in the place of their ego ideal and have consequently identified themselves with one another in their ego'.[39] While Freud's account of the 'genesis of male homosexuality' has its considerable problems, it should be noted that his description of the psychology of such social groups does not imply that its members are 'really' repressed homosexuals. The members of these groups may well have gone through a 'homosexual' period in their lives but this would have been neither their first nor their only previous stage. Thus if the kind of social group described by Freud resembles the homosocial groups which Lawrence imagines in his later novels, then it would follow that the homoeroticism of these groups, whatever its ambivalent relationship towards 'homosexuality', cannot be described as a kind of displaced or latent homosexuality. In a sense, we need to take Lawrence at his word.[40]

Of course the social groups described by Freud are not just a recent historical phenomenon. Nevertheless, according to Adorno, Freud's account of group psychology 'clearly foresaw the rise and nature of fascist mass movements in purely psychological categories'.[41] Thus Adorno argues that the 'egos' of the members of Freud's social group resemble those of the fascist followers, the 'object' which they 'put . . . in place of their ego ideal' is the fascist leader, and the 'mother' whom the members of Freud's social group must abandon corresponds to the fascist follower's 'outgroup'. These categories also match almost exactly the basic triangular structure of Lawrence's 'leadership novels'.

In *Aaron's Rod* the central protagonist, Aaron, leaves his working-class family and wife, Lottie, citing mysteriously the need for 'fresh air',[42] earns his living as a musician in London and then Italy, and finally meets and falls in love with the charismatic male writer, Lilly. Aaron's equivalent in Lawrence's next novel (*Kangaroo*), Somers, only desires, like Birkin and Gerald in *Women in Love*, a male love to complement rather than supplant the love in his marriage to Harriet while in the third leadership novel, *The Plumed Serpent*, Cipriano's devotion to his leader, Ramón, requires only that he find a submissive wife, Kate, who will worship him as he does Ramón.

Just as Aaron and Somers are restless questers, so Cipriano feels some kind of 'incompleteness',[43] a quality distinctly lacking in the three leader figures. Adorno comments that 'the leader has to appear himself as absolutely narcissistic', someone who is loved because 'he himself does not love'.[44] Thus according to one of his followers, 'Kangaroo could never have a mate . . . there's no female kangaroo of his species'.[45] Unlike Kangaroo, Lilly in *Aaron's Rod* is married but his wife is conveniently absent for most of the time while he remains, according to Aaron in one of his few sceptical moments, like 'the idol on the mountain top, worshipping [him]self'.[46] In *The Plumed Serpent* the leader figure, Ramón, marries twice but his first wife, an 'intense, almost exalted Catholic', dies after hysterically protesting her husband's revival of the pagan Indian gods and his desire to be 'worshipped' like a 'God'.[47] Ramón's sons remain loyal to their mother, unlike the matricide Paul Morel, and accuse their father of having murdered her. Ramón's equivalent of Freud's 'primal horde' are not his biological sons, even though they are no less oedipally struck than their father, but the soldiers who kill at his command. Only 'a couple of months or so' after the death of his first wife – a strikingly casual phrase – Ramón remarries, this time to a woman with 'an almost uncanny power, to make Ramón great and gorgeous in the flesh, whilst she herself became inconspicuous, almost *invisible*'.[48] Ramón has rescued this woman from insult and humiliation at the hands of her dissolute brothers, men who consider women only good 'for loose, soft, prostitutional sex', and in return she loves Ramón with 'fierce reverence' and a 'wild, virgin loyalty'.[49] Fathers, it would seem, have loyal and submissive wives whereas sons desire to prostitute their sisters. In reality, this second wife is both virginal and, as Kate observes, like a 'slave' or 'prostitute' in Ramón's 'harem' 'glorifying the blood male'.[50] As in *Sons and Lovers*, Lawrence remains both highly self-conscious about the so-called virgin/whore 'split' and powerless to avoid compulsively repeating it.

Ramón thinks he is the reincarnation of the Aztec god Quetzalcoatl, Kangaroo even more improbably wants to lead Australia out of the wilderness of democracy, and Lilly implies that he might be the kind of 'heroic soul'[51] to whom Aaron should submit but all are nevertheless vulnerable. Adorno argues that '[f]or the sake of those parts of the follower's narcissistic libido which have not been thrown into the leader image but remain attached to the follower's own ego, the superman must still resemble the follower' 'just as Hitler posed as a composite of King Kong and the suburban barber'.[52] So Ramón and Kangaroo receive wounds from their enemies, in the case of the latter fatally so, while Lilly, although apparently cast free of any specific class origins, is nevertheless poor.

This ambivalence in the leader is duplicated in the follower, the latter, according to Adorno, having the 'twofold wish to submit to authority and to be the authority himself'.[53] Aaron is searching for some man to whom he can submit himself and yet he considers that most men 'are insects and instruments, and their destiny is slavery';[54] Somers believes in 'the greater mystery of the dark God beyond a man' while expressing almost genocidal impulses towards most of the people he encounters; and Cipriano declares that 'Ramón is *more* than life' to him while his own soldiers cry out, 'We are Ciprianistas, we are his children'.[55]

The social group with which Lawrence is most preoccupied in the two later novels is the military since such an organisation not only structures this kind of ambivalence but also produces what Adorno calls the '[r]epressive egalitarianism' characteristic of the primal horde and the fascist community.[56] There may be no authoritarian homosocial community for Aaron to join but his fascination for Lilly is inseparable from his disgust for and renunciation of his wife and other female lovers. The bond of egalitarian male 'mateship' is offered to Somers by his friend Jack Callcott, one of the returned soldiers or 'Diggers' commanded by Kangaroo, and there is a 'deep communion of blood-oneness' between Ramón and Cipriano and their men.[57]

Of these followers, Cipriano is clearly the most unambiguously fascistic. Significantly, as a boy he was chosen by an English bishop, robbed by 'the Revolution', as a godson. 'I couldn't marry', he explains to his future wife Kate, 'because I always felt my god-father was there, and I felt I had promised him to be a priest'.[58] Instead, he becomes 'half a priest and half a soldier', later identifying his God-father with Ramón.[59] Although for most of his military life Cipriano has renounced women, his repressed desire returns as a lust for violence and ritualised killing. He is repeatedly and not unfavourably associated in the novel with the demonic and he thrives in the atmosphere of terror enveloping Mexico, tracking down and killing the bandits roaming the countryside for whom, like himself, 'the instriking thud of a heavy knife, stabbing into a living body . . . is the best. No lust of women can equal that lust. The clutching throp of gratification as the knife strikes in and the blood spurts out!'[60]

There is no place for women within these homosocial communities. Aaron's romance quest begins when he leaves his wife Lottie, Harriet is mockingly opposed in *Kangaroo* to her husband's political interests, and Kate in *The Plumed Serpent*, although offered a role as a goddess in the Quetzalcoatl cult, experiences a 'strange, heavy, *positive* passivity'[61] in her relationship with Cipriano and, like all the other women, must sit on the periphery of the circle of solemn male chanters and drum thumpers. The female body is partly the cause of such hostility and anxiety – Lottie is metonymically identified with and subsumed by her reproductive capacity and Cipriano denies Kate, like many Lawrence heroes, her orgasm – but the 'mental consciousness'[62] Lawrence spent his career attacking is also invariably gendered as feminine.

Thus in the leadership novels, the male/female opposition generates a series of crucial binaries: power/love; death/life; dark gods/ sky gods; war/peace; and the lower body/mind. Lilly declares:

The ideal of love . . . the ideal of liberty, the ideal of the brotherhood of man, the ideal of the sanctity of human life . . . all the whole beehive of ideals . . . had gone putrid, stinking – And when the ideal is dead and putrid, the logical sequence is only stink.[63]

That which is incorporeal, the ideal, becomes inevitably corporeal like decaying flesh just as the composite woman in Somer's dream – whose 'face reminded him of Harriet and his mother and of his sister and of girls he had known when he was younger' – turns into an old hag.[64] The idealisms against which Lawrence rages in these novels – Christianity, democracy, liberalism, socialism – are also invariably represented with images of engulfment, merging, claustrophobia and the viscous: Australia is described as 'treacly democratic' in *Kangaroo*;[65] social ideals in *Aaron's Rod* are 'the quicksands of woman'[66] and modern love is 'the degeneration into a sort of slime and merge'.[67] One side of the 'split' described in the letter about *Sons and Lovers* is inevitably accompanied by its other, feminine sexuality or, alternatively, what Judith Ruderman describes as the 'devouring mother'.[68]

In these three novels, women are fallen beings, standing for both a perverse sexuality and the various idealisms of the culture of bourgeois modernity. Alternatively, men – 'the rarest thing left in our sweet Christendom'[69] – possess, if they are not emasculated, both a physical or sensuous beauty as well as 'singleness' or individuality. But the realm of masculinity unifies more than just body and mind: all the followers come from working-class backgrounds whereas their corresponding leaders are from the top of the class hierarchy: Lilly is apparently classless but mixes with the cultural elites of Bohemia; Kangaroo is a lawyer and therefore at the top of the Australian colonial class hierarchy; and Ramón is a real or self-styled aristocrat. These fascist communities unite all levels of society. They also unite both Europe and its primitive other: Cipriano is almost 'pure Indian' whereas Ramón is 'almost pure Spaniard'.[70] Together they constitute a religious community, the antithesis of the calamitous 'mixed blood' of most Mexicans or of the 'great melting pot' of America where, Kate speculates, 'men from the creative continents were smelted back again not to a new creation, but down into the homogeneity of death'.[71]

In the contemporaneously written *Studies in Classic American Literature*, Lawrence speculates that when

> an Indian loves a white woman, and lives with her . . . [h]e will probably be very proud of it . . . But at the same time he will subtly jeer at his white mistress, try to destroy her white pride. He will submit to her, if he is forced to, with a kind of false, unwilling childishness, and even love her with the same childlike gentleness, sometimes beautiful. But at the bottom of his heart he is gibing, gibing, gibing at her.[72]

As Kate Millet observes, Lawrence virtually never considers love between a white man and a black woman.[73] When the paradigm of racial interaction is based upon the heterosexual relations of white women and black men, then the 'white man' and the 'red man' cannot 'mingle soothingly'.[74] The marriage between Cipriano the Indian and Kate the Irishwoman cannot succeed just as Aaron and Somers – who are physically small, working-class men like Cipriano and Lawrence himself – have somewhat unsuccessful relationships with, respectively, their upper-class lover and wife.

However, when the paradigm of racial interaction is between men rather than women and men, when the non-European male looks to a male white leader rather than a female white partner, then the 'nucleus of a new society' may be created 'beyond democracy', something like the 'immortal friendship of Chingachgook and Natty Bumppo' in Fenimore Cooper's novels,

> A stark, stripped human relationship of two men, deeper than the deeps of sex. Deeper than property, deeper than fatherhood, deeper than marriage, deeper than love.[75]

This is a homosocial bond which unites mind and body, leader and follower, individual and collective, European and non-European, the modern and the primitive, and it does so by scapegoating the feminine as either a form of sterile 'mental consciousness' or engulfing sexuality. Just as Pound represents rhetoric and usury as irremediably Jewish, so Lawrence figures the undifferentiated 'other' as feminine. And since Lawrence does not distinguish between the narcissism of heterosexual and homosexual love it is also implicitly homophobic. These men love each other but there are no actual homosexuals among their number.

The literary genre favoured by Lawrence to represent this 'new world-epoch' is that of popular romance. When Kangaroo confesses his love for Somers,

A sort of magnetic effusion seemed to come out of Kangaroo's body, and Richard's hand was almost drawn in spite of himself to touch the other man's body. He had deliberately to refrain from laying his hand on the near, generous stomach of the Kangaroo, because automatically his hand would have lifted and sought that rest. But he prevented himself, and the eyes of the two men met. Kangaroo searched Lovatt's [Somer's] eyes: but they seemed to be of cloudily blue like hell-smoke, impenetrable and devilish.[76]

Many familiar romance conventions are here, the lovers staring into each others' eyes, the magnetism between the dark beloved resisting the wooer's effusions almost as though Lawrence were daring the reader to imagine these two men as homosexual lovers. To do so, however, would be an error of taste of the same magnitude as translating a heterosexual romance into a sex manual. But where sex between the lovers of popular romance occurs elsewhere, or after the novel is finished, Lawrence can so explicitly, even outrageously, eroticise male friendships because homosexual sex is simply assumed not to be present anywhere. In a sense, Lawrence literalises romance conventions, the sublimated actions of the lovers no longer standing as metaphors for sex. When Lilly rubs Aaron's 'lower body – the abdomen, the buttocks, the thighs and knees . . . warm and glowing with camphorated oil'[77] we are not, I believe, meant to read this 'as really' about anal intercourse, an aestheticising of homosexual sex motivated by a desire to avoid the censors, but as simply a sensual activity between men in its own right, resonant, certainly, with much significance but not of a conventionally 'homosexual' kind. Love between men in Lawrence is so strong and eroticised not because it can never speak its name but precisely because it so insistently and stridently proclaims its identity.

The libidinal bonds which bind these men are both stimulated and gratified by various pseudo-religious ceremonies. Such a male romance may exercise a kind of spell over its participants and thus vicariously the reader but it is a spell, like the standardized propaganda techniques of the fascists, of what Adorno calls an essentially 'phoney' kind.[78] Towards the end of *The Plumed Serpent*, the ritualised execution of the men who try to kill Ramón is preceded by dialogue such as the following:

CIPRIANO: What man is that, limping?

GUARDS: It is Guillermo, overseer of Don Ramón, who betrayed Don Ramón, his master.

CIPRIANO: Why does he limp?

GUARDS: He fell from the window on to the rocks.

CIPRIANO: What made him wish to betray his master?

GUARDS: His heart is a grey dog, and a woman, a grey bitch, enticed him forth.

CIPRIANO: What woman enticed the grey dog forth?

. . .

GUARDS: This woman, Maruca, my Lord, with the grey bitch heart.

CIPRIANO: Is it she, indeed?

GUARDS: It is she.

CIPRIANO: The grey dog, and the grey bitch, we kill, for their mouths are yellow with poison. Is it well, Men of Huitzilopochtli?

GUARDS: It is very well, my Lord.[79]

With its main hero and answering chorus, this is clearly a ludicrous parody of Greek tragedy. Only by recognising it as such can we break the aesthetic spell Lawrence is attempting to cast and acknowledge that he is relishing the spectacle of the ritualised killing of human beings.

The extraordinary amount of violence found elsewhere in the novel is attributed to others – the spectators at bull fights in Mexico City, bandits and Bolshevists – but this truly depraved moment in Lawrence's writing career demonstrates that this violence is a projection of his own murderous fantasies. We should read, I think, the incessant anti-humanist sentiments expressed in all three novels, the repeated calls to exterminate the swarms of insect-like modern men and women crowding his mental space, not as the kind of cranky individualism so beloved by his many enamoured critics, but as the genocidal fantasies of a deeply wounded narcissistic personality.

However, strongly fascistic as certain aspects of Lawrence's writing are during this period, his homosocial communities are inherently unstable. Lawrence is fascinated by fascistic social structures and yet at the same time deeply sceptical. For one thing, Lawrence is hostile not only in the leadership novels but in his other contemporaneous writing to any kind of nationalist ideology, the extreme varieties of which provided precisely the kind of illusion of community so necessary for fascism. For another, he only accedes to the kind of rigid social hierarchies through which fascist communities regulate the deep ambivalence towards authority of their members with some reluctance. Only in *The Plumed Serpent* is the relationship between leader and follower entirely unproblematic. In the other two novels, there is not only considerable tension between leader and follower but it is the leader rather than the follower who is periodically feminised. When Lilly and Aaron set up house together like a married couple it is the leader, Lilly, who cooks, cleans, even darns socks, as though he were 'as efficient and unobtrusive a housewife as any woman'.[80] Similarly, while Kangaroo wants Somers to love him as a wife or child would her husband or his father, Somers is obsessed by Kangaroo's somewhat bizarre feminised body, particularly his large stomach which he periodically imagines as an actual kangaroo's pouch, the place where he is eventually shot, and something of course which only the female of the species possesses. Father figures become strangely maternalised – Somers at one point, for example, accusing Kangaroo of 'wanting to carry mankind in . . . [his] belly-pouch cosy'[81] – as though the leaders were being turned into their antithesis, the devouring female or mother.

The other axis of the triangular structure, that between follower and out-group, is similarly unstable, wives of the second and third novels being anything but submissive women. Indeed, as the masculinist doctrines of the novels become increasingly fascistic, authorial sympathy, paradoxically, shifts more towards the women or feminised out-group. Moving from *Aaron's Rod* to *The Plumed Serpent*, the leader figures become if not more charismatic then politically more powerful, Lilly a writer commanding no followers, Kangaroo a lawyer commanding a substantial political and paramilitary organisation, and Ramón a potential dictator. Similarly, although it is hard to say whether Somers is more enthralled by Kangaroo than Aaron is by Lilly, Cipriano's devotion to his leader is unquestioning unlike the two other follower figures. The novels also become increasingly detached from any convincing social and political reality: *Aaron's Rod* takes place in the socially ambiguous space of Bohemia, *Kangaroo* in the geographically further removed although English-speaking society of Australia, a country in which Lawrence lived for only 100 days, and *The Plumed Serpent* in the even more remote culture of

Mexico. Although there is hardly a practical political doctrine let alone policy espoused in the whole of that last novel, Ramón incredibly reminds his leader that he could effortlessly assume the presidency of Mexico if he so wanted.

However, the more purely fascistic the political organisation represented, the stronger the women. Aaron's wife is seen, at least by Aaron, as cloying and her voice is barely heard, while Somer's wife Harriet (based on Frieda) is a significant presence in *Kangaroo*, and the hero of *The Plumed Serpent* is not Ramón but Kate, the story being told largely from her point of view. The last two of these women are in fact so strong that they can break the phoney spell of the homosocial groups to which they are subjected. Harriet has the ability not only to mock Somers but even to make him capable of laughing at his own absurdity.[82] The heterogeneous style of the novel itself even releases repressed and narrowly channelled libidinal energy as the hectoring and politically strident voice of the narrator is supplanted, to mention only chapters VIII to X, by a popular song, an almost verbatim copy of a newspaper article on volcanoes, a mock philosophical discourse, an extended comical conceit about the 'good bark *Harriet and Lovatt*',[83] a nursery rhyme, and extended and rather loving descriptions of the Australian landscape. Another chapter called 'Bits' begins by quoting for a number of pages excerpts from the radical Australian magazine *The Bulletin*, passages which are described as 'the momentous life of the continent' without any 'consecutive thread'.[84] There is no such *bricolage* in *The Plumed Serpent*, the awfulness of all the chanted religious poetry only adding to the phoneyness of the novel, but at least a part of Kate is homesick for the normality of home, feeling as though Mexico were a bad dream and realising that the political doctrines of Ramón and Cipriano are 'high-flown bunk'.[85]

All of the leadership novels end ambiguously. Aaron's phallic rod, his flute, is broken in the bomb blast, a symbolic castration which allows for the possibility of what Lilly calls a 'deep, fathomless submission to the heroic soul in a greater man'[86] but we are left unsure as to whether he actually will substitute a leader, let alone Lilly, for his shattered ego ideal. By the end of *Kangaroo*, Somers rejects Kangaroo and his diggers, finding them indistinguishable from their socialist adversaries, standing as they do for the 'whole sticky stream of love, and the hateful will-to-love'[87] but is this insistence on that which belongs beyond love, the realm of power, a call for an even purer kind of fascism or simply the kind of conservatism or liberalism which refuses to distinguish between fascism and communism? Similarly, by the end of *The Plumed Serpent*, Kate and thus quite probably the implied author, appears to have rejected Cipriano and Ramón, but when the novel concludes with her saying to them 'You won't let me go', we are not only unsure whether this might be true, but whether Kate actually really wants to be enslaved. Do 'we' want this?

The same ambivalence marks the central doctrine of not just these novels but all of Lawrence's writing. Lawrence's repeated insistence on the single, isolated self, motivates his resistance to the idealisms of both the 'left' and the 'right' and yet the Mosaic proclamation which rings throughout his texts, 'I am I', is, in its tautological aspects, not only narcissistic but potentially megalomaniacal. Similarly, his strong identification with the feminine has led many of his readers to describe him as protofeminist, and yet such identification motivates his construction of an antithetical homosocial sphere, the narcissistic aspects of which are themselves partly the effect of his attempts to break out of his oedipal attachments.

In many ways *Kangaroo* is the most interesting of these novels because it explores at greater length the ways in which the competing ideologies of 'left' and 'right' mirror each other. In this novel Lawrence cannily represents and critiques the political reality of a period in which Mussolini could begin his career as a socialist and the German fascists could name themselves National Socialists. In his Australian novel Lawrence is both fascinated by a fascistic alternative to the bourgeois modernity of liberalism and its radical extension, communism, and also aware that such an alternative mirrors the modernity it would replace. There appears to be no third alternative. Certainly, in his next and final novel, *Lady Chatterley's Lover*, Lawrence rejects the father–son relationships of his leadership phase so as to explore a healthy heterosexual alternative to the virgin–whore relationships of *Sons and Lovers*. In *Lady Chatterley's Lover* the rejected 'ego ideal' represented by Clifford now has the primitive and modern qualities previously ascribed to women or feminised men but Mellors' relationship with Connie does not mirror that between the leaders and followers. In the leadership novels the follower figures attempt, albeit unsuccessfully, to repress not only their own mental individuality but any knowledge of the physical vulnerability of their partially feminised leaders but Mellors does not wish to suppress either his own intellectuality or Connie's physicality. Indeed that is the point of their relationship. *Lady Chatterley's Lover* is on the one hand both a rejection of the male homosocial communities of the leadership novels and on the other the 'split' subjectivity of *Sons and Lovers*.

However since the relationship between Connie and Mellors takes place in a pastoral world their sexual desire has no social or political correlative. Separated at the end of the novel, it is by no means certain that they will be able to marry or even resume their relationship. Thus while the leadership novels show that the 'left' must be rejected because its idealisations are as repressive as its primitivism is depraved and *Lady Chatterley's Lover* implies that the fascist alternative is equally unacceptable because it makes its followers mindless and its leaders bodiless, there is no final novel which explores the political reality of a third alternative. In a sense, Lawrence is an exemplary figure of the *entre guerre* period because he began as a socialist, then imagined alternative right-wing revolutions, but finished by rejecting the revolutions of either the left or the right, not so as to accept the middle ground of liberal democracy but, like so many others, in despair at any reasonable alternative.

CHAPTER 5

'Always à Deux': Wyndham Lewis and his doubles

Of all the reactionary modernists, Lewis was probably the most vociferous opponent of what would come to be known as 'mass culture'. In *Rude Assignment*, for example, he declares that he is 'what is described as a "highbrow"' living in a century 'badly-infected' by a '"lowbrow" virus' produced by 'monopoly-capital and mass-production' and 'transmitted' by, amongst other cultural institutions, 'the Moving Picture industry'.[1] But unlike the other reactionaries, Lewis does not express nostalgia for any kind of premodern culture. There is no equivalent in his writing of Yeats's Celtic Ireland, Eliot's period before the 'dissociation of sensibility', Pound's 'democratic aristocracy' of Twelfth Century Provence,[2] or Lawrence's New Mexico. Indeed possibly the most striking aspect of all Lewis's texts and paintings is his negative identification of 'mass' culture with the 'primitive' or 'pre-modern'. As Horace Zagreus says in *The Apes of God*, '[j]azz is the folk-music of the metropolitan mass – slum-peasant, machine-minder, – the heart-cry of the city-serf'.[3] This identification can be found in his earliest stories, where the 'peasants', 'primitive people' and 'wild children' are also described as 'puppets' and 'creaking men machines',[4] in his post-war paintings of savage yet mechanical 'tyros', in the satires of the menagerie of 'bourgeois-bohemia' and in such discursive texts as *Paleface: The Philosophy of the 'Melting Pot'*, where he excoriates the 'series of *backward*-cults, from primitivism or naturalism, to fairyhood' of the modern industrial world.[5]

Yet for all his abhorrence of these savage mechanicals, Lewis is also strangely attracted to them. In his early, pre-war 'play' 'Enemy of the Stars', for example, the relationship between the artist figure, Arghol, and the character who represents 'Humanity' or the primitive masses, Hanp, becomes reversed at crucial moments. Although Arghol is given to cursing Humanity for being imitative, parasitic

135

and promiscuous – all qualities conventionally attributed to mass culture – he always adopts in his physical interactions with Hanp the passive, feminine position, at the beginning of the play for example stretching 'elegantly, face over shoulder, like a woman' when Hanp wakes him with his boot.[6] 'Always a deux' [*sic*],[7] Arghol and Hanp are like an unhappy married couple. Thus at the end of the play Hanp drives a knife into Arghol's 'impious meat' and then throws himself from a bridge, 'his heart a sagging weight of stagnant hatred'.[8]

'We are two good old enemies, Edith [Sitwell] and I, *inseparable* in fact' Lewis mischievously informs us in *Blasting and Bombadiering*.[9] Yet while such perverse marriages can be found in virtually all of his texts, Lewis's enemies undergo some degree of change during the *entre guerre* period. Ideologically, his first but never dissolved marriage was to the romantic primitivism of liberal democracy. However, after the General Strike of 1926, Lewis became more preoccupied with communism and when Hitler came to power in 1933 he devoted much of his new ideological attention to fascism. Thus if during the 1920s and early 1930s Lewis both opposes and imitates the romantic primitivism of liberal democracy and its more radical extension, communism, in a way which can be described as fascistic, during the late 1930s his ambivalence towards the primitive and yet modernised masses of the fascist spectacle constitutes a form of reactionary modernism. Yet while he ended his career by rejecting the political avant-gardism of both the 'right' and the 'left', a strong modernist antipathy to ideologies of any kind characterises even his earliest writing. Lewis's flirtation with Nazi ideology was, therefore, not only brief but also less than committed.

The philosophical ground on which Lewis's 'duelling figures'[10] fight has been described by Bernard Lafourcade as a 'black Cartesianism'.[11] Curiously, however, Lewis's few references to Descartes in his most extended philosophical text, *Time and Western Man*, are dismissive:

Descartes called animals *machines*: they had no rational spark. But men use their rational spark so unequally, and are so much machines too, that, on the face of it, that generalization is a very superficial one.[12]

But Lewis does not express any concern with the basic Cartesian division of the mind and the mechanised body. What really bothers him is that, on the one hand, this 'rational spark' may be democratically distributed to others or that, on the other, the mechanised masses might threaten to extinguish his own.

Thus while Lewis is dismissive of Descartes he elsewhere favours the applied Cartesianism of the Fordist production line precisely because it enforces a rigid separation between the creative mind of the industrialist and the masses who, like the Little Tramp at the beginning of Chaplin's *Modern Times*, are merely cogs in the industrial machine. While Lewis maintains that '[i]t would be an insensitive man indeed who did not feel drawn towards such a man as Henry Ford, with his splendid energy and unsocial energy and unsocial character',[13] he also asserts

that a great deal of humanitarian sentiment is wasted on the 'terrible mechanical conditions' under which his employees work. He insists that from long experience he is convinced that they ask nothing better than to be given a quite mechanical and 'soulless' task. He himself, he says, could not bear it for a week; he finds it difficult to understand how *they* can bear it. But they not only can bear it, they like it, he is convinced.[14]

This is not unfair to Ford: as he writes in his autobiography of 1923, *My Life and Work*, the text to which Lewis is presumably referring, repetitive labour would be a terrifying prospect for him but for 'the majority of minds . . . [such] operations hold no terrors'.[15] Similarly, while Lewis expresses considerable animus towards the 'mechanical men' and mass culture of his own age, he never advocates a return to the economic and cultural conditions of pre-industrial societies. Mass culture is fine so long as it is for others. In fact 'mechanical men' are not only quite content with their lives of drudgery but, like the mouse who probably 'enjoys its half-hour with the cat when it is caught very much', they actually possess 'the profound instinct and wish . . . to be ruled'.[16]

Lewis's main adversary, then, is not modern-day science or the seventeenth-century materialist or empiricist philosophy from which it in part derives but the so-called 'time-philosophies', most recently and notably Bergson's, which attempt to bring the mechanised body to life by 'pumping it full of "time"' or spirit.[17] Such philosophies, he argues, '*hand back to*' the mechanical body 'this stolen, aristocratical monopoly of personality which we call the "mind"', dethroning the 'primitive king of the psychological world', the 'ego', and installing in his place the 'democratic' passions.[18] Instead, Lewis favours the philosophy of Berkeley, the kind of idealism which, he believes, keeps the world of objects '*solid*' and '*dead*' and yet also paradoxically, since the mind must preserve its ontological priority, not 'real'.[19]

Berkeley was also an important figure for Yeats, an Anglo-Irish antagonist of the 'filthy modern tide' which swept Europe when 'Locke sank into a swoon . . . [and] God took the spinning-jenny/ Out of his side'.[20] Yet whereas Yeats believes that 'The Garden died' after this fall into modernity, Lewis resists any nostalgic or vitalist impulse. As the eponymous hero of *Tarr* asserts,

> deadness is the first condition of art. The armoured hide of the hippopotamus, the shell of the tortoise, feathers and machinery, you may put in one camp; naked pulsing and moving of the soft inside of life – along with elasticity of movement and consciousness – that goes in the opposite camp. Deadness is the first condition for art: the second is absence of soul, in the human and sentimental sense. With the statue its lines and masses are its soul, no restless inflammable ego is imagined for its interior: it has *no inside*: good art must have no inside: that is capital.[21]

Such an aesthetic is virtually identical to the one described by Hulme in his 1914 essay 'Modern Art and its Philosophy'. In that essay Hulme also identifies deadness and the absence of interiority or flatness as the main characteristics of non-Western and medieval art and the new 'mechanical' art of those such as Epstein, Lewis and Gaudier-Brzeska. Thus just as Tarr conjoins the exotic or '[t]he armoured hide of the hippopotamus' and 'the shell of the tortoise' with the machinery of modern Europe by excluding the organic or living so Hulme conflates the art of 'primitive' cultures with the 'geometrical' art of post-Impressionism by rejecting the 'vitalism' of all European art since the Renaissance. Both aesthetics are parodic in the sense that they explicitly reject the emancipatory aspects of a modernity which they otherwise repeat.

Since there is little if any ironic distance between Tarr and his author, the former's aesthetic is also an accurate description of most of Lewis's own drawings and paintings. In the purely abstract paintings of his Vorticist period, for example, the mechanical forms have a fierce, vertiginous energy which could be felt as an assault either *on* or *by* a barbarous machine age.[22] Similarly in the drawings of the 'Timon of Athens' series the savage yet mechanical figures both constitute the anonymous crowds of the modern world and are its solitary antagonists. Some of Lewis's less abstract paintings do contrast individual figures in the foreground with the anonymous masses in the background. In 'A Battery Shelled' (1919), for example, the soldiers in the distance are both insect-like and reduced to a series of basic geometrical or mechanical forms whereas the three men in the foreground are individualised, almost realistic figures. (Lewis would later write that '[t]he insect world could be truly said to be a Machine World').[23] Nevertheless, these three figures are completely indifferent to the warscape only one of their number even bothers to view. Although detached from the carnage surrounding them, they are no more alive, at least emotionally, than the toiling insect figures.

But perhaps the painting which best exemplifies this doubling of the artist and his adversaries is Lewis's 1920–21 self-portrait of himself 'as a Tyro'. Like all his tyros, the self-portrait identifies the *beau monde* of contemporary life with a savage laughter, the mechanical and the primitive. The painting is somewhat unusual, however, since Lewis satirises himself rather than others, the two most prominent aspects of the tyro, his teeth and laughter, also characterising his own features. Nevertheless this identification with the mechanised other only serves to armour the self just as what might have been an expression of alienation is now one of menacing antagonism. Just as the Vorticist polemicist can declare that 'Our Vortex is proud of its polished sides', so the Cartesian self or tyro in this painting borrows from its mechanised other an armoured invulnerability.[24] The viewer of the painting is therefore placed in an ambiguous position: he or she might view the tyro as either a type of the barbarous modern world or as a figure who is sneering at his or her sentimental romanticism. A tyro or young soldier or recruit is both someone towards whom we might feel either the superiority of the experienced or the vulnerability of the citizen. Like his later and equally paradoxical description of himself as 'The Enemy', the tyro is both self and other.

Such doubling accounts for the peculiarly sterile nature of Lewis's satire and comedy. As is well known Lewis reverses Bergson's proposition that the comic occurs when people start behaving like objects,[25] arguing instead that '[t]he root of the Comic is to be sought in the sensations resulting from the observations of a *thing* behaving like a person'.[26] Lewis's own examples – of a sack of potatoes suddenly trundling down the street or a couple of trees walking[27] – show how wrong this reversal of Bergson is: what would be funny, rather than just odd, is if a person were to behave like a sack of potatoes or a walking couple like a pair of trees. Nevertheless, since according to Lewis the artist as satirist is on the side of death and the mechanical savages he ridicules are on the side of life, it must be the latter, the world of things, which comically behaves like the former, people or artists such as himself. The comic now occurs when one side of the Cartesian divide, the world of mechanical objects, *imitates* the other, the world of the mind or when, in the terms of his most famous satire, *The Apes of God*, the 'bourgeois bohemians' 'ape' the authentic artist.

However since the purpose of Lewis's satire is to return his puppets and automatons back to the life from which they foolishly tried to escape they often have a kind of vitality which their satirists lack. In a sense, Hanp is more alive than Arghol, Otto Kreisler a far more energetic character than Tarr. Such characters are comic scapegoats but their deaths do not allow for any kind of renewal. Thus a satire such as *The Apes of God* has a circular structure, its beginning (where we see ninety-six-year-old Lady Fredigonde at her toilette) mirroring its end (the same lady proposing to and being accepted by the much younger Horace Zagreus). These 'bourgeois-bohemians' will keep 'aping' the true artist-originals for the rest of eternity as though trapped in a circle of Hell (unless like Lady Fredigonde's husband they eventually wear out and stop) but their extraordinary albeit perverse persistence is also an indication of considerable energy. Alternatively the very frigidity of Lewis's heroes often turns them into the very machinic beings they so despise. Having spent most of his life being contemptuous of those around him, the hero of Lewis's last novel, *Self Condemned*, for example, becomes nothing more than 'a glacial shell of a man,' hardly distinguishable from the hollow academics with whom he works, his isolation eventually draining him of any interiority or humanity.[28] Lewis's machines come alive just as his satirists become the satirised.

Despite such doubling, however, the gender of the aesthetic remains essentially masculine. According to Tarr

God was man: the woman was a lower form of life. Everything started female and most so continued: a jellyish diffuseness spread itself and gaped upon all the beds and bas-fonds of everything: above a certain level sex disappeared, just as in highly-organized sensualism sex vanishes. On the other hand, *everything* beneath that line was female.[29]

Commenting on this passage, Fredric Jameson observes

that while women, the organic, and sex itself are here all identified within a mythic, clearly negative term, there is no correlative celebration of the male principle. The peculiarity of Lewis's sexual ideology is that, while openly misogynist, and sexist in the obvious senses of the word, it is not for all that phallocentric. The positive term which logically corresponds to the negative one of the female principle is not the male, as in D. H. Lawrence, but rather art, which is not the place of a subject, masculine or otherwise, but rather impersonal and inhuman, or, as Lewis likes to say, 'dead', spatial rather than temporal and existential.[30]

But this is not an entirely accurate description of *Tarr*, or at least of the relationships between its four main characters. In fact the axis of gender cuts across the axis which divides art from life. Thus while Kreisler and Anastasya are problematic characters – the former because he is on the side of life and yet a man, the latter because she is a woman and yet on the side of art – the artist-hero of the novel, Tarr, is no less of a man than his opposite, the kitsch-loving Bertha, is any more than a woman. Lewis does attack the cult of masculine virility in writers such as Ernest Hemingway and Lawrence but this does not degender the realm of 'art' any more than the artistic pretensions of the feminised realm of 'bourgeois bohemia' kills any vitalist impulse.

Nevertheless, although Tarr does have a reasonably successful relationship with Bertha (at least from his point of view!), his relationships with Anastasya and Kreisler are far more troubled. At one point in the novel Kreisler forcibly evicts the uninvited Tarr from his studio with a dog-whip, accusing him of 'hovering and fawning around' him all week at the Café[31] and later Tarr explains that 'such successful people as Anastasya and himself were by themselves: it was as impossible to combine or *wed* them as to compound the genius of two great artists'.[32] Tarr can neither marry Anastasya nor have an unproblematic male friendship with Kreisler. By contrast Tarr and Bertha, although complete opposites, actually marry by the end of the novel. As Tarr explains early on to another artist, 'no one could have a coarser, more foolish, slovenly taste than I have in women'.[33] Thus despite his contempt for Bertha, he becomes restless when temporarily separated from her and even decides to take a flat near where she lives so he might finish two paintings on which he is working.

However, although Tarr eventually decides that he cannot marry Anastasya his relationship with Kreisler is even more problematic. Indeed not only is this relationship the most significant in the novel but as most readers have recognised it is Kreisler rather than Tarr who becomes the main source and focus of the narrative's energy. There are some curious contrasts between Kreisler and Lewis.

Kreisler is thirty-six-years old – the same age as Lewis when the novel was published in 1918. Whereas Kreisler is a failed artist, Lewis had finally established a reputation as a painter by the outbreak of war. Kreisler is a bohemian; Lewis – who insisted that his fellow Vorticists wear business suits – a former bohemian. Kreisler is humiliated by his financial dependence upon his distant and dictatorial father. Lewis's parents had separated when he was eleven years old and according to his biographer, Jeffrey Meyers, Kreisler's 'formal and financial' relationship with his father was similar to Lewis's own;[34] but as though making light of their abandonment, Lewis in a letter to his mother of 1907 describes his father as 'the Old Rip'.[35] The main scandal of Kreisler's miserable existence is that his stepmother is his former fiancée. Lewis, however, would often boast in his letters to his mother of 'all . . . [his] female conquests'.[36] His relationship with his mother was so close that, from the evidence of his letters, it seems he sent his dirty washing from Paris where he was living to her in London![37] In the novel Kreisler rapes Bertha and makes her pregnant whereas the woman on whom she is modelled, a German woman with whom Lewis had a four-year relationship, was merely abandoned after she had had Lewis's child.[38] In short, Kreisler, a man humiliated by his father and abandoned by his mother/lover, seems to represent in part the negative aspects of Lewis's own oedipal relationships.[39]

Accordingly, although Lewis's avatar in the novel, Tarr, becomes almost mesmerised by Kreisler his troubling inability to leave Kreisler alone is never fully explored. The secondary plot, the one which concerns Kreisler's rivalry with Soltyk for Vokt's money, eventually takes over from the main plot, or Tarr's relationship with Kreisler and his trading of Bertha for Anastasya. Because Tarr has no role to play in this secondary plot, Lewis is able to develop its grotesquely oedipal potential to its full:

> Soltyk, who had got hold of Vokt, and was something that had interfered between that borrowable quantity and himself, occupied in his life now a position not dissimilar to his stepmother. Vokt and his father, who had kept him suspended in idleness, and who now both were withdrawing or had withdrawn like diminishing jets of water, did not attract the full force of his indolent tragic anger. Behind Ernst [Vokt] and his parent stood Soltyk and his stepmother.[40]

The classic oedipal scene is somewhat displaced since the son's rivalry is not with the father but with the 'mother'. Nevertheless

Kreisler's rivalry with Soltyk has a strong element of narcissistic identification: '[p]hysically,' the narrator explains, 'Soltyk even bore, distantly and with polish, a resemblance to Kreisler'.[41] As though bearing out Freud's problematic contention that the homosexual identifies with his mother so as to love another like himself, Kreisler's murderous rivalry with Soltyk also has a strong component of love. Kreisler for example offers to forgo the duel if Soltyk will give him a kiss and to that end he 'thrust his mouth forward amorously, his body in the attitude of the Eighteenth-Century gallant, right toe advanced and pointed, as though Soltyk had been a woman'.[42] And just before their ludicrous attempt at a duel, Kreisler sees Soltyk taking a sedative tablet and demands 'I want a jujube . . . [a]sk Herr Soltyk! [t]ell him not to keep them to himself!' as though the latter were both his rival brother and his mother.[43] Kreisler really is a quite extraordinary character. Yet while the dramatisation of his pathology gives the novel a *frisson* it would certainly not have possessed if Tarr had remained the main character, Kreisler is nevertheless to some extent quarantined: as the novel progresses, he becomes increasingly the double of Soltyk rather than Tarr, in the process allowing both Tarr and the author to disengage and distance themselves from his powerfully destructive and morbid energy.

Such disengagement is, however, only partial. At the end of the novel, Tarr decides to marry Bertha rather than Anastasya precisely because the former informs him that she is bearing Kreisler's child. Significantly, when the child is born it bears 'some resemblance to Tarr'.[44] While in a sense this makes Tarr a father since he tells Bertha that the child 'can always pass as mine',[45] he is not of course a 'real' or biological father. Indeed Kreisler's death represents the destruction of not only a humiliated son but also a potent father. Kreisler's acts of sexual violence, his rape of Bertha and obsessive pursuit of Anastasya, seem to be largely a reaction to his frequent humiliations. According to the denizens of the cafés he frequents, for example, Kreisler not only looks like the 'the sort of man . . . who would splice his sweet-heart with his papa', but it is also rumoured that he 'had to keep seventeen children in Munich alone; that he only had to look at a woman for her to become pregnant'.[46] Although frequently represented as a kind of overgrown child, Kreisler is also an 'antediluvian puppet of fecundity' and a kind of 'universal papa'.[47]

By contrast it is not until the final paragraph of the novel that we are informed that in the future Tarr will have 'three children by a lady of the name of Rose Fawcett'.[48] Similarly, although a brief reference is made to Tarr's 'childhood of mollycoddling' from his 'selfish vigorous little mother',[49] no mention is made of any father. Indeed this absence of either a father or of any paternal figures partly explains why Tarr appears, to use Hugh Kenner's mystificatory description of Lewis himself, as a 'man from nowhere'.[50] As Jameson observes, Tarr is positioned in the novel as a 'hypertrophied ego' and 'the psychic system of *Tarr* knows no superego'.[51] Although mesmerised by Kreisler for most of the narrative, Tarr is neither the son of any father nor the father of any son.

If Tarr's relationship with Kreisler suggests some kind of authorial anxiety about the identity of the male subject, then his relationship with Anastasya implies an anxiety about the female object. Anastasya tells Tarr that 'a high-brow girl such as me must be sexually . . . an abomination'[52] and, referring to her breasts, asks him whether he can 'respect such objects upon a person, right on top of a person?'[53] Tarr thinks of her as a 'milky ox' (that is as a cow and a castrated male) and when she seductively crosses her legs he sees 'two snowy stallion thighs'.[54] During this seduction scene Anastasya tells him that '[a] man's leg in Ladies' Hose is just as nice as a woman's leg'.[55] Tarr does not reply but somewhat later he calls her a 'great he-man of a german art-tart'.[56] Although Tarr attempts to degrade Anastasya by offering her twenty-five francs in return for sex, she returns the compliment, telling him that 'twenty-five francs to be your audience while you drivel about art'[57] is an insulting offer. They do have sex but Tarr needs to reassure himself that 'he would not be a pervert because he had slept with her'[58] and he finally comes to the conclusion that

he and Anastasya could not combine otherwise than at present: it was like a mother being given a child to bear the same size already as herself. Anastasya was in every way too big; she was too big physically, she was mentally outsize: in the sex department, she was a Juggernaut.[59]

By his own confession, therefore, Tarr has placed himself in the position of the mother so that – and in accord with Freud's account of homosexual desire – he loves someone who, because of their 'outsize' intellect, masculine characteristics and relative chastity (she has only ever had two old men as lovers), resembles himself. But these roles are reversible: Tarr feminises himself by desiring Anastasya while also asserting his masculinity by calling her 'a famous whore who becomes rather acid in her cups'[60] just as Anastasya behaves like an intellectual and a whore.

Yet despite these differences all four of the novel's major characters combine the primitive and the modern in various ways. Like all women, Bertha is 'a lower form of life' and therefore less evolved than men such as Tarr but she is also 'machine-like'[61] and the natural world with which she is associated produces jarring 'metallic tints'.[62] Similarly when Kreisler rapes Bertha he is both a 'mad beast' and someone who has 'revenged himself as a machine might do'.[63] Tarr combines, as Eliot puts it in his review of the novel, 'the thought of the modern and the energy of the cave-man'[64] and Anastasya, although a modern and independent woman from a middle-class family, appears to Kreisler as though 'bespangled and accoutred like a bastard princess or aristocratic concubine of the household of Peter the Great, jangling and rumbling like a savage raree show through abashed capitals'.[65]

Thus *Tarr* describes the 'resolution' of the opposition between the primitive and the modern in terms of all but one of the possible versions of the oedipal family romance. Tarr's most satisfactory relationship is with a degraded lover, Bertha, whose body is described as 'strung to heavy motherhood'.[66] A less satisfactory alternative is to identify with the mother and love another, Anastasya, as though she were Tarr's boyish self. And even more problematic is Kreisler's violent paternal relationship towards women such as Bertha or his filial submission to a hostile father. The only version of the oedipal family romance Lewis does not explore (apart from those of course in which a female is the main subject), is the Freudian comedy in which a male subject renounces his love for his mother and resolves his ambivalence towards his father so that he can love exogamously. During the modernist period the tension between the primitive and the modern, aesthetic modernity and bourgeois modernity, was often represented in oedipal terms, presumably because, as I suggested earlier, the Victorian or modern middle-class private/public division which partly overlaps these other divisions must have produced rather fraught father–son relationships and rather claustrophobic mother–son relationships. Certainly in their quite different and complex ways, the writing of Lawrence and Yeats seems to suggest this. However since Lewis is unable to provide a vision of exogamous desire such as Yeats provides at the end of 'Among School Children' it would follow that he is unable to resolve satisfactorily the conflicts of modernity.

That said, however, Lewis's career tends to defy easy ideological description. Jameson refers to Lewis's 'implacable lifelong opposition to Marxism itself'[67] but in his first major work of political philosophy, *The Art of Being Ruled*,[68] he is at times quite sympathetic towards Marxism and communism. Perhaps the only consistent aspect of Lewis's many and varied ideological pronouncements is their opposition to liberal democracy or what Hulme calls the 'democratic ideology' of the 'romantic movement'. Since like Hulme and Lasserre, Lewis does not distinguish between Romanticism and Enlightenment this ideology can embrace, on the one hand, the kinds of primitivism attacked in texts such as *Paleface* or, on the other, the 'phantom men' and abstractions of the Enlightenment.[69] In *The Art of Being Ruled*, for example, Lewis refers to 'the *poetry* of passive, more or less ecstatic, rhythmic, mechanical life' and 'the intoxicated dance of puppets'[70] as though the primitivism of Romanticism and the machinery of an enlightened progress were essentially the same.

The two main ideological adversaries of liberal democracy in *The Art of Being Ruled*, then, are fascism *and* communism. Lewis does claim to 'favour some form of *fascism* rather than communism' but then he immediately confesses that 'when two principles are opposed, and one of these is that of English liberalism, in most cases I should find myself on the other side, I expect'.[71] Although he favours fascism to communism he prefers communism to 'english liberalism'. Thus in 1925 when he completed *The Art of Being Ruled* 'the principal conflict' for Lewis is not between communism and fascism but 'between the democratic and liberal principle' and 'the principle of dictatorship of which Lenin was the protagonist and first great theorist'.[72] The former is an ideology for those who want to be 'ruled' whereas the later is an ideology of the 'rulers'. Furthermore,

[t]his division into rulers and ruled partakes of a sexual division; or rather, the contrast between the one class and the other is more like that between the sexes than anything else. The ruled are the females and the rulers the males, in this arrangement. A stupid, or slow-witted, not very ambitious, conventional, slothful person (what has been called aptly *homme moyen sensuel*, the human average) has necessarily a great many feminine characteristics. These involve him, too, in a great many childish ones. And the relation of the ruler to the ruled is always that of a man to a woman, or of an adult to a child.[73]

Lenin and Mussolini resemble Tarr whereas the democratised masses are like Bertha. In fact since '*fascismo* is merely a spectacular marinettian flourish put on to the tail, or, if you like, the head, of marxism'[74] then there is not much difference between the Italian and Soviet regimes:

[Mussolini's] government is doing for Italy – starting ostensibly from the other end – what the soviet has done for Russia. The more militant liberalist elements are being heavily discouraged in a very systematic way. They are not being physically wiped out, as happened in Russia, but they are being eliminated quite satisfactorily without recourse to murder on a large scale. What will shortly be reached will be a great socialist state such as Marx intended, rigidly centralized, working from top to bottom with the regularity and smoothness of a machine.[75]

When Lewis wrote *The Art of Being Ruled* the Soviet regime was less than a decade old and therefore one he could praise for its oppositional or anti-liberal and anti-democratic aspects. However in the year of its publication, 1926, the General Strike may have brought the reality of 'communist' or 'Marxist' revolution rather closer to home for him. Certainly in the conclusion to *Blasting and Bombardiering*, Lewis remembers that

in 1926 I began writing about politics, not because I like politics but everything was getting bogged in them and before you could do anything you had to deal with the politics with which it was encrusted. And I've got so bepoliticked myself in the process that in order to get at *me*, to-day, you have to get the politics off me first . . . However, when politics came on the scene I rang down the curtain; and that was in 1926. That was when politics began for me in earnest. I've never had a moment's peace since.[76]

Although he does not specify how the General Strike affected him, something of its impact can be gauged from the final chapter of *The Apes of God* (1930), which is titled 'The General Strike'. Interestingly, the strikers are never directly described:

The whole townland of London was up in arms and as silent as the grave and it was reported that in its eastern quarters, in the slum-wards such as Poplar, a Police-inspector and two Specials had been kicked to death and there were more and more violent riots in Hammersmith, where trams had been wrecked and street-rails torn up by the mob, and the Police stoned and injured: while it was confidently stated that in the North crowds had sacked the better quarters, in the big factory-towns, mines were flooded, mills were blazing, and troops were firing with machine-guns upon the populace. The absence of newspapers fostered every report of disorder.[77]

The strikers are responsible for most of the violence and while the rumours of their actions are yet to be confirmed the ending of the novel clearly implies that their violence, or at least its political and social effects, will soon surprise the culpably innocent bourgeois-bohemians whose revolutionary play-acting has in part incited it.

Whatever the reasons, after 1926 Lewis tended to oppose rather than conflate communism and fascism. However since Mussolini, who became dictator in the same year, was not in his eyes a particularly credible fascist alternative to communism, Lewis had to wait until 1930, when he visited Germany to write some newspaper articles about Hitler and the Nazi party, to discover a fascist party capable of combating the communist menace. Since the Nazis had not yet achieved complete political power, they could be both an oppositional force and a new rulers' ideology. Consequently in the book which resulted from his newspaper articles, *Hitler*, Lewis represents the communists as not only in league with the republican government but as propounding a doctrine which has all the essential characteristics previously ascribed only to liberal democracy:

> The Class-doctrine . . . demands a *clean slate*. Everything must be wiped off slick. A sort of colourless, featureless, automaton – *temporally* two-dimensional – is what is required by the really fanatical Marxist autocrat. Nothing but a mind *without backgrounds*, without any spiritual depth, a flat mirror for propaganda, a parrot-soul to give back the catchwords, an ego *without reflection*, in a word, a sort of Peter Pan Machine – the adult Child – will be tolerated.[78]

But for the fact that his target is Marxism rather than liberalism, Lewis's conflation of Romanticism and Enlightenment or the romantic cult of childhood with the *tabula rasa* of eighteenth-century empiricist philosophy is much the same as his equation of the primitive and the abstract in *The Art of Being Ruled*. Lewis's pre-1926 and post-1926 political positions remain much the same except that 'communism' changes from being an opponent of romantic primitivism to being an ideology which exemplifies it.

Yet by championing 'race' rather than the 'Class-doctrine' of the Marxists and the 'productive' and 'concrete' capital of both the peasant and the industrialist rather than the 'intangible' and 'speculative' 'Loan-capital' of capitalism and communism, Lewis comes close to repeating the kind of romanticism which he finds so abominable. Like Hitler he believes that since the 'interest of the industrialist . . . is in many ways identical with that of the peasant' the western economies could recover from economic depression 'if only the incubus of *Das Leihkapital* could be removed'.[79] Although Lewis mischievously identifies Eliot as a fellow 'credit-crank' his views on the financial sphere are therefore probably much closer to Pound's. However whereas Pound's *initial* impulse tends to be anti-modern Lewis's tends to be anti-primitive. Thus by attacking a modern phenomenon such as *Leihkapital* Lewis finds himself, albeit with some degree of cantankerous amusement, enthusing about the '*Golden Age*' which would return if only '*Das Leihkapital* could be removed'.[80] Lewis's opposition to the abstract and quantifying tendencies of the Enlightenment brings him perilously close to nostalgic romanticism.

This apparent difficulty is perhaps even more evident when he discusses Nazi concepts of 'race'. By contrast to the Marxist emphasis on class, the intention of the Nazi doctrine of *Blutsgefühl* is 'to *draw in* and to *concentrate*, rather than to diffuse, disperse and mix'.[81] Nevertheless it is a paradoxical doctrine since it 'provides us with a passionate *exclusiveness*' by desiring a '*closer and closer* drawing together of the people of one race and culture, by means of bodily attraction'.[82] Alternatively, although the Marxist concept of class tends romantically to dissolve boundaries between self and other it is also a fundamentally warlike doctrine and therefore one which erects boundaries between the self and its others. Lewis even claims that all the violence in Berlin is initiated by 'Marxist murder-gangs' in league with the government and that Hitler, who is frequently referred to as a 'Man of Peace', allows his Nazis only 'fists or sticks to defend' themselves.[83] In practice therefore it is almost impossible to distinguish between his concepts of race and class since both are exclusive *and* inclusive. Lewis does concede that '[t]he *extreme* interpretation of the Race-doctrine would be liable to leave you with a romantic snob on your hands: the extreme interpretation of the Class-doctrine with a simple Robot'[84] but his fictional snobs are anonymous robots and his identity-less machines violently exclusive.

Lewis's primary strategy for avoiding such doubling in *Hitler* is to represent his adversaries as comically married to their obsessions. Apart from 'Loan-capital' the Nazis' main targets are Jews and 'perverts' but Lewis's satire is largely directed towards the liberal Englishman's relationships with such people. Because the 'average political Anglo-saxon' 'always falls in love with what he *ought not to do*',[85] Lewis decides to take his innocent reader for a tour of a 'characteristic Nachtlokal' in Berlin's '*quartier-général* of dogmatic Perversity – the Perverts' Paradise, the Mecca of both Lesb and So'.[86] At first the Anglo-Saxon 'sightseer might be disappointed' or feel that 'he had been misled into visiting a respectable resort' but then

elegant and usually eyeglassed young women will receive him, with an expensive politeness, and he will buy one of these a drink, and thus become at home. Still, he will have to be a sightseer of some penetration not to think that his sightseeing eyes may not this time be destined to gloat, upon what he had promised them they should find there. Then these bland Junos-gone-wrong, bare-shouldered and braceleted (as statuesque as feminine show-girl guardees), after a drink or two, will whisper to the outlandish sightseer that they are *men*. Oh dear – so, after all, the sightseeing eyes are going to be satisfied! And they will goggle at the slightly smiling bland edwardian 'tart' at their side – still disposed to regard this as hoax after all, for it is *too* like, it is too true to nature by far.

But his companion will invite the sceptical tourist to pass his disbelieving paw beneath her chin. She will catch hold of it without coyness and drag it under this massively fashioned feature. All doubt is then at an end. There, sure enough, the fingers of the sightseer will encounter a bed of harsh unshaven bristles as stiff as those of a tooth-brush.[87]

One might suspect that Lewis is vicariously enjoying his imaginary sightseer's experience but since he adopts the role of tour guide there can be no question of him being suddenly erotically surprised. The comedy lies in our observing an innocent not only experiencing perversion for the first time but perhaps also enjoying it. Since Lewis-as-tourist-guide has seen it all before the reader-as-sightseer is unlikely to discover him staring at any of these 'Junos-gone-wrong' with undue fascination. Lewis is watching the sightseer, not the 'pervert'.

In contrast to such 'women', Lewis represents the Jews as women who play at being men:

the Jews . . . govern England to the complete satisfaction of everybody, and without a hitch, or so much as a single rift in the lute! But that would not be quite true: for if indeed, wearing the trousers, the Jew is the brilliant and bossy Hausfrau of this stolid english hubby, the latter has at least, in his quiet way, succeeded in influencing her, decidedly for the good.[88]

But the main point of such satire is to warn the 'Hitlerite' against taking 'the Jew too seriously'.[89] Although Lewis is clearly antisemitic he also wants to be anti-antisemitic:

The Hitlerite must understand that, when talking to an Englishman or an American about the 'Jew' (as he is prone to do), he is apt to be talking about that gentleman's *wife!* Or anyhow *Chacun son Jew!* is a good old english saying. So if the Hitlerite desires to win the ear of England he must lower his voice and coo (rather than shout) *Juda verrecke!* – if he *must* give expression to such a fiery intolerant notion. Therefore – a pinch of malice certainly, but no 'antisemitism' for the love of Mike![90]

A Hitlerite only 'prone' to talk about 'the "Jew"' and one who might be trained to 'coo' a vicious curse or threat is clearly as much a figure of ridicule as the Anglo-Saxon who is happily married to a Jew. Lewis is far more concerned to distance himself from the Nazis' antisemitism than he is to distance himself from their homophobia. Indeed he claims that Berlin's nightlife leaves 'the Nazis cold'[91] and that for them '[t]*he Bank is more important than the Backside'.*[92] Nevertheless he does inform us that Hitler's Berlin offices are 'round the corner' from an institution called 'the *Domino Bar*'[93] and he does speculate that

all these Bars and Dancings, with their Kaffir bands, are for him [the Nazi] the squinting, misbegotten, paradise of the *Schiebertum*. 'Juda verrecke!' he would no doubt mutter, or shout, if he got into one. Sooner or later he would desire to be at the head, or in the midst, of his *Sturmabteilung* – to roll this nigger-dance luxury-spot up like a verminous carpet, and drop it into the Spree – with a heartfelt *Pfui!* at its big sodden splash.[94]

Whereas the Nazi 'takes the Jew too seriously' there is only a suggestion in this passage that he is rather too interested in perversion. Indeed although he desires 'to roll this nigger-dance', this imaginary Nazi seems less interested in perversion as such than the fact that it is a manifestation of Judaism.

Thus while 'the pervert' and 'the Jew' are associated and even interchangeable in his polemics and novels of the 1930s, the latter is, arguably, of greater political significance. It is perhaps not surprising, then, that when Lewis finally attacked German fascism in *The Hitler Cult* (1939) he also chose to publish in the same year *The Jews: Are They Human?* Despite its vicious title the latter is primarily an attack on the figure of the antisemite rather than 'the Jew'. Nevertheless it utilises the same comic strategies as *Hitler*:

The antisemite can be, especially in England, quietly studious. That is another type. I once, when I was a schoolboy, went with one to the East End of London. He took up his position under a lamppost in the Commercial Road upon a foggy night. He 'put his pipe on,' wiped his glasses, and got ready to enjoy himself. He gazed at the Jewish passers-by in a kind of rapt and gloating way. *He* now was rather like a Philatelist. These specimens of an accursed race were his postage-stamps. He caught his breath when a particular 'beauty' passed – he plucked my sleeve or nudged me and muttered rapturously, 'I say! Look at that one!'[95]

Chacun son hobby or obsession, we might say. Yet while the satire is clearly directed at the antisemite it is obviously not written from the point of view of the Jews of the East End. Lewis is watching the antisemite who is watching the Jews but the gaze of neither is returned. Lewis's anti-antisemitism is not a form of philosemitism and for that reason barely disturbs the crudest of antisemitic stereotypes:

A man begins by disliking instinctively a waddling strut just ahead of him as he walks down the street – those board-like horizontal shoulders, those protruding ears. Next he resents the arrogance so provokingly painted upon the 'oily' countenance – for like the Dago, the Jew is 'oily' to Anglo-Saxon eyes. The smell of the cheap cigar puts the final touch. He feels he could have forgiven anything except that acrid whiff of cheap self-satisfaction – and, before you can say knife, antisemitism has lifted up its ugly head![96]

Elsewhere in *The Jews* Lewis either attributes the same attributes to the antisemite as the latter attributes to the Jews or he uses a stereotype to the disadvantage of the antisemite but not to himself. Since 'nearly every disobliging thing that is said about the Jew can with equal truth be said about the Gentile',[97] the latter can be as 'sentimental' as any woman,[98] his slums as ugly as any Jewish ghetto[99] and his 'Dollar Diplomacy' just as invidious as Jewish usury.[100] Alternatively, although '[t]he *average* intellectual endowment of the Jew is much more considerable than is the case with his Gentile neighbour' it is nevertheless also true that 'we', 'being more stupid in the mass . . . shoot up higher, when we do shoot up, in dazzling concentrations of intellectual power'.[101] The average antisemite might be less intelligent than the average Jew but the latter is obviously less intelligent than Lewis.

Although *The Jews* makes only a few passing references to Hitler and the Nazis it is a kind of companion text to *The Hitler Cult*. As the former attempts to show how the antisemite doubles the figure of the Jew so the latter demonstrates the ways in which German fascism doubles not just communism but liberal democracy. Whereas in *Hitler* the communists were represented as childlike automatons the *Führer* is now described as a proponent of the 'medieval' and 'mystical' doctrine of *Blut und Boden* and as an 'engine for producing mass-emotion'.[102] Similarly, the Nuremberg rallies are compared to the 'intoxicated', 'chanting and rolling chains' of Berlin nightclub-bers (who are themselves compared to 'a Negro congregation') and also described as 'a gala of abstract *numbers*'.[103]

However perhaps the most striking aspect of *The Hitler Cult* is its obsession with Hitler's and the Nazis' literal and figurative stature:

> The very scale of Germany economically and industrially is the work of Jewish bankers and business men, who taught the German to *think big*. Wagner teaches Hitler to feel big. Rhinehardt (at second-hand) teaches him to *look* big.
>
> But there is a further thing to be noted about *bigness*. This cult of the Kolossal is the symptomatic expression of the new barbarity of machine-age man. The vast face of the *Massenmensch* – the enormously magnified visage of the Little Man – is a degeneracy.[104]

Lewis must therefore stress 'the *smallness*' of Hitler's 'personality'.[105] He is 'a crude puppet',[106] a 'male Joan of Arc',[107] a 'human violet',[108] a 'monster of shyness' with a 'feminine strain',[109] 'a pedestrian and highly respectable member of the Rousseau class',[110] an 'hysterical *prima donna*',[111] 'a dreamy-eyed hairdresser, who reads Schiller, without understanding him, in between haircuts, and wallows in the obvious at the slightest provocation',[112] an 'orderly corporal',[113] someone who is 'soft',[114] 'not quite real',[115] 'irration-al',[116] 'childish',[117] 'stupid',[118] and 'genuinely servile'[119] – to mention only some of the characteristics ascribed to him.

As for the reasons why such a *small* man should think himself so *large*, Lewis looks towards his resentment of the Jews. '[T]he "Nordic" business of the Nazis', he argues, is merely 'a childish retort to the Jews only, and their "Chosen People" complex'[120] and in general 'Hitler's Germanism . . . has an extraordinary family likeness with the privileges enjoyed by the Chosen People'.[121] Yet while Lewis dismisses German fascism as merely a parody, he also expresses his distaste for what it parodies. Of the Jews' 'many faults', he asserts, the 'exasperating idea that they have been especially picked out by the All-father as his favourite race is not the least, and is not rendered any more endearing by reason of the Nazi "Aryan" imitation'.[122]

Despite such claims, though, there is a sense in which Lewis's anti-fascism repeats the Nazis' antisemitism. Just as the Nazis assert that the Jews are racially inferior while at the same time imitating their idea of a Chosen People, so Lewis devotes almost an entire book to the subject of Hitler's 'smallness' while at the same time repeating the Nazi claim to be above or beyond politics. In 1926 when the Soviet regime was still in its infancy, Lewis could voice some sympathy with communism as a way of attacking European liberalism without aligning himself with a mass movement within his own country. However as communism became more popular within Britain, particularly after the 1926 General Strike, Lewis discovered Hitler, in part because he was a violently anti-liberal and anti-communist figure but also because he was still someone who represented the aspirations of a country which had not only been recently defeated but forced to pay reparations to the Allies. As he later confessed

when I first learned [in 1930] what had happened I was sorry for the Germans . . . I said to myself that to be 'humbled to the dust,' 'starved,' 'robbed,' and 'enslaved' cannot be pleasant. And I saw the point of Hitler – as that gentleman must appear to a humbled, starved, robbed and enslaved German.[123]

But since he has now transformed himself into a 'would-be conqueror',[124] Lewis must ridicule Hitler just as he had previously ridiculed the romantic liberal and the communist. In effect, the authentic artist cannot subscribe to any ideology.[125] As Reed Way Dasenbrock argues in his discussion of *The Revenge for Love* (1937) since 'one of the keys to fascism's success was its ability to present itself not just as an alternative to liberal politics but as an alternative to politics itself', even Lewis's distrust of certain fascist parties reproduces the kind of distain for politics which 'is central to the fascist worldview'.[126]

However if Lewis's attempt to position himself outside politics duplicates such a world-view, it also parodies the so-called 'Chosen People' status of the Jews to which he so objects. In *The Jews* he claims that

'[t]he advantage of my book is that I am not a Jew. I have not so much as a drop of the blood of the Chosen People in my veins to bias me. God did not choose *me* – and I am not sorry. I am an outsider.[127]

Apart from its tone of resentment, the most significant aspect of this curious assertion is Lewis's refusal to recognise that as an 'outsider' he must himself resemble 'the Chosen People'. Elsewhere he claims that 'the Jews' have an ambiguous status, arguing that while 'the Jews are responsible for our religion, they were also responsible for the Crucifixion'.[128] However in this passage, as indeed for almost all of *The Jews*, he is more than prepared to ridicule the Jews and consign them to the position of degraded other without recognising that, like the figure of the scapegoat, such a position also accords its occupants the kind of privilege which he claims for himself. Throughout all his texts of the 1920s and 1930s Lewis attacks snobbery of one kind or another but never from the position of the 'masses'. 'The Jews' and 'snobs' are alike since – at least in his eyes – they claim a kind of status or privilege that is rightfully only the authentic artist's.

But such violence towards the 'other' also requires the repression of any form of identification. It is always others who are comically married to their obsessions and enemies, never Lewis. Accordingly, Lewis can claim in a book-length study of antisemitism that he has 'no animus against the antisemite, except for the tinge of resentment one must feel at the memory of hours of acute boredom'.[129] Similarly, it is always other people who want to control the machines and puppets of the modern jungle. Dasenbrock points out that Lewis's lofty disdain for ideological commitments of any kind stems from his belief that the 'modern world is a kind of puppet show, and we are naive children thinking the puppets are real, ignoring the puppet masters pulling the strings, pulling our strings'.[130] Thus in *The Art of Being Ruled*, Lewis argues that certain, usually unnamed, interests benefit from inciting what he calls the 'sex-war', the 'class-war' and the 'age-war' and in his novels, from his first and only posthumously published *Mrs Dukes' Million* to *The Revenge for Love*, published soon after the outbreak of the Spanish Civil War, there is accordingly an emphasis on what Dasenbrock calls 'deceiving surfaces and false bottoms'.[131] But the image of a conspirator who always escapes detection is merely the other of a self which must continually distance itself from any kind of political engagement. Lewis's satirical manipulation of his duelling puppets and married couples doubles the more sinister machinations of some unnameable conspirator.

Nevertheless Lewis's politics cannot simply be labelled fascist. Adorno's contention that the fascist has a 'twofold wish to submit to authority and to be the authority himself'[132] is one that Lewis himself makes on several occasions in *The Hitler Cult*. Although he obsessively points out Hitler's feminine aspects and servility he also argues that Hitler 'hates the sight' of the ' "masses" '.[133] Hitler is a comically divided character:

I am aware that many people will regard this insistence upon his native humility – now that he has acquired a 'Napoleonic strut' – as a paradox. I am not quite sure that the orderly corporal entirely approves of Herr Hitler, the great *Führer*. I think we can detect something of that sort in the *Führer*'s eye.[134]

But Lewis will not recognise such a comic division within himself. By denying himself the masochistic pleasure of submission Lewis also denies political authority of any kind. If his 'chronic opposition-alism', to use Jameson's phrase,[135] originally drew him towards Hitler it also ensured that he would become a vociferous anti-fascist. As Arghol says 'Anything but yourself is dirt. Anybody that is'[136] – including fascists.

Notes

INTRODUCTION

1 T. S. Eliot, *Selected Essays*, 3rd edn (London: Faber and Faber, 1951), p. 16.

2 For a history of the idea of modernity see Matei Calinescu, *Five Faces of Modernity: Modernism, Avant-Garde, Decadence, Kitsch, Postmodernism* (Durham: Duke University Press, 1987), to whom I am much in debt.

3 Some critics such as Michael North in *The Political Aesthetic of Yeats, Eliot, and Pound* (Cambridge University Press, 1991), pp. 1–2 and Calinescu in *Five Faces*, p. 41, date this rift somewhat later while at the same time extending 'modernism' back into the mid-to-late nineteenth century. However I follow those, such as Raymond Williams, *Culture and Society 1850–1950* (London: Chatto, 1958), Terry Eagleton, *The Ideology of the Aesthetic* (Oxford: Blackwell, 1990) and Peter Bürger, *Theory of the Avant-Garde*, trans. Michael Shaw (Minneapolis: University of Minnesota Press, 1984), who situate 'modernism' within an aesthetic modernity which extends back to the late eighteenth century while at the same time preserving the Anglo-American use of the term 'modernism' to designate a period which begins during the first decade of the twentieth century.

4 Eliot, *Selected Essays*, p. 29.

5 T. S. Eliot, Rev. of *Tarr*, by Wyndham Lewis, *The Egoist* (Sept. 1918), 105–6.

6 Bürger, *Theory of the Avant-Garde*, p. 27.

7 Eric J. Hobsbawm, *The Age of Empire 1875–1914* (New York: Pantheon, 1987), p. 9.

8 Nevertheless, Jackson Lears argues that 'antimodern sentiments' had taken hold amongst many in the American middle and upper classes towards the end of the nineteenth century in *No Place of Grace: Antimodernism and the Transformation of American Culture 1880–1920* (New York: Pantheon, 1981) and according to George Dangerfield's classic *The Strange Death of Liberal England* (1935; New York: Capricorn, 1961) 'Liberal England' suffered a 'strange death' in the few years before the outbreak of the First World War.

9 Lawrence Rainey, *Institutions of Modernism: Literary Elites and Public Culture* (New Haven, Conn.: Yale University Press, 1998), pp. 41, 39, 76. Other recent scholarship by Joyce Piell Wexler, *Who Paid for Modernism? Art, Money, and the Fiction of Conrad, Joyce, and Lawrence* (Fayetteville: University of Arkansas Press, 1997), and the contributors to *Modernist Writers and the Marketplace*, ed. Ian Willison, Warwick Gould and Warren Chernaik (London: Macmillan, 1996) and *Marketing Modernism: Self-Promotion, Canonization, Rereading*, ed. Kevin J. H. Dettmar and Stephen Watt (Ann Arbor: University of Michigan Press, 1996) also explore the many and complex ways in which modernist writing was marketed.

10 Andreas Huyssen, *After the Great Divide: Modernism, Mass Culture, Postmodernism* (Bloomington: Indiana University Press, 1986), p. vii.

11 See, for example, Pierre Bourdieu, 'Flaubert's Point of View', trans. Priscilla Ferguson, *Critical Inquiry* 14 (1988), 539–62.

12 Similarly the arguments of Michael Tratner, *Modernism and Mass Politics: Joyce, Woolf, Eliot, Yeats* (Stanford University Press, 1995) – who describes the ways in which modernism was an attempt to engage with and speak for a mass mind – and those of the contributors to *High and Low Moderns: Literature and Culture, 1889–1939*, ed. Maria DiBattista and Lucy McDiarmid (New York: Oxford University Press, 1996) – who show how 'the division between the aestheticist high moderns and the materialist low moderns was not as marked, nor even as secure, as literary culture then and has since presumed', p. 4, – also complement rather than contradict Huyssen.

13 Eliot, *Selected Essays*, p. 17.

14 On the issue of the gender of modernism, see Sandra M. Gilbert and Susan Gubar, *No Man's Land*, 3 vols. (New Haven, Conn.: Yale University Press, 1988–94), Bonnie Kime Scott, *The Gender of Modernism* (Bloomington: Indiana University Press, 1990) and Suzanne Clark, *Sentimental Modernism: Women Writers and the Revolution of the Word* (Bloomington: Indiana University Press, 1991). Similarly, although those such as Klaus Theweleit, *Male Fantasies*, 2 vols., trans. Stephen Conway, Jessica Benjamin and Anson Rabinbach (Minneapolis: University of Minnesota Press, 1987) stress the hyper-masculinity of fascism, Alice Kaplan persuasively argues that while fascist subjects are 'virile, phallic, their devotion to the language they learn is total, boundaryless, and the language itself is a maternal one', *Reproductions of Banality: Fascism, Literature and French Intellectual Life* (Minneapolis: University of Minnesota Press, 1986), p.10. Significantly, while in his *The Founding and Manifesto of Futurism* Marinetti advocates 'scorn for women', when his automobile runs off the road it is reborn out of a 'maternal ditch', *Futurist Manifestos*, ed. Umbrio Apollonio (London: Thames & Hudson, 1973), p. 21.

15 Bürger, *Theory of the Avant-Garde*, p. 22.

16 Ibid., p. 34.

17 Eliot, *Selected Essays*, pp. 442–3.
18 Ibid., pp. 420, 438.
19 Wyndham Lewis, *Tarr*, revised edn (1928; London: Calder and Boyars, 1968), p. 45.
20 Bürger, *Theory of the Avant-Garde*, p. 52.
21 Lucy R. Lippard (ed.), *Dadas on Art* (Englewood Cliffs, N.J.: Prentice-Hall, 1971), p. 143.
22 Jean Arp, 'Dadaland' in *Dadas on Art*, ed. Lippard, p. 143.
23 W. H. Auden, *Collected Shorter Poems 1927–1957* (London: Faber and Faber, 1969), p. 142.
24 Bürger, *Theory of the Avant-Garde*, 25.
25 Walter Benjamin, *Illuminations*, ed. Hannah Arendt, trans. Harry Zohn (London: Fontana, 1973), p. 243.
26 Ibid., p. 244.
27 See Jürgen Habermas, 'Modernity – An Incomplete Project', in *Postmodern Culture*, ed. Hal Foster (London: Pluto, 1985) and *The Philosophical Discourse of Modernity*, trans. Frederick G. Lawrence (Cambridge, Mass: MIT Press, 1987).
28 Bürger, *Theory of the Avant-Garde*, p. 244. As Marjorie Perloff speculates in *The Futurist Moment: Avant-Garde, Avant Guerre, and the Language of Rupture* (University of Chicago Press, 1986), pp. 34–5, it might be that *all* revolutionary movements have an aesthetic goal.
29 Bürger, *Theory of the Avant-Garde*, p. 49.
30 Benjamin, *Illuminations*, p. 243.
31 Ernst Nolte, *Three Faces of Fascism: Action Française, Italian Fascism, National Socialism*, trans. Leila Vennewitz (London: Weidenfeld and Nicolson, 1965), pp. 30, 433.
32 George L. Mosse, 'Ernst Nolte on *Three Faces of Fascism*', *Journal of the History of Ideas* 27 (1966), 623.
33 Henry A. Turner, 'Fascism and Modernization', *Reappraisals of Fascism*, ed. Henry A. Turner (New York: New Viewpoints, 1975), p. 126.
34 Renzo De Felice, *Fascism: An Informal Introduction to Its Theory and Practice*, interview with Michael A. Ledeen (New Brunswick, N.J.: Transaction, 1976), pp. 48, 56.
35 Stanley G. Payne, *A History of Fascism 1914–1945* (Madison: University of Wisconsin Press, 1995), p. 485.
36 Roger Griffin, *The Nature of Fascism* (New York: St Martin's Press, 1991), pp. 36, 35.
37 Walter Laqueur, *Fascism: Past, Present, Future* (New York: Oxford University Press), p. 9, and A. James Gregor, *Interpretations of Fascism* (Morristown, N.J.: General Learning Press, 1974).
38 Jeffrey Herf, *Reactionary Modernism: Technology, Culture and Politics in Weimar and the Third Reich* (Cambridge University Press, 1984), p. 224.
39 Apollonio (ed.), *Futurist Manifestos*, p. 22.
40 W. B. Yeats, *Explorations* (London: Macmillan, 1962), p. 425.

41 George Steiner, *In Bluebeard's Castle: Some Notes Towards the Re-Definition of Culture* (London: Faber and Faber, 1971), p. 40.

42 George Steiner, *The Portage to San Cristobal of A. H.* (London: Faber and Faber, 1981), p. 122.

43 Theodor Adorno and Max Horkheimer, *Dialectic of Enlightenment* (1944; London: Verso, 1979), p. 9.

44 Joseph Conrad, *Heart of Darkness*, ed. Robert Kimbrough (New York: Norton, 1988), p. 38.

45 Conrad, *Heart of Darkness*, p. 75.

46 Ibid., p. 79.

47 Similarly just as there is no postcolonial site outside what Edward Said describes as 'the perfect closure' of the novel, *Culture and Imperialism* (London: Vintage, 1994), p. 26, then neither is there any pre-colonial site. The colonial nightmare does direct and observable violence, but the 'other' remains, like the 'continent' into which the French man-of-war insanely fires (17), always unnameable. Thus while critics from Chinua Achebe, 'An Image of Africa: Racism in Conrad's *Heart of Darkness*,' *Massachusetts Review* 18 (1977), 782–94, to Brook Thomas, 'Preserving and Keeping Order by Killing Time in *Heart of Darkness*', *Joseph Conrad, 'Heart of Darkness': A Case Study in Contemporary Criticism*, ed. Ross C. Murfin (New York: St Martin's Press, 1989), pp. 237–58, have argued that Conrad merely projects Europe's own darkness on to the African 'other', the novel's structure also draws the reader's attention to the fact that such darkness *is* a projection. For a critique of modernist claims for any 'affinity' or 'kinship' between the 'modern' and the 'primitive' see the analysis of William Rubin's *'Primitivism' in 20th Century Art: Affinity of the Tribal and the Modern* (New York: MOMA, 1984) by James Clifford in *The Predicament of Culture: Twentieth-Century Ethnography, Literature, and Art* (Cambridge, Mass.: Harvard University Press, 1988), pp. 189–214 and Hal Foster's *Recodings: Art, Spectacle, Cultural Politics* (Washington: Bay Press, 1985), pp. 181–207.

48 On Woolf and the androgynous see Nancy Toping Bazin, *Virginia Woolf and the Androgynous Vision* (New Brunswick, N.J.: Rutgers University Press, 1973) and Elaine Showalter, *A Literature of Their Own: British Women Novelists from Brontë to Lessing* (London: Virago, 1982), pp. 263–97.

49 Elizabeth Abel, *Virginia Woolf and the Fictions of Psychoanalysis* (University of Chicago Press, 1989), p. 14.

50 Although Mary Lou Emery notes that the 'theft and the exclusion of Mrs. McNab is necessary to the readers' perceptions of Lily Briscoe's "birth" as an artist and necessary to Woolf's achievement of aesthetic unity', '"Robbed of Meaning": The Work at the Center of *To The Lighthouse*', *Modern Fiction Studies* 38 (1992), 228, it should be remembered that Woolf intended, as Jane Marcus points out in *Virginia Woolf and the Languages of Patriarchy* (Bloomington: Indiana University Press, 1987), p. 12, the 'Time Passes' section to be presented as Mrs McNab's interior

monologue, and that while the final version is somewhat patronising towards Mrs McNab, she is affectionately treated for all that and does not seem to occasion any great authorial anxiety or animus.

51 Virginia Woolf, *To the Lighthouse*, ed. Susan Dick (Oxford: Blackwell, 1992), p. 16.
52 Woolf, *To the Lighthouse*, p. 16.
53 Ibid., p. 17.
54 Ibid., p. 18.
55 Jean-François Lyotard, *The Postmodern Condition: A Report on Knowledge*, trans. Geoff Bennington and Brian Massumi (Manchester University Press, 1984), p. 81. For an analysis of how the fascism of several contemporary French writers can be 'treated as an extreme but logical development of a number of fundamental aesthetic concepts or cultural ideals: namely, the notion of the integrity of "Man" . . . the totalized organic unity of the artwork . . . and . . . culture considered as the model for the positive form of political totalization', see David Carroll, *French Literary Fascism: Nationalism, Anti-Semitism, and the Ideology of Culture* (Princeton University Press, 1995), p. 7.
56 Woolf, *To the Lighthouse*, p. 166.
57 T. S. Eliot, *The Complete Poems and Plays* (London: Faber and Faber, 1969), p. 45.
58 Eliot, *Complete Poems*, p. 68
59 W. B. Yeats, *The Poems*, ed. Richard Finneran (New York: Macmillan, 1989), p. 108.
60 On modernism as a 'hostile reaction to the unprecedentedly large reading public created by the late nineteenth-century education reforms', see John Carey's *The Intellectuals and the Masses: Pride and Prejudice Among the Literary Intelligentsia, 1880–1939* (London: Faber and Faber, 1992), p. vii.
61 What follows has been more extensively analysed in my 'The *New Age* and the Emergence of Reactionary Modernism before the Great War', *Modern Fiction Studies* 38 iii (1992), 653–67.
62 Hilaire Belloc, 'The Servile State,' *New Age* (26 May 1910), p. 77.
63 J. M. Kennedy, *The Quintessence of Nietzsche* (London: Laurie, 1909), p. 101. *A Defence of Conservatism* by Anthony M. Ludovici, one of the *New Age* Nietzscheans, was favourably reviewed by Eliot, 'Recent Books', *The Monthly Criterion* 6 (1927), 69–73.
64 Maurice B. Reckitt, *As It Happened: An Autobiography* (London: Dent, 1941), p. 112.
65 A. J. Orage, 'Unedited Opinions (vi): Modern Novels' *New Age* (29 Dec. 1910), 204.
66 J. M. Kennedy, *English Literature, 1880–1905* (London: Swift, 1912), p. 202.
67 Wyndham Lewis, *Rude Assignment: A Narrative of My Career Up-To-Date* (London: Hutchinson, 1950), p. 128.

68 Quoted in Wallace Martin, *The* New Age *Under Orage: Chapters In English Cultural History* (Manchester University Press, 1967), p. 4.

69 Jay P. Corrin, *G. K. Chesterton and Hilaire Belloc: The Battle Against Modernity* (Athens, Ohio: Ohio University Press, 1981), p. 195. In July of 1915, Lawrence wrote to Bertrand Russell, '[y]ou *must* work out the idea of a new state, not go on criticising this old one. Get anybody and everybody to help – Orage, Shaw, anybody, but it must be a *new State*. And the idea is, that every man shall vote according to his understanding, and that the highest understanding must dictate for the lower understandings'. *The Letters of D. H. Lawrence*, vol. ii, ed. George J. Zytaruk and James T. Boulton (Cambridge University Press, 1981), p. 366.

70 Hilaire Belloc, *The Servile State* (London: Foulis, 1912), pp. 112, 108. Some of the Guild Socialists such as G. D. H. Cole and S. G. Hobson did advocate harnessing various aspects of the existing economic order but even amongst the Guild Socialists there were some, such as Arthur J. Penty, who advocated the total abolition of 'machine production' and industrialism, 'Medievalism and Modernism', *New Age* (23 Apr. 1914), 39, and others, like the Spanish writer Ramiro de Maeztu, who argued that the 'two great principles of the Guild are limitation and hierarchy', 'The Jealousy of the Guilds', *New Age* (29 Apr. 1915), 687. Most of the *New Age* writers simply inverted the concept of historical 'progress' they were challenging, believing, like Penty, that people should 'come to connect the Golden Age with the past again rather than with the future', 'The Restoration of the Guild System', *New Age* (4 Sept. 1914), 547.

71 A. J. Orage, Preface to *National Guilds*, by S. G. Hobson (London: Bell, 1919), pp. v–vi.

72 Georges Sorel, *Reflections on Violence*, trans. T. E. Hulme (1916; London: Collier, 1961), p. 106.

73 Lewis, *Rude Assignment*, p. 37.

74 On the alliance between the extreme right and extreme left in France, see Zeev Sternhell's *La Droite Révolutionnaire, 1885–1914: Les Origines Françaises du Fascisme* (Paris: Seuil, 1978), *Neither Right nor Left: Fascist Ideology in France*, trans. David Maisel (Berkeley: University of California Press, 1986) and Paul Mazgaj, *The Action Française and Revolutionary Syndicalism* (Chapel Hill: University of North Carolina Press, 1979).

75 T. E. Hulme, *Speculations: Essays on Humanism and the Philosophy of Art*, ed. Herbert Read (New York: Harcourt, 1924), p. 258.

76 Hulme, *Speculations*, p. 256.

77 Hulme, *Further Speculations*, ed. Samuel Hynes (Lincoln: University of Nebraska Press, 1962), p. 34.

78 Hulme, 'Notes on Bergson II' *New Age* (26 Oct. 1911), 610–11. On the influence of Lasserre, see Michael H. Levenson, *A Genealogy of Modernism: A Study in English Literary Doctrine, 1908–1922* (Cambridge University Press, 1984), pp. 82–6.

79 Alan Robinson, *Poetry, Painting and Ideas, 1885–1914* (London: Macmillan, 1985), p. 90.

80 Pierre Lasserre, *Le Romantisme Français: Essai sur la Révolution dans les Sentiments et dans les Idées au XIX Siècle*, Nouvelle Edition (1907; Paris: Calmann, 1928), p. xxvi.

81 Hulme, *Further Speculations*, p. 116.

82 A. R. Orage, 'Readers and Writers', *New Age* (23 Dec. 1915), 181.

83 Wilhelm Worringer, *Abstraction and Empathy: A Contribution to the Psychology of Style*, trans. Michael Bulloch (1908; New York: International University Press, 1953), pp. 15, 129.

84 G. K. Chesterton, Introduction, in Philip Mairet, *A. R. Orage: A Memoir* (London: Dent, 1936), p. vi.

85 Because of their obscurity it is almost impossible to determine the class background of many of the *New Age* writers. Wallace Martin, *The New Age Under Orage*, p. 8, improbably maintains that the readership of the paper was comprised mainly of an 'intelligentsia' with no particular class or political affiliations.

86 Mairet, *A. R. Orage: A Memoir*, pp. 1–9.

87 Anthony Quinton, Introduction, in Michael Roberts, *T. E. Hulme*, (1938; Manchester: Carcanet, 1982), p. i.

88 William M. Chace, *The Political Identities of Ezra Pound and T. S. Eliot* (Stanford University Press, 1973), p. 19.

89 Charles Harrison, *English Art and Modernism, 1900–1939* (Bloomington: Indiana University Press, 1981), p. 90.

90 Peter Ackroyd, *T. S. Eliot* (London: Hamish Hamilton, 1984), p. 19.

91 Terry Eagleton, *Exiles and Émigrés: Studies in Modern Literature* (London: Chatto, 1970), p. 15.

1. W. B. YEATES AND THE FAMILY ROMANCE OF IRISH NATIONALISM

1 Donald Torchiana, *W. B. Yeats and Georgian Ireland* (Evanston, Ill.: Northwestern University Press, 1966), p. 159.

2 Paul Scott Stanfield, *Yeats and Politics in the 1930s* (New York: St Martin's Press, 1988), p.187.

3 Grattan Freyer, *W. B. Yeats and the Anti-Democratic Tradition* (Dublin: Gill & Macmillan, 1981).

4 George Watson, *Irish Identity and the Literary Revival* (London: Croom Helm, 1979), p. 122.

5 Elizabeth Cullingford, *Yeats, Ireland and Fascism* (New York University Press, 1981), pp. 234–5. One of Bernard G. Krimm's explicit aims in *W. B. Yeats and the Emergence of the Irish Free State* (Troy, N.Y.: Whitson, 1981) is a refutation of O'Brien's essay but his detailed account of Yeats's political activities after 1918 does not label the writer's ideological position.

6 Declan Kiberd, *Inventing Ireland: The Literature of the Modern Nation* (London: Jonathan Cape, 1995), p. 320.

7 Edward Said, *Culture and Imperialism* (London: Vintage, 1994), p. 278.

8 George Orwell, 'W. B. Yeats,' *Collected Essays* (London: Secker & Warburg, 1961), p. 195.

9 Malcolm Brown, *The Politics of Irish Literature: From Thomas Davis to W. B. Yeats* (London: Allen & Unwin, 1972), p. 321.

10 Seamus Deane, *Celtic Revivals: Essays in Modern Irish Literature 1880–1980* (London: Faber and Faber, 1985), p. 37.

11 F. S. L. Lyons, *Culture and Anarchy in Ireland, 1890–1939* (Oxford: Clarendon, 1979), p. 28.

12 Conor Cruise O'Brien, 'Passion and Cunning: An Essay on the Politics of W. B. Yeats', *In Excited Reverie: A Centenary Tribute to William Butler Yeats, 1865–1939*, ed. A. Norman Jeffares and K. G. W. Cross (London: Macmillan, 1965), p. 211.

13 W. B. Yeats, *The Letters of W. B. Yeats*, ed. Allan Wade (London: Rupert Hart-Davis, 1954), p. 715.

14 W. B. Yeats, *Autobiographies*, ed. William H. O'Donnell and Douglas N. Archibald (New York: Scribner, 1999), p. 545.

15 C. L. Innes, *Woman and Nation in Irish Literature and Society, 1880–1935* (Athens, Ga.: University of Georgia Press, 1993), p. 76.

16 René Girard, *Deceit, Desire and the Novel: Self and Other in Literary Structure*, trans. Yvonne Freccero (Baltimore: Johns Hopkins University Press, 1976).

17 Joseph Chadwick, 'Family Romance as National Allegory in Yeats's *Cathleen ni Houlihan* and *The Dreaming of the Bones*', *Twentieth Century Literature* 32 (1986), 155–68.

18 Yeats, *Autobiographies*, p. 559. R. F. Foster argues that '[i]n later years WBY was to launch the myth that an attempt to create a national literary culture arose after the shattering fall of Parnell in 1891, and thus led inevitably to political separatism. But . . . the effort was being made from 1885 – stimulated by the apparent imminence of Home Rule and a triumphant constitutional nationalism. The agenda was not about creating an alternative to politics; it concerned what to do when politics had delivered national autonomy', *W. B. Yeats; A Life, Vol. I: The Apprentice Mage* (Oxford University Press, 1997), p. 41.

19 W. B. Yeats, *The Variorum Edition of the Plays of W. B. Yeats*, ed. Russell K. Alspach (London: Macmillan, 1966), p. 173.

20 Chadwick, 'Family Romance as National Allegory', p. 156.

21 W. B. Yeats, *The Poems*, ed. Richard Finneran (New York: Macmillan, 1989), p. 345.

22 Yeats, *The Plays*, p. 232.

23 Cullingford, *Yeats, Ireland and Fascism*, p. 17.

24 Yeats, *Autobiographies*, pp. 91–2.

25 Yeats, *The Plays*, p. 231.

26 Ibid., p. 233.
27 W. B. Yeats, *Uncollected Prose by W. B. Yeats*, vol. I, ed. John P. Prayne (London: Macmillan, 1970), p. 150.
28 W. B. Yeats (ed.), *Fairy and Folk Tales of Ireland* (London: Pan, 1979), p. 385.
29 Patrick J. Keane, *Terrible Beauty: Yeats, Joyce, Ireland and the Myth of the Devouring Female* (Columbia: University of Missouri Press, 1988), pp. 94–5.
30 W. B. Yeats, *Memoirs*, ed. Denis Donoghue (London: Macmillan, 1972) pp. 63, 65.
31 Yeats, *Memoirs*, p. 192.
32 Ibid., p. 176.
33 Yeats, *The Poems*, p. 107.
34 Ibid., p. 108.
35 Yeats, *Memoirs*, p. 156.
36 Ibid., p. 226.
37 Ibid., p. 95.
38 Ibid., p. 226.
39 Yeats, *The Poems*, p. 96.
40 Ibid., p. 108.
41 Yeats, *The Plays*, p. 229.
42 Yeats, *The Poems*, p. 108.
43 Ibid., p. 109.
44 Ibid., p. 182.
45 Ibid., pp. 181–2.
46 Yeats, *Memoirs*, p. 232.
47 Yeats, *The Poems*, p. 182.
48 Chadwick, 'Family Romance as National Allegory', p. 164.
49 Ibid., p. 162.
50 Yeats, *The Poems*, pp. 183, 184.
51 Yeats, *The Plays*, p. 222.
52 Yeats, *The Poems*, p. 184.
53 A. Norman Jeffares, *A New Commentary on the Poems of W. B. Yeats* (London: Macmillan, 1984), p. 195.
54 Yeats, *Memoirs*, pp. 41, 61.
55 Yeats, *The Poems*, p. 233.
56 Ibid., pp. 189, 188.
57 Ibid., p. 190.
58 Harold Bloom, *Yeats* (Oxford University Press, 1970), p. 326.
59 Yeats, *The Poems*, pp. 93, 339. In a diary entry of 21 June 1908, Yeats maintains that '[o]f old she [Gonne] was a phoenix & I feared her, but she is my child more than my sweetheart', quoted in Foster, *W. B. Yeats*, p. 407.
60 Yeats, *The Poems*, p. 216.
61 Ibid., p. 216.

62 Ibid., p. 309.
63 Ibid., p. 280.
64 W. B. Yeats, *The Senate Speeches of W. B. Yeats*, ed. Donald Pearce (London: Faber and Faber, 1961), p. 99.
65 Deane, *Celtic Revivals*, p. 30.
66 Yeats, *Speeches*, p. 99.
67 W. B. Yeats, *Explorations* (London: Macmillan, 1962), p. 345.
68 Yeats, *The Poems*, p. 337.
69 Yeats, *Explorations*, p. 942.
70 Ibid., pp. 347–9.
71 Frank Kermode, *Romantic Image* (London: Routledge and Kegan Paul, 1957), pp. 138–61.
72 Yeats, *Autobiographies*, p. 180.
73 W. B. Yeats, *A Critical Edition of Yeats's 'A Vision'*, ed. George Mills Harper and Walter Kelly Hood (1925; London: Macmillan, 1978), p. 131.
74 Yeats, *A Vision*, p. 137.
75 Ibid., p. 61.
76 Yeats, *The Poems*, p. 181.
77 Ibid., p. 91.
78 Yeats, *A Vision*, p. 134.
79 Yeats, *The Poems*, p. 650.
80 Yeats, *A Vision*, pp. 72–73.
81 Ibid., p. 130.
82 Kiberd, *Inventing Ireland*, p. 318.
83 Yeats, *Letters*, p. 851.
84 Ibid., pp. 806, 811.
85 O'Brien, 'Passion and Cunning', p. 254.
86 Yeats, *The Poems*, p. 319.
87 Ibid., p. 348.
88 Yeats, *Letters*, p. 812.
89 Ibid., p. 812.
90 Yeats, *Letters*, p. 809.
91 W. B. Yeats, *The Variorum Edition of the Poems of W. B. Yeats*, ed. Peter Allt and Russell K. Alspach (New York: Macmillan, 1957), p. 544.
92 Ibid.
93 Yeats, *Variorum Edition of the Poems*, p. 545.
94 A. Norman Jeffares and A. S. Knowland, *A Commentary on the Collected Plays of W. B. Yeats* (Stanford University Press, 1975), p. 246.
95 Yeats, *The Plays*, p. 987.
96 Ibid., p. 1002.
97 Yeats, *The Poems*, p. 257.
98 Ibid., p. 259.
99 Yeats, *Letters*, pp. 815, 817.
100 Yeats, *Explorations*, p. 423.

101 Ibid., p. 413.
102 Jeffares and Knowland, *A Commentary on the Collected Plays*, p. 275.
103 Yeats, *The Plays*, p. 1049.
104 Ibid., p. 1048.
105 Ibid., p. 1049.
106 Bloom, *Yeats*, p. 427.
107 O'Brien, 'Passion and Cunning', p. 211.

2. EZRA POUND AND THE POETICS OF LITERALISM

1 Ezra Pound, *Literary Essays of Ezra Pound*, ed. T. S. Eliot (London: Faber and Faber, 1960), p. 5.
2 Pound, *Essays*, p. 12.
3 William Wordsworth and Samuel Taylor Coleridge, *Lyrical Ballads 1805*, ed. Derek Roper (London: Collins, 1968), pp. 26, 27.
4 Pound, *Essays*, p. 5.
5 Wordsworth, *Lyrical Ballads*, p. 27.
6 Ibid., p. 35.
7 Pound, *Essays*, p. 42.
8 Northrop Frye, *The Great Code: The Bible and Literature* (London: Ark, 1983), p. 23.
9 Ibid.
10 Ezra Pound, *Selected Poems* (London: Faber and Faber, 1977), p. 103.
11 Thus when Herbert Schneidau approvingly quotes D. S. Carne-Ross's conclusion that 'Pound's whole effort is not to be polysemous but to give back to the literal first level its full significance, its old significance' in 'Wisdom Past Metaphor: Another View of Objective Verse', *Paideuma* 5 (1976), 19, neither distinguish between modern prose, in which the figurative is secondary to the literal, and primitive poetry, in which there is no distinction between the figurative and the literal.
12 Richard Sieburth, 'In Pound We Trust: The Economy of Poetry/The Poetry of Economics', *Critical Inquiry* 14.4 (1987), 150.
13 Robert Casillo, *The Genealogy of Demons: Anti-Semitism, Fascism, and the Myths of Ezra Pound* (Evanston, Ill.: Northwestern UP, 1988), p. 325. In practice, however, these critics do not distinguish between Pound's animus towards metaphor and his hostility towards history. See also Stephen Hartnett, 'The Ideologies and Semiotics of Fascism: Analysing Pound's *Cantos* 12–15', *Boundary 2* 20.1 (1993), 65–93, and Andrew Parker, 'Ezra Pound and the "Economy" of Anti-Semitism,' *Boundary 2* 11 (1982), 103–28.
14 See also Peter Nicholls, *Ezra Pound: Politics, Economics and Writing* (London: Macmillan, 1984), p. 2. Even a critic as hostile towards poststructuralism as Paul Morrison can characterise Pound's poetics as one of 'tropological stability, of fixed addresses and proper names', *The Poetics of Fascism: Ezra Pound, T. S. Eliot, Paul de Man* (New York: Oxford

University Press, 1996), p. 36. Both Jean-Michel Rabaté, *Language, Sexuality and Ideology in Ezra Pound's* Cantos (London: Macmillan, 1986, p. 1), and Alan Durant, *Ezra Pound, Identity in Crisis* (Brighton: Harvester, 1981) concede that there are forms of totalitarian closure in Pound's poetry and yet they argue, in the words of the former, that we can recover a 'new space of writing where anarchy and difference come into play' from his poetry.

15 Frye, *The Great Code*, p. 13.
16 Pound, *Essays*, p. 86.
17 Parker argues that '[o]ur discovery of Pound's general association of figurative language with a particular notion of Judaism will enable us finally to reject the currently prevailing position which considers Pound's anti-Semitism as merely a 'contingent' phenomenon, ancillary to his poetic achievement'. 'Pound and "The Economy" of Anti-Semitism', p. 104.
18 For useful discussions of the relationship between poetry and science in Pound's writing, see Martin A. Kayman, *The Modernism of Ezra Pound: The Science of Poetry* (London: Macmillan, 1986), pp. 66–109, and Ian F. A. Bell, *Critic as Scientist: The Modernist Poetics of Ezra Pound* (London: Methuen, 1981).
19 Ernest Fenollosa, *The Chinese Written Character as a Medium for Poetry*, ed. Ezra Pound (San Francisco: City Lights, 1936), p. 8.
20 Ibid., p. 12.
21 Ibid., p. 23.
22 Ibid., p. 28.
23 Ezra Pound, *ABC of Reading* (London: Routledge, 1934), pp. 6–7.
24 See Michael Bernstein's discussion of Fenollosa, *The Tale of the Tribe: Ezra Pound and the Modern Verse Epic* (Princeton University Press, 1980), pp. 37–9, to which I am indebted.
25 Frye, *The Great Code*, p. 13.
26 Ezra Pound, *The Spirit of Romance* (1910; London: Owen, 1952), p. 126.
27 George Kennedy, 'Fenollosa, Pound and the Chinese Character', *Yale Literary Magazine* 126.1 (1958), 24–36.
28 Pound, *ABC*, p. 5.
29 Ken Ruthven, *Ezra Pound as Literary Critic* (London: Routledge, 1990), pp. 1–39, especially 20.
30 Quoted in Ruthven, *Ezra Pound as Literary Critic*, p. 243.
31 Ezra Pound, *Jefferson And/Or Mussolini: Fascism As I Have Seen It* (New York: Liveright, 1970), p. 33.
32 Nicholls, *Ezra Pound*, p. 191.
33 See David Murray, 'Pound-signs: Money and Representation in Ezra Pound', *Ezra Pound: Tactics for Reading*, ed. Ian Bell (London: Vision, 1982) and Richard Godden, 'Icons, Etymologies, Origins and Monkey Puzzles in the Languages of Upward and Fenollosa', *Ezra Pound: Tactics*

for Reading, ed. Bell, Terri Brint Joseph, 'Peirce, Pound, and Fenollosa', *Poetics 1984*, ed. John Deely (Lanham, Md.: University Press of America, 1985), and Sieburth, 'In Pound We Trust', pp. 155–6.

34 Ezra Pound, *Selected Prose 1909–1965*, ed. William Cookson (London: Faber and Faber, 1973), p. 299.

35 Ibid., p. 224.

36 Ibid., p. 265.

37 Ibid., p. 285.

38 Ezra Pound, *Cantos* (London: Faber and Faber, 1975), p. 190.

39 Of course printing more money might create the kind of inflation which Germany had just experienced, but Pound argues that the 'term "inflation" is used as a bogey to scare people away from any expansion of money at all', *Selected Prose*, p. 265. Since 'currency is merely a convention and a bit of paper with 10 on it is no more difficult to provide than a bit of paper with 5 or 20', *Selected Prose*, p. 211, then the reverse is also the case: it is merely convention which determines how much a particular commodity is worth. If we can change what money can buy and how much commodities are worth we can also fix or stabilise the relationship between money and commodities. Thus Pound wants to resurrect 'the canonist doctrine of the just price' but in a modern form, *Selected Prose*, p. 263. 'STATE AUTHORITY behind the printed note', he argues, 'is the best means of establishing a JUST and HONEST currency', *Selected Prose*, p. 262.

40 Ibid., p. 286.

41 Ibid., pp. 214, 221.

42 Pound, *Cantos*, pp. 63, 65.

43 Ibid., pp. 61, 62, 64.

44 Pound, *Selected Prose*, p. 264.

45 Sieburth, 'Pound We Trust', p. 150.

46 Pound, *Selected Prose*, p. 209.

47 Pound, *Jefferson And / Or Mussolini*, p. 36.

48 Pound, *Selected Prose*, pp. 211–12.

49 Ibid., p. 233.

50 Ibid., p. 235.

51 Sieburth, 'In Pound We Trust', p. 170.

52 Pound, *Selected Prose*, pp. 316–17.

53 For a discussion of these debates see Tim Redman, *Ezra Pound and Italian Fascism* (Cambridge University Press, 1991), pp. 37–40, 52–3, 55–6, 130–1, 134–5.

54 Ezra Pound, *Guide to Kulchur* (London: Owen, 1960), p. 36.

55 Pound, *Selected Prose*, p. 300.

56 Ibid., p. 261.

57 Ibid., p. 261.

58 Pound, *Selected Prose*, p. 204.

59 Ibid., p. 179.

60 David Murray, 'Pound-signs: Money and Representation in Ezra Pound', p. 63.

61 Pound, *Spirit of Romance*, p. 95.

62 Hyam Maccoby, 'The Jew As Anti-Artist: The Anti-Semitism of Ezra Pound', *Midstream* 22 (1976), 69.

63 Pound, *Essays*, p. 431.

64 Pound, *Cantos*, pp. 172–3.

65 Ibid., p. 172.

66 Ibid., p. 173.

67 Ibid., p. 174.

68 Ibid.

69 Pound, *Cantos*, p. 173.

70 Casillo, *The Genealogy of Demons*, p. 210.

71 Zygmunt Baumann, 'Allosemitism: Premodern, Modern, Postmodern' in *Modernity, Culture and 'the Jew'*, ed. Bryan Cheyette and Laura Marcus (Cambridge: Polity Press, 1998), p. 144. See also Baumann's *Modernity and the Holocaust* (Ithaca, N. Y.: Cornell University Press, 1989).

72 Baumann, 'Allosemitism: Premodern, Modern, Postmodern', p. 149. See also *Between 'Race' and Culture: Representations of 'the Jew' in English and American Literature*, ed. Bryan Cheyette (Stanford University Press, 1996), and Bryan Cheyette, *Construction of 'the Jew' in English Literature and Society: Racial Representations, 1875–1945* (Cambridge University Press, 1993).

73 Steiner, *In Bluebeard's Castle: Some Notes towards the Re-Definition of Culture* (London: Faber and Faber, 1971), p. 47.

74 Daniel Pearlman, 'E P as Wandering Jew', *Ezra Pound*, ed. Harold Bloom (New York: Chelsea, 1987), pp. 87–104, and Casillo, *The Genealogy of Demons*, p. 300.

75 Massimo Bacigalupo, *The Forméd Trace: The Later Poetry of Ezra Pound* (New York: Columbia University Press, 1980), p. 59.

76 Pound, *Cantos*, pp. 230, 250, 798.

77 Herbert Schneidau, 'Wisdom Past Metaphor: Another View of Objective Verse', *Paideuma* 5 (1976), 20. See also Max Nänny, 'Context, Contiguity and Contact in Ezra Pound's *Personae*', in *Ezra Pound*, ed. Harold Bloom, pp. 75–86.

78 Roman Jakobson, 'Two Aspects of Language and Two Types of Aphasic Disturbance', in *Fundamentals of Language* (The Hague: Mouton, 1956), pp. 53–82.

79 Quoted in David Lodge, *The Modes of Modern Writing: Metaphor, Metonymy, and the Typology of Modern Literature* (London: Arnold, 1977), p. 75.

80 Ibid.

81 Carol F. Terrell, *A Companion to the Cantos of Ezra Pound*, vol. 1 (Berkeley: University of California Press, 1980–84), p. 77.

82 Pound, *Cantos*, pp. 84–5.

83 Ibid., p. 84.

84 Ibid., p. 85.
85 Ibid., p. 233.
86 Terrell, *A Companion to the Cantos*, vol. i, p. 181.
87 Pound, *Selected Prose*, p. 281.
88 Pound, *Cantos*, p. 232.
89 Ibid., p. 234.
90 Pound, *Selected Prose*, p. 243.
91 Pound, *Cantos*, p. 235.
92 Frye, *The Great Code*, p. 56.
93 Terrell, *A Companion to the Cantos*, vol. i, p. 183.
94 Ezra Pound,'*Ezra Pound Speaking': Radio Speeches of World War II*, ed. Leonard W. Doob (Westport, Conn.: Greenwood, 1978), p. 254. Also quoted in Parker, 'Ezra Pound and the Economy of Anti-Semitism', p. iii.
95 Hugh Kenner, 'The Broken Mirrors and the Mirror of Memory', *Motive and Method in the Cantos of Ezra Pound*, ed. Lewis Leary (New York: Columbia University Press, 1961), p. 22.
96 Chace, *The Political Identities of Ezra Pound and T. S. Eliot*, p. 68.
97 Pound, *Cantos*, p. 251.
98 Ibid., p. 230.
99 Ibid., pp. 222, 246.
100 Ibid., p. 257.
101 Pound,'*Ezra Pound Speaking*', p. 113.
102 Pound, *Selected Prose*, p. 270n.
103 Jacques Derrida, *Dissemination*, translated by Barbara Johnson (University of Chicago Press, 1981), p. 133. Drawing upon the work of René Girard, Casillo – to whom I am in debt – has also discussed at length scapegoating in Pound.
104 Pound, *Cantos*, p. 172.
105 Humphrey Carpenter, *A Serious Character: The Life of Ezra Pound* (London: Faber and Faber, 1988), pp. 848, 874 and Charles Norman, *Ezra Pound* (London: Macdonald, 1969), p. 458.
106 Carpenter, *A Serious Character*, p. 899.
107 Pound, *Cantos*, p. 460.
108 Carpenter, *A Serious Character*, pp. 679–80.
109 Terrell, *A Companion to the Cantos*, vol. ii, p. 398.
110 Pound, *Cantos*, p. 522.
111 Ibid., p. 802.
112 Ibid., p. 425.
113 Terrell, *A Companion to the Cantos*, vol. ii, p. 362.
114 Casillo, *The Genealogy of Demons*, pp. 16–18.
115 Pound, *Cantos*, pp. 439, 443.
116 Casillo, *The Genealogy of Demons*, p. 400n.
117 Pound, *Cantos*, p. 434.
118 Ibid., pp. 427, 436.

119 Donald Hall, *Remembering Poets: Reminiscences and Opinions* (New York: Harper and Row, 1978), p. 242.
120 Pound, *Cantos*, p. 482.
121 Ibid., p. 430.
122 Girard, *Deceit, Desire and the Novel*, p. 32.
123 Pound, *Cantos*, p. 430.
124 Ibid., p. 478.
125 Ibid., p. 802.
126 Bernstein, *The Tale of the Tribe*, p. 120.
127 Pound, *Cantos*, p. 795.
128 Ibid., p. 479.
129 Terrell, *A Companion to the Cantos*, vol. II, p. 417.

3. 'NEITHER LIVING NOR DEAD': T. S. ELIOT AND THE UNCANNY

1 T. S. Eliot, *The Use of Poetry and the Use of Criticism* (London: Faber, 1933), p. 148.
2 Eliot, *The Use of Poetry*, p. 148.
3 Sigmund Freud, 'The Uncanny', vol. XVII of *The Standard Edition of the Complete Psychological Works*, ed. James Strachey (London: Hogarth, 1955) p. 368.
4 Ibid., pp. 362–3.
5 Ibid., p. 357.
6 James Longenbach, 'Uncanny Eliot', *T. S. Eliot: Man and Poet*, ed. Laura Cowan, vol. I (Orono, Maine: The National Poetry Foundation, 1990), pp. 47–69. Maud Ellmann, *The Poetics of Impersonality: T. S. Eliot and Ezra Pound* (Brighton: Harvester, 1987), pp. 101–2, has also briefly discussed the uncanny aspects of Eliot's poetry.
7 Freud, 'The Uncanny', p. 358.
8 The phrase is A. D. Moody's, *T. S. Eliot, Poet* (Cambridge University Press, 1979), p. 38, but Christopher Ricks also talks about the 'psychological *dédoublement*' of Eliot's poems, *T. S. Eliot and Prejudice* (London: Faber and Faber, 1988), p. 6, and virtually all readers of these poems have observed some kind of psychological doubleness. Longenbach's claim that 'Prufrock does not face the possibility of his dual existence . . . [and] expends all his energy keeping that threatening double suppressed', 'Uncanny Eliot', p. 57, is one which my following discussion will attempt to refute.
9 T. S. Eliot, *The Complete Poems and Plays* (London: Faber and Faber, 1969), p. 30.
10 Ibid., p. 27.
11 Ibid., p. 29.
12 Ibid., p. 24.
13 Ibid., p. 21.
14 Ibid., pp. 14, 24.

15 Freud, 'The Uncanny', p. 352.
16 Eliot, *Complete Poems*, p. 19.
17 Ibid., p. 15.
18 Ibid., p. 29.
19 Ibid., p. 20.
20 Ibid., pp. 19, 21.
21 Ibid., p. 21.
22 Ibid., p. 15.
23 Ibid., p. 14.
24 Ibid., p. 15.
25 Although according to Hugh Kenner, Eliot 'once referred casually to Prufrock . . . as a young man', *The Invisible Poet: T. S. Eliot* (London: Allen, 1960), p. 40.
26 Quoted in Mary Ann Gillies, *Henri Bergson and British Modernism* (Montreal: McGill-Queens University Press, 1996), p. 62.
27 Eliot, *Complete Poems*, p. 24.
28 Ibid.
29 Eliot, *Complete Poems*, pp. 13, 14
30 Ibid., p. 13.
31 The most recent and exhaustive condemnation is by Anthony Julius, *T. S. Eliot, Anti-Semitism, and Literary Form* (Cambridge University Press, 1995), pp. 41–74.
32 Eliot, *Complete Poems*, p. 38.
33 For a discussion of the woman as a kind of *vagina dentata* see Tony Pinkney, *Women in the Poetry of T. S. Eliot: A Psychoanalytic Approach* (London: Macmillan, 1986), pp. 18–24.
34 Eliot, *Complete Poems*, pp. 37–8.
35 Ibid., p. 55.
36 Curiously, the poems written in French lack the animus of the English poems. The disgust felt by the customer for the waiter in 'Dans le Restaurant', for example, is clearly dissipated by the poem's final section.
37 Eliot, *Complete Poems*, pp. 50, 53, 54.
38 Ibid., p. 41.
39 Ibid., p. 45.
40 Ibid., p. 57.
41 Julius, *T. S. Eliot*, pp. 77, 28.
42 Ricks, *T. S. Eliot and Prejudice*, p. 11.
43 Quoted in B. C. Southam, *A Student's Guide to* The Selected Poems of T. S. Eliot, 5th edn (London: Faber and Faber, 1990), p. 63.
44 Eliot, *Complete Poems*, pp. 40–41.
45 Ricks, *T. S. Eliot and Prejudice*, p. 67.
46 T. S. Eliot, *The Waste Land: A Facsimile and Transcript of the Original Drafts including the Annotations of Ezra Pound*, ed. Valerie Eliot (New York: Harcourt, 1971), p. 39.
47 Eliot, *The Waste Land: Facsimile*, pp. 43, 51.

48 Ibid., p. 119.
49 F. O. Matthiessen, *The Achievement of T. S. Eliot; An Essay on the Nature of Poetry*, 3rd edn (New York: Oxford University Press, 1958), p. 39.
50 Cleanth Brooks, *Modern Poetry and the Tradition* (London: Poetry London, 1948), p. 145. See also A. D. Moody, 'T. S. Eliot: The American Strain', in *The Placing of T. S. Eliot*, ed. Jewel Spears Brooker (Columbia: University of Missouri Press, 1991), p. 82.
51 Eliot, *Complete Poems*, pp. 62–3.
52 Southam, *A Student's Guide*, p. 109.
53 Eliot, *Complete Poems*, p. 76.
54 Ibid., p. 62.
55 Ibid., p. 76.
56 Ibid., p. 210.
57 Ibid., p. 62.
58 Ibid., pp. 73, 62.
59 David Chinitz, 'T. S. Eliot and the Cultural Divide', *PMLA* 110 (1995), 243.
60 Southam, *A Student's Guide*, p. 119.
61 Paper delivered at the 1998 MLA conference in Toronto.
62 Eliot, *Complete Poems*, pp. 65–6.
63 Ibid., p. 67.
64 Ibid., p. 74.
65 Ibid., p. 61.
66 Eliot, *The Waste Land: Facsimile*, p. 67.
67 Ibid.
68 Eliot, *The Waste Land: Facsimile*, pp. 69 and 68.
69 Ellmann, *The Poetics of Impersonality*, p. 95.
70 Freud, 'The Uncanny', p. 367.
71 Eliot, *The Complete Poems*, p. 64.
72 Ibid., pp. 56, 57.
73 Ibid., pp. 76, 78.
74 Ibid., p. 77.
75 T. S. Eliot, '*Ulysses*, Order and Myth', *James Joyce: The Critical Heritage*, vol. 1, ed. Robert H. London (London: Routledge, 1970), p. 270.
76 T. S. Eliot, *On Poetry and Poets* (London: Faber and Faber, 1957), pp. 109, 110.
77 *The Letters of T. S. Eliot*, ed. Valerie Eliot, vol. 1 (London: Faber and Faber, 1988), p. 498.
78 Eliot, *The Letters*, p. 504.
79 Ibid., pp. 480, 486.
80 Ibid., p. 498.
81 Eliot, *The Complete Poems*, p. 62.
82 Eliot, *The Use of Poetry*, pp. 153–4.
83 Eliot, *The Complete Poems*, pp. 119, 120.
84 Ibid., pp. 121, 122.

85 Lyndall Gordon, *Eliot's New Life* (New York: Farrar Straus & Giroux, 1988), p.60.
86 Eliot, *The Complete Poems*, p. 124.
87 Ibid., p. 13, 14, 65, 121.
88 Ibid., pp. 62 and 61.
89 Ibid., pp. 67, 69, 126.
90 Ibid., p. 79.
91 Ibid., p. 83.
92 Ricks, *T. S. Eliot and Prejudice*, p. 210.
93 Eliot, *Complete Poems*, p. 96.
94 Ibid., p. 85.
95 Ibid., p. 68.
96 Ibid., pp. 37, 61, 62.
97 Ibid., p. 61.
98 Ibid., p. 62.
99 Ibid., pp. 94, 98.
100 Ibid., p. 189.
101 Ibid., p. 190.
102 Ibid., p. 189–90.
103 Eliot, *The Letters*, p. 321.
104 T. S. Eliot, *After Strange Gods: A Primer of Modern Heresy* (London: Faber, 1934), p. 28.
105 Ronald Schuchard, 'Eliot and Hulme in 1916: Toward a Revaluation of Eliot's Critical and Spiritual Development', *PMLA* 88 (1973), 1083–94.
106 Quoted in John D. Margolis, *T. S. Eliot's Intellectual Development, 1922–1939* (University of Chicago Press, 1972), p. 95. James S. J. Torrens has also usefully analysed the influence of Maurras on Eliot in 'Charles Maurras and Eliot's "New Life"', *PMLA* (1974), 312–22.
107 T. S. Eliot, 'A Commentary', *The Criterion* 2 (1924), 231.
108 Quoted in Ronald Schuchard, 'T. S. Eliot as an Extension Lecturer, 1916–1919', *Review of English Studies* 25. 98 (1974), 165.
109 Schuchard, 'T. S. Eliot as an Extension Lecturer', p. 165.
110 T. S. Eliot, 'A Commentary', *The Criterion* 13 (1934), 453.
111 T. S. Eliot, Rev. of *Reflections on Violence*, by Georges Sorel, trans. T. E. Hulme, *Monist* (27 July 1917), 478.
112 Ibid., p. 479.
113 Ibid., p. 478.
114 Margolis, *T. S. Eliot's Intellectual Development*, pp. 92–3.
115 Ibid., pp. 94–5.
116 Quoted in Schuchard, 'T. S. Eliot as an Extension Lecturer', p. 116.
117 T. S. Eliot, *To Criticize the Critic, and Other Writings* (New York: Farrar, Straus & Giroux, 1972), p. 143.
118 T. S. Eliot, 'The Literature of Fascism', *The Criterion* 8 (1928), 290 and 282.

119 C. K. Stead, *Pound, Yeats, Eliot and the Modernist Movement* (London: Macmillan, 1986), pp. 205, 219.

120 T. S. Eliot, *For Lancelot Andrewes: Essays on Style and Order* (New York: Doubleday, 1929), p. vii.

121 Eliot, *The Letters*, pp. 416, 417.

122 Eliot, 'A Commentary' (1924), 231.

123 Eliot's ambivalence towards romanticism has been discussed by a great many critics. I have been particularly influenced by Frank Kermode, *Romantic Image* (London: Routledge and Kegan Paul, 1957), pp. 138–61; George Bornstein, *Transformations of Romanticism in Yeats, Eliot, and Stevens* (University of Chicago Press, 1976), pp. 94–162; and Perry Meisel, *The Myth of the Modern: A Study in British Literature and Criticism after 1850* (New Haven, Conn.: Yale University Press, 1987), pp. 69–120.

124 Eliot, *The Use of Poetry*, p. 13.

125 Ibid., pp. 32–3.

126 Ibid., p. 34.

127 Ibid., pp. 144–5.

128 Ibid., pp. 145, 146.

129 Ibid., p. 34.

130 Ibid., p. 36.

131 Ibid., p. 69.

132 Eliot, *Selected Essays*, p.17.

133 Carol Christ's interesting argument that Eliot imagines 'the literary past as a woman, whom he deserts, dishonours, even murders while he appropriates her voice', 'Gender, Voice, and Figuration in Eliot's Early Poetry', *The Modernist in History*, ed. Ronald Bush (Cambridge University Press, 1991), p. 27, rather overstates both his hostility and the extent of his volition.

134 Eliot, *Selected Essays*, p. 14.

135 Ibid., p. 145.

136 Ibid., pp. 145–6.

137 Ibid., p. 144.

138 T. S. Eliot, Introduction, in Charlotte Eliot, *Savonarola: A Dramatic Poem* (London: R. Cobden-Sanderson, 1926), p. viii.

139 Grover Smith (ed.), *Josiah Royce's Seminar, 1913–1914; As Recorded in the Notebooks of Harry T. Costello* (New Brunswick, N.J.: Rutgers University Press, 1963) p. 121. Eliot praises descriptive anthropology in his Rev. of *The Elementary Forms of the Religious Life*, by Emile Durkheim, *The Saturday Westminster Gazette* (19 Aug. 1916), 24–5 and 'A Prediction in Regard to Three English Authors', *Vanity Fair* (Feb. 1924), 98.

140 Eliot, *Selected Essays*, p. 142.

141 T. S. Eliot, Rev. of *Poems* and *Marriage*, by Marianne Moore, *Dial* (Dec. 1923), 597.

142 Eliot, *Selected Essays*, p. 146.

143　Eliot, *The Use of Poetry*, p. 155.
144　Ibid., pp. 152, 153.
145　Eliot, Rev. of *The Elementary Forms of the Religious Life*, 24.
146　Carol H. Smith, *T. S. Eliot's Dramatic Theory and Practice, from* Sweeney Agonistes *to* The Elder Statesman (Princeton University Press, 1963), pp. 44–6, 62–72.
147　Robert Crawford, *The Savage and the City in the Work of T. S. Eliot* (Oxford: Clarendon Press, 1987), p. 162.
148　Quoted in ibid., p. 164.
149　Eliot, *The Use of Poetry*, p. 42.
150　Quoted in Crawford, *The Savage and the City*, p. 212.
151　Eliot, Rev. of *Tarr*, p. 105.
152　T. S. Eliot, 'War-Paint and Feathers', *The Athenæum* (17 Oct. 1919), 1036.
153　Eliot, '*Ulysses*, Order and Myth', pp. 270–1. For a discussion of Eliot's own mythical method, see Grover Smith's 'The Structure and Mythical Method of *The Waste Land*', *T. S. Eliot's* The Waste Land, ed. Harold Bloom (New York: Chelsea, 1986), pp. 97–114.
154　T. S. Eliot, Rev. of *The Growth of Civilisation* and *The Origin of Magic and Religion*, by W. J. Perry, *The Criterion* 2 (1924), 490.
155　Marc Manganaro, '"Beating a Drum in a Jungle": T. S. Eliot on the Artist as "Primitive"', *Modern Language Quarterly* 47 (1986), 398.
156　T. S. Eliot, *The Sacred Wood: Essays on Poetry and Criticism* (London: Methuen, 1960), pp. viii, x.
157　Ibid., p. 160.
158　Ibid., pp. 160, 161.
159　Ibid., p. 160. See also Eliot, *Selected Essays*, pp. 237–77.
160　Eliot, *Selected Essays*, pp. 442, 420.
161　Eliot, *The Use of Poetry*, p. 26.
162　Eliot, *Selected Essays*, p. 476.
163　Ibid., p. 472.
164　Ibid., p. 440.
165　Eliot, *The Use of Poetry*, p. 128.
166　Eliot, *Sacred Wood*, p. viii.
167　T. S. Eliot, *Notes towards the Definition of Culture* (London: Faber and Faber, 1962), p. 28.
168　Eliot, *The Complete Poems*, pp. 189–90.
169　Eliot, *Notes*, p. 68.
170　Bornstein, *Transformations of Romanticism*, pp. 133, 139.
171　Eliot, *Notes*, p. 47.
172　Ibid., p. 58.
173　Eliot, *Selected Essays*, p. 27.
174　Eliot, *After Strange Gods*, p. 55.
175　T. S. Eliot, *The Idea of a Christian Society* (London: Faber, 1939), p. 21.
176　T. S. Eliot, Rev. of *Son of Woman: The Story of D. H. Lawrence*, by John Middleton Murray, *The Criterion* 10 (1931), 772.

177 Raymond Williams, *Culture and Society 1780–1950* (London: Chatto, 1958), pp. 297–300.
178 Eliot, *The Complete Poems*, pp. 28, 45, 27.
179 Ibid., p. 62.
180 Ibid., p. 73.
181 Crawford, *The Savage and the City*, p. 145.
182 Eliot, *The Complete Poems*, p. 137.
183 Jeffrey M. Pearl's sophisticated argument that Eliot's scepticism undermines even his own anti-liberalism tends to downplay the ideological aspects of such scepticism, *Skepticism and Modern Enmity* (Baltimore: Johns Hopkins University Press, 1989).
184 T. S. Eliot, 'Recent Books', *The Monthly Criterion* 6 (1927), 70, 73.
185 T. S. Eliot, 'Mr Barnes and Mr Rowse.' *The Criterion* 8 (1929), 690–1.
186 As Michael North points out, '[f]ascism was *more* modern than Eliot was willing to be in his social and political opinions', *The Political Aesthetic of Yeats, Eliot, and Pound* (Cambridge University press, 1991), p. 118.
187 T. S. Eliot, 'A Commentary', *The Criterion* 9 (1930), 590.
188 Eliot, 'The Literature of Fascism' (1928), 282.
189 Eliot, 'Recent Books', 179.
190 Eliot, *The Idea of a Christian Society*, p. 50.
191 Ibid., pp. 15–16.
192 T. S. Eliot, 'A Commentary', *The Criterion* 11 (1931), 69.
193 Theodor Adorno and Max Horkheimer, *Dialectic of Enlightenment* 1944; (London: Verso, 1979), p. xvi.
194 Eliot, 'A Commentary', (1928), 579.
195 Eliot, 'A Commentary', (1930), 590.
196 T. S Eliot, 'A Commentary,' *The Criterion* 15 (1936), 268.
197 Eliot, letter to his mother, 2 October 1919, *Letters*, p. 337. Eleanor Cook, 'T. S. Eliot and the Carthaginian Peace', *T. S. Eliot's* The Waste Land, ed. Harold Bloom, pp. 81–96, provides a full account of Eliot's opposition to the Treaty of Versailles's 'Carthaginian Peace' and shows how crucial this is to *The Waste Land*.
198 Eliot, 'A Commentary' (1936), p. 268.
199 T. S. Eliot, 'A Commentary', *The Criterion* 16 (1937), 290.
200 Ibid., p. 289.
201 T. S. Eliot, 'A Commentary', *The Criterion* 18 (1938), 60.
202 Eliot, *After Strange Gods*, p. 30.

4. THE HOMOSOCIAL AND FASCISM IN D. H. LAWRENCE

1 Eve Kosofsky Sedgwick, *Between Men: English Literature and Male Homosocial Desire* (New York: Columbia University Press, 1985), p. 216.
2 Cornelia Nixon, *Lawrence's Leadership Politics and the Turn Against Women* (Berkeley: University of California Press, 1986), p. 10. See also Paul

Delany, *D. H. Lawrence's Nightmare: The Writer and His Circle in the Years of the Great War* (New York: Basic, 1978).

3 Nixon, *Lawrence's Leadership Politics*, p. 163.

4 Other critics who have discussed or mentioned Lawrence's attitudes towards homosexuality are Kate Millet, *Sexual Politics* (New York: Doubleday, 1970), pp. 266–83; Jeffrey Meyers, *Homosexuality and Literature 1890–1930* (London: Athlone, 1977), pp. 131–61; Gregory Woods, *Articulate Flesh: Male Homo-Eroticism and Modern Poetry* (New Haven, Conn.: Yale University Press, 1987), pp. 126–39; Margaret Bolsterli, 'Studies in Context: The Homosexual Ambience in Twentieth Century Literary Culture', *D. H. Lawrence Review* 6 (1973), 71–85; and Emile Delaveney, *D. H. Lawrence and Edward Carpenter: A Study in Edwardian Transition* (London: Heinemann, 1971). All assume that there was a strong component of homosexuality in his sexuality identity. By contrast Mark Kinkead-Weekes argues that while '[t]he simple temptation is to see his depression and misery, perhaps even the renewed illness, as psychosomatic reaction against his own latent homosexuality', in fact for Lawrence 'homosexuality seemed to go with brittle and irreverent talk, self-enclosure, sensationalism, promiscuity. *That* – no simple homophobia – was what Lawrence felt was "a form of inward corruption"', *D. H. Lawrence: Triumph to Exile 1912–1922* (Cambridge University Press, 1996), pp. 212, 215. However I am not sure that there is such a phenomenon as 'simple homophobia'. And is it possible for a prejudice such as homophobia to 'go with' or be ancillary to a world-view or philosophy? Surely where prejudice exists it must be in part responsible for or what produces a world-view or set of opinions.

5 D. H. Lawrence, *Sons and Lovers*, ed. Helen Baron and Carl Baron (1913; Cambridge University Press, 1992), p. 15.

6 See for example H. M. Daleski, *The Forked Flame: A Study of D. H. Lawrence* (London: Faber and Faber, 1968), p. 43, and Terry Eagleton, *Literary Theory: An Introduction* (Oxford: Blackwell, 1983), p. 177.

7 Lawrence, *Sons and Lovers*, p. 298.

8 Ibid., p. 235.

9 Ibid., p. 92.

10 D. H. Lawrence, *The Letters of D. H. Lawrence*, vol. 1, ed. James T. Boulton (Cambridge University Press, 1979), p. xlv.

11 Lawrence, *Sons and Lovers*, p. 437.

12 Ibid., p. 361.

13 Ibid., p. 314.

14 Ibid., p. 410.

15 Ibid., p. 423.

16 Ibid., p. 451.

17 D. H. Lawrence, *The Rainbow*, ed. Mark Kinkead-Weekes (1915; Cambridge University Press, 1989), pp. 40, 51.

18 Lawrence, *The Rainbow*, p. 99.

19 Ibid., p. 391.
20 Graham Holderness, *D. H. Lawrence: History, Ideology and Fiction* (Dublin: Gill & Macmillan, 1982), p. 183.
21 D. H. Lawrence, *The Letters of D. H. Lawrence*, vol. II, ed. George J. Zytaruk and James T. Boulton (Cambridge University Press, 1981), p. 371.
22 Delany, *D. H. Lawrence's Nightmare*, pp. 28–9.
23 D. H. Lawrence, *The Complete Poems of D. H. Lawrence*, ed. Vivian de Sola Pinto and Warren Roberts, vol. II (London: Heinemann, 1964), p. 742.
24 Lawrence, *The Letters*, vol. I, p. 425.
25 Lawrence, *The Letters*, vol. II, p. 321.
26 Ibid., p. 331.
27 Sigmund Freud, 'Group Psychology and the Analysis of the Ego' (1920), vol. XIX of *The Standard Edition of the Complete Psychological Works of Sigmund Freud*, ed. James Strachey, 24 vols. (London: Hogarth, 1955), p. 136.
28 D. H. Lawrence, *Women in Love*, ed. David Farmer, Lindeth Vasey and John Worthen (1920; Cambridge University Press, 1987), p. 501.
29 Lawrence, *Women in Love*, pp. 503–4.
30 Meyers, *Homosexuality and Literature*, p. 131.
31 Lawrence, *The Complete Poems*, vol. I, p. 447.
32 Lawrence, *The Letters*, vol. II, p. 285.
33 Kinkead-Weekes makes a similar point in his discussion of *The Rainbow* and *Women in Love*, *D. H. Lawrence*, pp. 204, 330.
34 D. H. Lawrence, *Studies in Classic American Literature* (Penguin, 1977), p. 178.
35 Freud, 'Group Psychology', p. 108.
36 See for example, Jeffrey Weeks, *Coming Out: Homosexual Politics in Britain from the Nineteenth Century to the Present* (London: Quartet, 1977).
37 Lawrence, *Studies in Classic American Literature*, p. 178.
38 Ibid., p. 176.
39 Freud, 'Group Psychology', p. 116.
40 As Andrew Hewitt argues in another context, we must resist the idea that 'the fascist fears homosexuality because he somehow "is" – or fears he will become, or reveal himself to have always already been – homosexual', *Political Inversions: Homosexuality, Fascism, & the Modernist Imaginary* (Stanford University Press, 1996), p. 11.
41 Theodor W. Adorno, 'Freudian Theory and the Pattern of Fascist Propaganda,' *The Essential Frankfurt School Reader*, ed. Andrew Arato and Eike Gebhardt (Oxford: Blackwell, 1978), p. 120.
42 D. H. Lawrence, *Aaron's Rod*, ed. Mara Kalnins (1922; Cambridge University Press, 1988), p. 66.
43 D. H. Lawrence, *The Plumed Serpent*, ed. L. D. Clark (1926; Cambridge University Press, 1987), p. 188.
44 Adorno, 'Freudian Theory', pp. 126, 127.
45 D. H. Lawrence, *Kangaroo*, ed. Bruce Steele (Cambridge University Press, 1994), p. 104.

46 Lawrence, *Aaron's Rod*, p. 105.
47 Lawrence, *The Plumed Serpent*, pp. 156, 165.
48 Ibid., pp. 395, 398.
49 Ibid., p. 396.
50 Ibid., p. 399.
51 Lawrence, *Aaron's Rod*, p. 299.
52 Adorno, 'Freudian Theory', p. 127.
53 Ibid.
54 Lawrence, *Aaron's Rod*, p. 281.
55 Lawrence, *The Plumed Serpent*, p. 362.
56 Adorno, 'Freudian Theory', p. 131.
57 Lawrence, *The Plumed Serpent*, p. 417.
58 Ibid., p. 70.
59 Ibid., p. 82.
60 Ibid., p. 135.
61 Ibid., p. 421.
62 Lawrence, *Kangaroo*, p. 263.
63 Lawrence, *Aaron's Rod*, pp. 280–1.
64 Lawrence, *Kangaroo*, p. 108.
65 Ibid., p. 66.
66 Lawrence, *Aaron's Rod*, p. 290.
67 Ibid., p. 166.
68 Judith Ruderman, *D. H. Lawrence and the Devouring Mother: The Search for a Patriarchal Ideal of Leadership* (Durham, N.C.: Duke University Press, 1984).
69 Lawrence, *Aaron's Rod*, p. 213.
70 Lawrence, *The Plumed Serpent*, p. 64.
71 Ibid., p. 77.
72 Lawrence, *Studies in Classic American Literature*, p. 42.
73 Millet, *Sexual Politics*, p. 287.
74 Ibid., p. 57.
75 Lawrence, *Studies in Classic American Literature*, p. 59.
76 Lawrence, *Kangaroo*, p.136.
77 Lawrence, *Aaron's Rod*, p. 96.
78 Adorno, 'Freudian Theory', p. 133.
79 Lawrence, *The Plumed Serpent*, pp. 377–8.
80 Lawrence, *Aaron's Rod*, p. 98.
81 Lawrence, *Kangaroo*, p. 210.
82 Ibid., pp. 69, 274.
83 Ibid., p. 171.
84 Ibid., p. 272.
85 Lawrence, *The Plumed Serpent*, p. 371.
86 Lawrence, *Aaron's Rod*, p. 299.
87 Lawrence, *Kangaroo*, p. 209.

5. '*ALWAYS À DEUX*': WYNDHAM LEWIS AND HIS DOUBLES

1 Wyndham Lewis, *Rude Assignment: A narrative of My Career Up-To-Date* (London: Hutchinson, 1950), pp. 13, 21, 14.

2 Ezra Pound, *The Spirit of Romance* (London: Owen, 1952), p. 39.

3 Wyndham Lewis, *The Apes of God* (1930; London: Grayson, 1931), p. 422.

4 Wyndham Lewis, *The Complete Wild Body*, ed. Bernard Lafourcade (Santa Barbara, Calif.: Black Sparrow Press, 1982), p. 150.

5 Wyndham Lewis, *Paleface: The Philosophy of the 'Melting-Pot'* (London: Chatto & Windus, 1929), p. 241.

6 Wyndham Lewis (ed.), *Blast 1* (1914; Berkeley: Black Sparrow Press, 1981), p. 65.

7 Ibid., p. 80.

8 Ibid., pp. 84, 85.

9 Wyndham Lewis, *Blasting and Bombardiering*, 1937 (Berkeley, Calif.: University of California Press, 1967), p. 91.

10 David Ayers, *Wyndham Lewis and Western Man* (New York: St Martin's Press, 1992), p. 26.

11 Bernard Lafourcade, 'The Taming of the Wild Body.' *Wyndham Lewis: A Revaluation*, ed. Jeffrey Meyers (London: Athlone, 1980), p. 79.

12 Wyndham Lewis, *Time and Western Man* (London: Chatto & Windus, 1927), p. 323.

13 Ibid., p. 139.

14 Ibid., p. 43.

15 Henry Ford, *My Life and Work* (London: Heinemann, 1923), p. 103.

16 Lewis, *Time and Western Man*, p. 92.

17 Ibid., p. 170.

18 Ibid., p. 318.

19 Ibid., p. 479.

20 Yeats, *The Poems*, ed. Richard Finneran (New York: Macmillan, 1989), p. 214.

21 Wyndham Lewis, *Tarr*, revised edn 1928 (London: Calder and Boyars, 1968), pp. 279–80.

22 See Walter Michel, *Wyndham Lewis: Paintings and Drawings* (London: Thames & Hudson, 1971).

23 Lewis, *Paleface*, p. 251.

24 Lewis (ed.), *Blast 1*, p. 149.

25 Henri Bergson, 'Laughter', *Comedy*, ed. and introduction Wylie Sypher (New York: Doubleday, 1956).

26 Lewis, *The Wild Body*, p. 158.

27 Ibid., p. 159.

28 Wyndham Lewis, *Self Condemned* (1954; Toronto: Canadian Publishers, 1974), p. 407.

29 Lewis, *Tarr*, pp. 293–4.

30 Fredric Jameson, *Fables of Aggression: Wyndham Lewis, the Modernist as Fascist* (Berkeley, Calif.: University of California Press, 1979), p. 97.

31 Lewis, *Tarr*, p. 219.

32 Ibid., p. 293.

33 Ibid., p. 19.

34 Jeffrey Meyers, *The Enemy: A Biography of Wyndham Lewis* (London: Routledge and Kegan Paul, 1980), p. 15.

35 Wyndham Lewis, *The Letters of Wyndham Lewis*, ed. W. K. Rose (London: Methuen, 1963), p. 38.

36 Ibid., p. 28.

37 Ibid., pp. 16, 31.

38 Meyers, *The Enemy*, p. 22.

39 Strangely, Kreisler bears some similarities to Lewis's early friend Augustus John. Kreisler at one point is described as a 'universal papa' since it is rumoured that he 'only had to look at a woman for her to become pregnant', *Tarr*, p. 85. In early letters to his mother, Lewis describes John surrounded by his wives' children as a 'deity of Masculinity' and as an 'artistic personality' so 'strong' that it prevents him from painting, *Letters*, p. 31. Perhaps Lewis displaces the paternal characteristics of the older, successful John on to the rebellious son, Kreisler. For a discussion of Lewis's relationship to John, see Timothy Materer, 'Lewis and the Patriarchs: Augustus John, W. B. Yeats, T. Sturge Moore', *Wyndham Lewis: A Revaluation*, ed. Jeffrey Meyers (London: Athlone, 1980).

40 Lewis, *Tarr*, p. 121.

41 Ibid., p. 81.

42 Ibid., p. 252.

43 Ibid., p. 250.

44 Ibid., p. 299.

45 Ibid., p. 291.

46 Ibid., p. 93.

47 Ibid., p. 85.

48 Ibid., p. 299.

49 Ibid., p. 28.

50 Hugh Kenner, *Wyndham Lewis* (Norfolk, Conn.: New Directions, 1954), p. 9.

51 Jameson, *Fables of Aggression*, pp. 96, 98.

52 Lewis, *Tarr*, p. 275.

53 Ibid., p. 272.

54 Ibid., p. 274.

55 Ibid., p. 275.

56 Ibid., p. 285.

57 Ibid., p. 286.

58 Ibid., p. 294.

59 Ibid., p. 293.

60 Ibid., p. 286.

61 Ibid., p. 181.
62 Ibid., p. 51.
63 Ibid., p. 181.
64 T. S. Eliot, Rev. of *Tarr*, by Wyndham Lewis, *The Egoist* (Sept. 1918), pp. 105–6.
65 Lewis, *Tarr*, p. 122.
66 Ibid., p. 43.
67 Jameson, *Fables of Aggression*, p. 18.
68 Wyndham Lewis, *The Art of Being Ruled*, ed. Reed Way Dasenbrock (1926; Santa Rosa: Black Sparrow Press, 1989).
69 Ibid., p. 259.
70 Ibid., p. 142.
71 Ibid., p. 27.
72 Ibid., p. 69.
73 Ibid., p. 96.
74 Ibid., p. 369.
75 Ibid., p. 370.
76 Lewis, *Blasting and Bombardiering*, p. 303.
77 Lewis, *Apes of God*, p. 618.
78 Wyndham Lewis, *Hitler* (London: Chatto & Windus, 1931), p. 84.
79 Ibid., pp. 176, 184.
80 Ibid., p. 184.
81 Ibid., p. 108.
82 Ibid., p. 107.
83 Ibid., pp. 16, 19.
84 Ibid., p. 85.
85 Ibid., p. 22.
86 Ibid., pp. 23, 21.
87 Ibid., p. 24.
88 Ibid., p. 40.
89 Ibid., p. 41.
90 Ibid., p. 42.
91 Ibid., p. 21.
92 Ibid., p. 22.
93 Ibid., p. 23.
94 Ibid., p. 28.
95 Wyndham Lewis, *The Jews: Are They Human?* (London: Allen & Unwin, 1939), p. 32.
96 Ibid., p. 40.
97 Ibid., p. 61.
98 Ibid., p. 59.
99 Ibid., p. 20.
100 Ibid., p. 99.
101 Ibid., p. 68.
102 Wyndham Lewis, *The Hitler Cult* (London: Dent, 1939), p. 37.

103 Ibid., pp. 235, 234.
104 Ibid., p. 63.
105 Ibid., p. 101.
106 Ibid., p. 37.
107 Ibid., p. 76.
108 Ibid.
109 Ibid.
110 Lewis, *The Hitler Cult*, p. 77.
111 Ibid., p. 78.
112 Ibid., p. 103.
113 Ibid., p. 107.
114 Ibid., p. 41.
115 Ibid., p. 47.
116 Ibid., p. 50.
117 Ibid., p. 78.
118 Ibid., p. 105.
119 Ibid., p. 106.
120 Ibid., p. 123.
121 Ibid.
122 Lewis, *The Hitler Cult*, p. 19.
123 Lewis, *The Jews*, p. 29.
124 Lewis, *The Hitler Cult*, p. 29.
125 As Lewis himself confessed, '[i]f I am asked, "what are your Politics?"
    I can truly answer I have none', quoted in Julian Symons, 'Intro-
    duction', *The Essential Wyndham Lewis: An Introduction to His Work*, ed.
    Julian Symons (London: Deutsch, 1989), pp. 8–9. A corollary of
    Lewis's claim to be both beyond and devoid of politics is, as Ayers
    argues, the 'tension' in his work 'between his assumption that the self
    is really almost nothing at all, and his perception that the survival of
    European culture – Western Man – depends on the stability and
    coherence of the self', *Wyndham Lewis and Western Man*, p. 3.
126 Reed Way Dasenbrock, 'Wyndham Lewis's Fascist Imagination',
    Fascism, Aesthetics, and Culture, ed. Richard J. Golsan (Hanover, N.H.:
    University Press of New England, 1992), p. 93.
127 Lewis, *The Jews*, p. 11.
128 Ibid., p. 54.
129 Ibid., p. 28.
130 Dasenbrock, 'Wyndham Lewis's Fascist Imagination', p. 88.
131 Ibid., p. 94.
132 Adorno, 'Freudian Theory', p. 127.
133 Lewis, *The Hitler Cult*, p. 115.
134 Ibid., p. 107.
135 Jameson, *Fables of Aggression*, p. 5.
136 Lewis, *Blast 1*, p. 70.

Works cited

Abel, Elizabeth. *Virginia Woolf and the Fictions of Psychoanalysis*. University of Chicago Press, 1989.

Achebe, Chinua. 'An Image of Africa: Racism In Conrad's *Heart of Darkness*', *Massachusetts Review* 18 (1977), 782–94.

Ackroyd, Peter. *T. S. Eliot*. London: Hamish Hamilton, 1984.

Adorno, Theodor W. 'Freudian Theory and the Pattern of Fascist Propaganda', *The Essential Frankfurt School Reader*. Ed. Andrew Arato and Eike Gebhardt. Oxford: Blackwell, 1978.

Adorno, Theodor and Max Horkheimer. *Dialectic of Enlightenment*. 1944; London: Verso, 1979.

Apollonio, Umbrio (ed.). *Futurist Manifestos*. London: Thames, 1973.

Auden, W. H. *Collected Shorter Poems, 1927–1957*. London: Faber and Faber, 1969.

Ayers, David. *Wyndham Lewis and Western Man*. New York: St Martin's Press, 1992.

Bacigalupo, Massimo. *The Forméd Trace: The Later Poetry of Ezra Pound*. New York: Columbia University Press, 1980.

Baumann, Zygmunt. 'Allosemitism: Premodern, Modern, Postmodern', *Modernity, Culture and 'the Jew'*. Ed. Bryan Cheyette and Laura Marcus. Cambridge: Polity Press, 1998.

Modernity and the Holocaust. Ithaca, N. Y: Cornell University Press, 1989.

Bazin, Nancy Topping. *Virginia Woolf and the Androgynous Vision*. New Brunswick, N.J.: Rutgers University Press, 1973.

Bell, Ian F. A. *Critic as Scientist: The Modernist Poetics of Ezra Pound*. London: Methuen, 1981.

Bell, Ian F. A. (ed.) *Ezra Pound: Tactics for Reading*. London: Vision, 1982.

Belloc, Hilaire. 'The Servile State'. *New Age* 26 May 1910, 77–9.

The Servile State. London: Foulis, 1912.

Benjamin, Walter. *Illuminations*. Ed. Hannah Arendt. Trans Harry Zohn. London: Fontana, 1973.

Bergson, Henri. 'Laughter', *Comedy*. Ed. and intro. Wylie Sypher. New York: Doubleday, 1956.

Bernstein, Michael André. *The Tale of the Tribe: Ezra Pound and the Modern Verse Epic*. Princeton University Press, 1980.

Bloom, Harold. *Yeats*. Oxford University Press, 1970.

Bloom, Harold (ed.). *T. S. Eliot's 'The Waste Land'*. New York: Chelsea, 1986. *Ezra Pound*. New York: Chelsea, 1987.

Bolsterli, Margaret. 'Studies in Context: The Homosexual Ambience in Twentieth Century Literary Culture', *D. H. Lawrence Review* 6 (1973), 71–85.

Bornstein, George. *Transformations of Romanticism in Yeats, Eliot, and Stevens*. University of Chicago Press, 1976.

Bourdieu, Pierre. 'Flaubert's Point of View', Trans. Priscilla Ferguson, *Critical Inquiry* 14 (1988), 539–62.

Brooks, Cleanth. *Modern Poetry and the Tradition*. London: Poetry London, 1948.

Brown, Malcolm. *The Politics of Irish Literature: From Thomas Davis to W. B. Yeats*. London: Allen & Unwin, 1972.

Bush, Ronald (ed.). *T. S. Eliot: The Modernist in History*. Cambridge University Press, 1991.

Bürger, Peter. *Theory of the Avant-Garde*. Trans. Michael Shaw. Minneapolis: University of Minnesota Press, 1984.

Calinescu, Matei. *Five Faces of Modernity: Modernism, Avant-Garde, Decadence, Kitsch, Postmodernism*. Durham: Duke University Press, 1987.

Carey, John. *The Intellectuals and the Masses: Pride and Prejudice Among the Literary Intelligentsia, 1880–1939*. London: Faber and Faber, 1992.

Carpenter, Humphrey. *A Serious Character: The Life of Ezra Pound*. London: Faber and Faber, 1988.

Carroll, David. *French Literary Fascism: Nationalism, Anti-Semitism, and the Ideology of Culture*. Princeton University Press, 1995.

Casillo, Robert. *The Genealogy of Demons: Anti-Semitism, Fascism, and the Myths of Ezra Pound*. Evanston, Ill.: Northwestern University Press, 1988.

Chace, William M., *The Political Identities of Ezra Pound and T. S. Eliot*. Stanford University Press, 1973.

Chadwick, Joseph. 'Family Romance as National Allegory in Yeats's *Cathleen ni Houlihan* and *The Dreaming of the Bones*', *Twentieth Century Literature* 32 (1986), 155–68.

Chesterton, G. K. Introduction. *A. R. Orage: A Memoir*, by Philip Mairet. London: Dent, 1936.

Cheyette, Bryan. *Constructions of 'the Jew' in English Literature and Society: Racial Representations, 1875–1945*. Cambridge University Press, 1993.

Cheyette, Bryan (ed.) *Between 'Race' and Culture: Representations of 'the Jew' in English and American Literature*. Stanford University Press, 1996.

Cheyette, Bryan and Laura Marcus (eds.) *Modernity, Culture and 'the Jew'*. Cambridge: Polity Press, 1998.

Chinitz, David. 'T. S. Eliot and the Cultural Divide', *PMLA* 110 (1995), 236–47.

Christ, Carol. 'Gender, Voice, and Figuration in Eliot's Early Poetry', *The Modernist in History*. Ed. Ronald Bush. Cambridge University Press, 1991.

Clark, Suzanne. *Sentimental Modernism: Women Writers and the Revolution of the Word*. Bloomington: Indiana University Press, 1991.

Clifford, James. *The Predicament of Culture: Twentieth-Century Ethnography, Literature, and Art*. Cambridge, Mass.: Harvard University Press, 1988.

Conrad, Joseph. *Heart of Darkness*. Ed. Robert Kimbrough. New York: Norton, 1988.

Cook, Eleanor. 'T. S. Eliot and the Carthaginian Peace', *T. S. Eliot's 'The Waste Land'*. Ed. Harold Bloom. New York: Chelsea House Publishers, 1986.

Corrin, Jay P. *G. K. Chesterton and Hilaire Belloc: The Battle Against Modernity*. Athens, Ohio: Ohio University Press, 1981.

Crawford, Robert. *The Savage and the City in the Work of T. S. Eliot*. Oxford: Clarendon Press, 1987.

Cullingford, Elizabeth. *Yeats, Ireland and Fascism*. New York University Press, 1981.

Daleski, H. M. *The Forked Flame: A Study of D. H. Lawrence*. London: Faber and Faber, 1968.

Dangerfield, George. *The Strange Death of Liberal England*. 1935. New York: Capricorn, 1961.

Dasenbrock, Reed Way. 'Wyndham Lewis's Fascist Imagination', *Fascism, Aesthetics, and Culture*. Ed. Richard J. Golsan. Hanover, N.H.: University Press of New England, 1992.

Deane, Seamus. *Celtic Revivals: Essays in Modern Irish Literature 1880–1980*. London: Faber and Faber, 1985.

De Felice, Renzo. *Fascism: An Informal Introduction to Its Theory and Practice*. Interview with Michael A. Ledeen. New Brunswick, N.J.: Transaction, 1976.

Delany, Paul. *D. H. Lawrence's Nightmare: The Writer and His Circle in the Years of the Great War*. New York: Basic, 1978.

Delavenay, Emile. *D. H. Lawrence and Edward Carpenter: A Study in Edwardian Transition*. London: Heinemann, 1971.

De Maeztu, Ramiro. 'The Jealousy of the Guilds', *New Age* (29 Apr. 1915), 687–8.

Derrida, Jacques. *Dissemination*. Trans. Barbara Johnson. University of Chicago Press, 1981.

Dettmar, Kevin J. H. and Stephen Watt (eds.). *Marketing Modernism: Self-Promotion, Canonization, Rereading*. Ann Arbor: University of Michigan Press, 1996.

DiBattista, Maria and Lucy McDiarmid (eds.). *High and Low Moderns: Literature and Culture, 1889–1939*. New York: Oxford University Press, 1996.

Durant, Alan. *Ezra Pound, Identity in Crisis*. Brighton: Harvester, 1981.

Eagleton, Terry. *Exiles and Émigrés: Studies In Modern Literature*. London: Chatto, 1970.

    The Ideology of the Aesthetic. Oxford: Blackwell, 1990.

Literary Theory: An Introduction. Oxford: Blackwell, 1983.

Eliot, T. S. *After Strange Gods: A Primer of Modern Heresy*. London: Faber, 1934.

'A Commentary', *The Criterion* 2 (1924), 231–5.

'A Commentary', *The Criterion* 8 (1928), p. 579.

'A Commentary', *The Criterion* 8 (1929), 576–9.

'A Commentary', *The Criterion* 9 (1930), 586–90.

'A Commentary', *The Criterion* 11 (1931), 65–72.

'A Commentary', *The Criterion* 13 (1934), 451–4.

'A Commentary', *The Criterion* 15 (1936), 265–9.

'A Commentary', *The Criterion* 16 (1937), 289–93.

'A Commentary', *The Criterion* 18 (1938), 58–62.

The Complete Poems and Plays. London: Faber and Faber, 1969.

To Criticize the Critic, and Other Writings. New York: Farrar, Straus & Giroux, 1972.

For Lancelot Andrewes: Essays on Style and Order. New York: Doubleday, 1929.

The Idea of a Christian Society. London: Faber, 1939.

Introduction. *Savonarola: A Dramatic Poem*, by Charlotte Eliot. London: R. Cobden-Sanderson, 1926, pp. vii–xii.

The Letters of T. S. Eliot. Ed. Valerie Eliot. Vol. 1. London: Faber and Faber, 1988.

'The Literature of Fascism', *The Criterion* 8 (1928), 280–90.

'Mr Barnes and Mr Rowse', *The Criterion* 8 (1929), 682–91.

Notes towards the Definition of Culture. London: Faber and Faber, 1962.

On Poetry and Poets. London: Faber and Faber, 1957.

'A Prediction in Regard to Three English Authors', *Vanity Fair* (Feb. 1924) 29.

'Recent Books', *The Monthly Criterion* 6 (1927), 69–73.

'A Reply to Mr Ward', *The Criterion* 7 (1928), 84–8.

Rev. of *The Elementary Forms of the Religious Life*, by Emile Durkheim. *The Monist* 27.2 (1918), 158–9.

Rev. of *The Elementary Forms of the Religious Life*, by Emile Durkheim, *The Saturday Westminster Gazette* (19 Aug. 1916), 24–5.

Rev. of *The Growth of Civilisation* and *The Origin of Magic and Religion*, by W. J. Perry, *The Criterion* 2 (1924), 489–90.

Rev. of *Poems* and *Marriage*, by Marianne Moore, *Dial* (Dec. 1923), 594–7.

Rev. of *Reflections on Violence*, by Georges Sorel and trans. T. E. Hulme, *Monist* (27 July 1917), 478–9.

Rev. of *Son of Woman: The Story of D. H. Lawrence*, by John Middleton Murray, *The Criterion* 10 (1931), 768–74.

Rev. of *Tarr*, by Wyndham Lewis, *The Egoist* (Sept. 1918), 105–6.

The Sacred Wood: Essays on Poetry and Criticism. London: Methuen, 1960.

Selected Essays. London: Faber and Faber, 1951.

'*Ulysses*, Order and Myth', *James Joyce: The Critical Heritage*. Vol. 1. Ed. Robert H. London: Routledge, 1970.

The Use of Poetry and the Use of Criticism. London: Faber and Faber, 1933.

'War-Paint and Feathers', *The Athenæum* (17 Oct. 1919), 1036.

'The Waste Land': A Facsimile and Transcript of the Original Drafts including the Annotations of Ezra Pound. Ed. Valerie Eliot. New York: Harcourt, 1971.

Ellmann, Maud. *The Poetics of Impersonality: T. S. Eliot and Ezra Pound.* Brighton: Harvester, 1987.

Emery, Mary Lou. '"Robbed of Meaning": The Work at the Center of *To The Lighthouse*', *Modern Fiction Studies* 38 (1992), 217–34.

Fenollosa, Ernest. *The Chinese Written Character as a Medium for Poetry.* Ed. Ezra Pound. San Francisco: City Lights, 1936.

Ferrall, Charles. 'The *New Age* and the Emergence of Reactionary Modernism before the Great War', *Modern Fiction Studies* 38. iii (1992), 653–67.

Ford, Henry. *My Life and Work.* London: Heinemann, 1923.

Foster, Hal. *Recodings: Art, Spectacle, Cultural Politics.* Washington: Bay Press, 1985.

Foster, R. F. *W. B. Yeats: A Life, Vol 1: The Apprentice Mage.* Oxford University Press, 1997.

Freud, Sigmund. *The Standard Edition of the Complete Psychological Works of Sigmund Freud*, vol. xviii, *Group Psychology and the Analysis of the Ego.* 1920. Ed. James Strachey. 24 vols. London: Hogarth, 1955.

The Standard Edition of the Complete Psychological Works, vol. xvii, 'The Uncanny'. Ed. James Strachey. London: Hogarth, 1955.

Freyer, Grattan. *W. B. Yeats and the Anti-Democratic Tradition.* Dublin: Gill & Macmillan, 1981.

Frye, Northrop. *The Great Code: The Bible and Literature.* London: Ark, 1983.

Gilbert, Sandra M. and Susan Gubar. *No Man's Land.* 3 vols. New Haven, Conn.: Yale University Press, 1988–94.

Gillies, Mary Ann. *Henri Bergson and British Modernism.* Montreal: McGill-Queen's University Press, 1996.

Girard, René. *Deceit, Desire and the Novel: Self and Other in Literary Structure.* Trans. Yvonne Freccero. Baltimore: Johns Hopkins University Press, 1976.

Godden, Richard. 'Icons, Etymologies, Origins and Monkey Puzzles in the Languages of Upward and Fenollosa', *Ezra Pound: Tactics for Reading.* Ed. Ian Bell. London: Methuen, 1981.

Gordon, Lyndall. *Eliot's New Life.* New York: Farrar Straus Giroux, 1988.

Gregor, A. James. *Interpretations of Fascism.* Morristown, N.J.: General Learning Press, 1974.

Griffin, Roger. *The Nature of Fascism.* New York: St Martin's Press, 1991.

Habermas, Jürgen. 'Modernity – An Incomplete Project', *Postmodern Culture.* Ed. Hal Foster. London: Pluto, 1985.

The Philosophical Discourse of Modernity. Trans. Frederick G. Lawrence. Cambridge, Mass.: MIT Press, 1987.

Hall, Donald. *Remembering Poets: Reminiscences and Opinions.* New York: Harper and Row, 1978.

Harrison, Charles. *English Art and Modernism, 1900–1939.* Bloomington: Indiana University Press, 1981.

Hartnett, Stephen. 'The Ideologies and Semiotics of Fascism: Analysing Pound's *Cantos* 12–15', *Boundary 2* 20.1 (1993), 65–93.

Herf, Jeffrey. *Reactionary Modernism: Technology, Culture, and Politics in Weimar and the Third Reich.* Cambridge University Press, 1984.

Hewitt, Andrew. *Political Inversions: Homosexuality, Fascism, & the Modernist Imaginary.* Stanford University Press, 1996.

Hobsbawm, E. J. *The Age of Empire 1875–1914.* New York: Pantheon, 1987.

Holderness, Graham. *D. H. Lawrence: History, Ideology and Fiction.* Dublin: Gill & Macmillan, 1982.

Hulme, T. E. *Further Speculations.* Ed. Samuel Hynes. Lincoln: University of Nebraska Press, 1962.

'Mr Balfour, Bergson, and Politics', *New Age* (9 Nov. 1911), 38–40.

'Notes on Bergson II', *New Age* (26 Oct. 1911), 610–11.

Speculations: Essays on Humanism and the Philosophy of Art. Ed. Herbert Read. New York: Harcourt, 1924.

Huyssen, Andreas. *After the Great Divide: Modernism, Mass Culture, Postmodernism.* Bloomington: Indiana University Press, 1986.

Innes, C. L. *Woman and Nation in Irish Literature and Society, 1880–1935.* Athens, Ga.: University of Georgia Press, 1993.

Jakobson, Roman. 'Two Aspects of Language and Two Types of Aphasic Disturbance', *Fundamentals of Language.* The Hague: Mouton, 1956, pp. 53–82.

Jameson, Fredric. *Fables of Aggression: Wyndham Lewis, the Modernist as Fascist.* Berkeley: University of California Press, 1979.

Jeffares, A. Norman. *A New Commentary on the Poems of W. B. Yeats.* London: Macmillan, 1984.

Jeffares, A. Norman, and A. S. Knowland. *A Commentary on the Collected Plays of W. B. Yeats.* Stanford University Press, 1975.

Joseph, Terri Brint. 'Peirce, Pound, and Fenollosa', *Poetics 1984.* Ed. John Deely. Lanham, Md.: University Press of America, 1985.

Julius, Anthony. *T. S. Eliot, Anti-Semitism, and Literary Form.* Cambridge University Press, 1995.

Kaplan, Alice Yaeger. *Reproductions of Banality: Fascism, Literature and French Intellectual Life.* Minneapolis: University of Minnesota Press, 1986.

Kayman, Martin A. *The Modernism of Ezra Pound: The Science of Poetry.* London: Macmillan, 1986.

Keane, Patrick J. *Terrible Beauty: Yeats, Joyce, Ireland and the Myth of the Devouring Female.* Columbia: University of Missouri Press, 1988.

Kennedy, George. 'Fenollosa, Pound and the Chinese Character', *Yale Literary Magazine*, 126.1 (1958), 24–36.

Kennedy, J. M. *English Literature, 1880–1905.* London: Swift, 1912.

The Quintessence of Nietzsche. London: Laurie, 1909.

Kenner, Hugh. 'The Broken Mirrors and the Mirror of Memory', *Motive and Method in the Cantos of Ezra Pound.* Ed. Lewis Leary. New York: Columbia University Press, 1961.

The Invisible Poet: T. S. Eliot. London: Allen, 1960.

Wyndham Lewis. Norfolk, Conn.: New Directions, 1954.

Kermode, Frank. *Romantic Image.* London: Routledge and Kegan Paul, 1957.

Kiberd, Declan. *Inventing Ireland: The Literature of the Modern Nation.* London: Jonathan Cape, 1995.

Kinkead-Weekes, Mark. *D. H. Lawrence: Triumph to Exile 1912–1922.* Cambridge University Press, 1996.

Krimm, Bernard G. *W. B. Yeats and the Emergence of the Irish Free State.* Troy, N.Y.: Whitson, 1981.

Lafourcade, Bernard. 'The Taming of the Wild Body', *Wyndham Lewis: A Revaluation.* Ed. Jeffrey Meyers. London: Athlone, 1980.

Laquer, Walter. *Fascism: Past, Present, Future.* New York: Oxford University Press, 1996.

Lasserre, Pierre. *Le Romantisme Français: Essai sur la Révolution dans les Sentiments et dans les Idées au XIX Siècle.* Nouvelle Edition. 1907. Paris: Calmann, 1928.

Lawrence, D. H. *Aaron's Rod.* 1922. Ed. Mara Kalnins. Cambridge University Press, 1988.

The Complete Poems of D. H. Lawrence. Ed. Vivian de Sola Pinto and Warren Roberts. 2 vols. London: Heinemann, 1964.

Kangaroo. 1923. Ed. Bruce Steele. Cambridge University Press, 1994.

The Letters of D. H. Lawrence, vol. I. Ed. James T. Boulton. Cambridge University Press, 1979.

The Letters of D. H. Lawrence, vol. II. Ed. George J. Zytaruk and James T. Boulton. Cambridge University Press, 1981.

The Plumed Serpent. 1926. Ed. L. D. Clark. Cambridge University Press, 1987.

The Rainbow. 1915. Ed. Mark Kinkead-Weekes. Cambridge University Press, 1989.

Sons and Lovers. 1913. Ed. Helen Baron and Carl Baron. Cambridge University Press, 1992.

Studies in Classic American Literature. Penguin, 1977.

Women in Love. 1920. Ed. David Farmer, Lindeth Vasey and John Worthen. Cambridge University Press, 1987.

Lears, Jackson. *No Place of Grace: Antimodernism and the Transformation of American Culture 1880–1920.* New York: Pantheon, 1981.

Levenson, Michael H. *A Genealogy of Modernism: A Study in English Literary Doctrine, 1908–1922.* Cambridge University Press, 1984.

Lewis, Wyndham. *The Apes of God.* 1930. London: Grayson, 1931.

The Art of Being Ruled. Ed. Reed Way Dasenbrock. 1926. Santa Rosa: Black Sparrow Press, 1989.

Blasting and Bombardiering. 1937. Berkeley: University of California Press, 1967.

The Complete Wild Body. Ed. Bernard Lafourcade. Santa Barbara: Black Sparrow Press, 1982.

Hitler. London: Chatto & Windus, 1931.

The Hitler Cult. London: Dent, 1939.

The Jews: Are They Human? London: Allen & Unwin, 1939.

The Letters of Wyndham Lewis. Ed. W. K. Rose. London: Methuen, 1963.

Paleface: The Philosophy of the 'Melting-Pot'. London: Chatto & Windus, 1929.

Rude Assignment: A Narrative of My Career Up-To-Date. London: Hutchinson, 1950.

Self Condemned. 1954. Toronto: Canadian Publishers, 1974.

Tarr. Revised edn of 1928. London: Calder and Boyars, 1968.

Time and Western Man. London: Chatto & Windus, 1927.

(ed.). *Blast 1.* 1914. Berkeley: Black Sparrow Press, 1981.

Lippard, Lucy R. (ed.). *Dadas on Art.* Englewood Cliffs, N.J.: Prentice-Hall, 1971.

Lodge, David. *The Modes of Modern Writing: Metaphor, Metonymy, and the Typology of Modern Literature.* London: Arnold, 1977.

Longenbach, James. 'Uncanny Eliot'. *T. S. Eliot: Man and Poet*, vol. 1. Ed. Laura Cowan. Orono, Maine: The National Poetry Foundation, 1990, pp. 47–69.

Lyons, F. S. L. *Culture and Anarchy in Ireland, 1890–1939.* Oxford: Clarendon, 1979.

Lyotard, Jean-François. *The Postmodern Condition: A Report on Knowledge.* Trans. Geoff Bennington and Brian Massumi. Manchester University Press, 1984.

Maccoby, Hyam. 'The Jew As Anti-Artist: The Anti-Semitism of Ezra Pound', *Midstream* 22 (1976), 59–71.

Mairet, Philip. *A. R. Orage: A Memoir.* London: Dent, 1936.

Manganaro, Marc. ' "Beating a Drum in a Jungle": T. S. Eliot on the Artist as "Primitive" ', *Modern Language Quarterly* 47 (1986), 393–421.

Marcus, Jane. *Virginia Woolf and the Languages of Patriarchy.* Bloomington: Indiana University Press, 1987.

Marcuse, Herbert. *Negations: Essays in Critical Theory.* London: Penguin, 1969.

Margolis, John D. *T. S. Eliot's Intellectual Development, 1922–1939.* University of Chicago Press, 1972.

Martin, Wallace. *The 'New Age' Under Orage: Chapters in English Cultural History.* Manchester University Press, 1967.

Materer, Timothy. 'Lewis and the Patriarchs: Augustus John, W. B. Yeats, T. Sturge Moore'. *Wyndham Lewis: A Revaluation.* Ed. Jeffrey Meyers. London: Athlone, 1980.

Matthiessen, F. O. *The Achievement of T. S. Eliot; An Essay on the Nature of Poetry.* 3rd edn. New York: Oxford University Press, 1958.

Mazgaj, Paul. *The Action Française and Revolutionary Syndicalism.* Chapel Hill: University of North Carolina Press, 1979.

Meisel, Perry. *The Myth of the Modern: A Study in British Literature and Criticism after 1850*. New Haven, Conn.: Yale University Press, 1987.

Meyers, Jeffrey. *The Enemy: A Biography of Wyndham Lewis*. London: Routledge and Kegan Paul, 1980.

Homosexuality and Literature 1890–1930. London: Athlone, 1977.

Meyers, Jeffrey (ed.). *Wyndham Lewis: A Revaluation*. London: Athlone, 1980.

Michel, Walter. *Wyndham Lewis: Paintings and Drawing*. London: Thames & Hudson, 1971.

Millet, Kate. *Sexual Politics*. New York: Doubleday, 1970.

Moody, A. D. 'T. S. Eliot: The American Strain', In *The Placing of T. S. Eliot*. Ed. Jewel Spears Brooker. Columbia: University of Missouri Press, 1991.

T. S. Eliot, Poet. Cambridge University Press, 1979.

Morrison, Paul. *The Poetics of Fascism: Ezra Pound, T. S. Eliot, Paul de Man*. New York: Oxford University Press, 1996.

Mosse, George L. 'Ernst Nolte on *Three Faces of Fascism*', *Journal of the History of Ideas* 27 (1966), 621–5.

Murray, David. 'Pound-signs: Money and Representation in Ezra Pound', *Ezra Pound: Tactics for Reading*. Ed. Ian Bell. London: Vision, 1982.

Nänny, Max. 'Context, Contiguity and Contact in Ezra Pound's *Personae*', *Ezra Pound*. Ed. Harold Bloom. New York: Chelsea, 1987, pp. 75–86.

Nicholls, Peter. *Ezra Pound: Politics, Economics and Writing*. London: Macmillan, 1984.

Nixon, Cornelia. *Lawrence's Leadership Politics and the Turn Against Women*. Berkeley: University of California Press, 1986.

Nochlin, Linda and Tamar Garb (eds.). *The Jew in the Text: Modernity and the Construction of Identity*. London: Thames & Hudson, 1995.

Nolte, Ernst. *Three Faces of Fascism: Action Française, Italian Fascism, National Socialism*. Trans. Leila Vennewitz. London: Weidenfeld and Nicolson, 1965.

Norman, Charles. *Ezra Pound*. London: Macdonald, 1969.

North, Michael. *The Political Aesthetic of Yeats, Eliot, and Pound*. Cambridge University Press, 1991.

O'Brien, Conor Cruise. 'Passion and Cunning: An Essay on the Politics of W. B. Yeats', *In Excited Reverie: A Centenary Tribute to William Butler Yeats, 1865–1939*. Ed. A. Norman Jeffares and K. G. W. Cross. London: Macmillan, 1965.

Orage, A. J. Preface to *National Guilds*, by S. G. Hobson. London: Bell, 1919.

'Readers and Writers', *New Age* (23 Dec. 1915), p. 181.

'Unedited Opinions (VI): Modern Novels', *New Age* (29 Dec. 1910), p. 204.

Orwell, George. 'W. B. Yeats', *Collected Essays*. London: Secker & Warburg, 1961.

Parker, Andrew. 'Ezra Pound and the "Economy" of Anti-Semitism', *Boundary 2* 11 (1982), 103–28.

Payne, Stanley G. *A History of Fascism 1914–1945*. Madison: University of Wisconsin Press, 1995.

Pearl, Jeffrey M. *Skepticism and Modern Enmity.* Baltimore: Johns Hopkins University Press, 1989.

Pearlman, Daniel. 'E P as Wandering Jew', *Ezra Pound.* Ed. Harold Bloom. New York: Chelsea, 1987, pp. 87–104.

Penty, Arthur J. 'Medievalism and Modernism', *New Age* (23 Apr. 1914), 776–7. 'The Restoration of the Guild System', *New Age* (4 Sept. 1914), 544–7.

Perloff, Marjorie. *The Futurist Moment: Avant-Garde, Avant Guerre, and the Language of Rupture.* University of Chicago Press, 1986.

Pinkney, Tony. *Women in the Poetry of T. S. Eliot: A Psychoanalytic Approach.* London: Macmillan, 1986.

Pound, Ezra. *ABC of Reading.* London: Routledge, 1934.

Cantos. London: Faber and Faber, 1975.

'Ezra Pound Speaking': Radio Speeches of World War II. Ed. Leonard W. Doob. Westport, Conn.: Greenwood, 1978.

'A Few Don'ts by an Imagiste', *Poetry* (Mar. 1913), 200–6.

Guide to Kulchur. London: Owen, 1960.

Jefferson And / Or Mussolini: Fascism As I Have Seen It. New York: Liverwight, 1970.

Literary Essays of Ezra Pound. Ed. T. S. Eliot. London: Faber and Faber, 1960.

Personae: The Collected Poems of Ezra Pound. New York: Boni & Liverwight, 1926.

Selected Poems. London: Faber and Faber, 1977.

Selected Prose 1909–1965. Ed. William Cookson. London: Faber and Faber, 1973.

The Spirit of Romance. 1910. London: Owen, 1952.

Quinton, Anthony. Introduction to *T. E. Hulme,* by Michael Roberts. 1938; Manchester: Carcanet, 1982.

Rabaté, Jean-Michel. *Language, Sexuality and Ideology in Ezra Pound's 'Cantos'.* London: Macmillan, 1986.

Rainey, Lawrence. *Institutions of Modernism: Literary Elites and Public Culture.* New Haven, Conn.: Yale University Press, 1998.

Reckitt, Maurice B. *As It Happened: An Autobiography.* London: Dent, 1941.

Redman, Tim. *Ezra Pound and Italian Fascism.* Cambridge University Press, 1991.

Ricks, Christopher. *T. S. Eliot and Prejudice.* London: Faber and Faber, 1988.

Robinson, Alan. *Poetry, Painting and Ideas, 1885–1914.* London: Macmillan, 1985.

Rubin, William (ed.). *'Primitivism' in 20th Century Art: Affinity of the Tribal and the Modern.* New York: MOMA, 1984.

Ruderman, Judith. *D. H. Lawrence and the Devouring Mother: The Search for a Patriarchal Ideal of Leadership.* Durham N.C.: Duke University Press, 1984.

Ruthven, Ken. *Ezra Pound as Literary Critic*. London: Routledge, 1990.

Said, Edward. *Culture and Imperialism*. London: Vintage, 1994.

Schneidau, Herbert. 'Wisdom Past Metaphor: Another View of Objective Verse', *Paideuma* 5 (1976), 15–29.

Schuchard, Ronald. 'T. S. Eliot as an Extension Lecturer, 1916–1919', *Review of English Studies* 25. 98 (1974), 163–73; 25.99 (1974), 292–304.

'Eliot and Hulme in 1916: Toward a Revaluation of Eliot's Critical and Spiritual Development', *PMLA* 88 (1973), 1083–94.

Scott, Bonnie Kime. *The Gender of Modernism*. Bloomington: Indiana University Press, 1990.

Sedgwick, Eve Kosofsky. *Between Men: English Literature and Male Homosocial Desire*. New York: Columbia University Press, 1985

Showalter, Elaine. *A Literature of Their Own: British Women Novelists from Brontë to Lessing*. London: Virago, 1982.

Sieburth, Richard. 'In Pound We Trust: The Economy of Poetry/The Poetry of Economics', *Critical Inquiry* 14.4 (1987), 142–72.

Smith, Carol H. *T. S. Eliot's Dramatic Theory and Practice, from 'Sweeney Agonistes' to 'The Elder Statesman'*. Princeton University Press, 1963.

Smith, Grover. 'The Structure and Mythical Method of *The Waste Land*'. *T. S. Eliot's 'The Waste Land'*. Ed. Harold Bloom. New York: Chelsea, 1987, pp. 97–114.

Smith, Grover (ed.). *Josiah Royce's Seminar, 1913–1914; As Recorded in the Notebooks of Harry T. Costello*. New Brunswick, N.J.: Rutgers University Press, 1963.

Sorel, Georges. *Reflections on Violence*. Trans. T. E. Hulme. 1916; London: Collier, 1961.

Southam, B. C. *A Student's Guide to 'The Selected Poems of T. S. Eliot'*. 5th edn London: Faber and Faber, 1990.

Stanfield, Paul Scott. *Yeats and Politics in the 1930s*. New York: St Martin's Press, 1988.

Stead, C. K. *Pound, Yeats, Eliot and the Modernist Movement*. London: Macmillan, 1986.

Steiner, George. *In Bluebeard's Castle: Some Notes towards the Re-Definition of Culture*. London: Faber and Faber, 1971.

The Portage to San Cristobal of A. H. London: Faber and Faber, 1981.

Sternhell, Zeev. *La Droite Révolutionnaire, 1885–1914: Les Origines Françaises du Fascisme*. Paris: Seuil, 1978.

Neither Right nor Left: Fascist Ideology in France. Trans. David Maisel. Berkeley: University of California Press, 1986.

Symons, Julian. Introduction. *The Essential Wyndham Lewis: An Introduction to His Work*. Ed. Julian Symons. London: Deutsch, 1989.

Terrell, Carol F. *A Companion to the 'Cantos' of Ezra Pound*. 2 Vols. Berkeley: University of California Press, 1980–84.

Theweleit, Klaus. *Male Fantasies*. 2 vols. Trans. Stephen Conway, Jessica

Benjamin and Anson Rabinbach. Minneapolis, University of Minnesota Press, 1987 and Cambridge: Polity, 1989.

Thomas, Brook. 'Preserving and Keeping Order by Killing Time In *Heart of Darkness*', *Joseph Conrad, 'Heart of Darkness': A Case Study in Contemporary Criticism*. Ed. Ross C. Murfin. New York: St Martin's Press, 1989, pp. 237–58.

Torchiana, Donald. *W. B. Yeats and Georgian Ireland*. Evanston, Ill.: Northwestern University Press, 1966.

Torrens, James S. J. 'Charles Maurras and Eliot's "New Life"', *PMLA* (1974), 312–22.

Tratner, Michael. *Modernism and Mass Politics: Joyce, Woolf, Eliot, Yeats*. Stanford University Press, 1995.

Turner, Henry A. 'Fascism and Modernization', *Reappraisals of Fascism*. Ed. Henry A. Turner. New York: New Viewpoints, 1975.

Watson, George. *Irish Identity and the Literary Revival*. London: Croom Helm, 1979.

Weeks, Jeffrey. *Coming Out: Homosexual Politics in Britain from the Nineteenth Century to the Present*. London: Quartet, 1977.

Wexler, Joyce Piell. *Who Paid for Modernism? Art, Money, and the Fiction of Conrad, Joyce, and Lawrence*. Fayetteville: University of Arkansas Press, 1997.

Williams, Raymond. *Culture and Society 1780–1950*. London: Chatto, 1958.

Willison, Ian, Warwick Gould and Warren Chernaik (eds.). *Modernist Writers and the Marketplace*. London: Macmillan, 1996.

Woods, Gregory. *Articulate Flesh: Male Homo-Eroticism and Modern Poetry*. New Haven, Conn.: Yale University Press, 1987.

Woolf, Virginia. *To the Lighthouse*. Ed. Susan Dick. Oxford: Blackwell, 1992.

Wordsworth, William and Samuel Taylor Coleridge. *Lyrical Ballads 1805*. Ed. Derek Roper. London: Collins, 1968.

Worringer, Wilhelm. *Abstraction and Empathy: A Contribution to the Psychology of Style*. Trans. Michael Bulloch. 1908; New York: International University Press, 1953.

Yeats, W. B. *Autobiographies*. Ed. William H. O'Donnell and Douglas N. Archibald. New York: Scribner, 1999.

A Critical Edition of Yeats's 'A Vision' (1925). Ed. George Mills Harper and Walter Kelly Hood. London: Macmillan, 1978.

Explorations. London: Macmillan, 1962.

The Letters of W. B. Yeats. Ed. Allan Wade. London: Rupert Hart-Davis, 1954.

Memoirs. Ed. Denis Donoghue. London: Macmillan, 1972.

The Poems. Ed. Richard Finneran. New York: Macmillan, 1989.

The Senate Speeches of W. B. Yeats. Ed. Donald Pearce. London: Faber, 1961.

Uncollected Prose by W. B. Yeats, Vol. I. Ed. John P. Prayne. London: Macmillan, 1970.

The Variorum Edition of the Plays of W. B. Yeats. Ed. Russell K. Alspach. London: Macmillan, 1966.

The Variorum Edition of the Poems of W. B. Yeats. Ed. Peter Allt and Russell K. Alspach. New York: Macmillan, 1957.

A Vision (1937) New York: Macmillan, 1956.

Yeats, W. B. (ed.). *Fairy and Folk Tales of Ireland*. London: Pan, 1979.

Index